Networkologies

A Philosophy of Networks for a
Hyperconnected Age – A Manifesto

Networkologies

A Philosophy of Networks for a
Hyperconnected Age – A Manifesto

Christopher Vitale

Winchester, UK
Washington, USA

First published by Zero Books, 2014
Zero Books is an imprint of John Hunt Publishing Ltd., Laurel House, Station Approach,
Alresford, Hants, SO24 9JH, UK
office1@jhpbooks.net
www.johnhuntpublishing.com
www.zero-books.net

For distributor details and how to order please visit the 'Ordering' section on our website.

Text copyright: Christopher Vitale 2013

ISBN: 978 1 78099 238 9

A CIP catalogue record for this book is available from the British Library.

Design: Lee Nash

Printed and bound by CPI Group (UK) Ltd, Croydon, CR0 4YY

We operate a distinctive and ethical publishing philosophy in all
areas of our business, from our global network of authors to
production and worldwide distribution.

CONTENTS

practics, metaleptics, sync, understanding, evolution, meta-
evolution, hyper-evolution, thinking, critique, deconstruction,
reconstruction,post-foundation, refraction, diagram, difference,
distributedness, histriography, psychology, panpsychism,
liberation, commons, oppression, economics, political economy,
politics, transviduality, post-anarchism, pantheism, theophanic
post-theology, erotics, praxis, aesthetics, nothing, philosophy,
meta-philosophy, history of philosophy, beginning, dream

Reference Matter   220

Note to the Reader

This book is a short introduction to the task of producing a philosophy of networks for our hyperconnected age. The book has two primary parts. The *Introduction* explains why we might want a philosophy of networks, and the basics of what this could mean. This is done by sketching the technological, cultural, and historical contexts of this project, including the scientific and philosophical sources of its inspiration, while articulating many of the project's primary concerns in the process. The *Manifesto* which follows then presents, in hypercondensed and programmatic form, the project as a whole, describing in microcosm what it might mean to view the world and everything in it as composed of networks of networks, and the implications this can have for a wide variety of fields.

While the *Introduction* emphasizes accessibility and explanation, the *Manifesto* emphasizes compactness, intensity, and scope. Minor repetitions of core notions between these texts allow each to be comprehensive in what it sets out to do, such that the *Introduction* and *Manifesto* can be read either together or separately, and the notes are designed to be separable for each part for this reason. Those who wish to read the book from front to back, however, will find that any topic explained in the *Introduction* is always, after a brief recap, dealt with in greater depth and breadth in the *Manifesto*. In addition, the notes for both sections emphasize, whenever possible, sources which, like this book, aim to speak to both general readers and specialists, in the hope that readers who are new to any of the topics mentioned can learn about them for themselves.

Because of the brevity of this book, the task of grounding, explaining, and describing the ramifications of many of the claims made are necessarily left to future texts of what I have come to call "the networkological project." At present, three additional books in the *Networkologies* series are nearly complete, and more are already in progress. While it is unusual to work on several books at once rather than publish them in series, I found that this fit the networked nature of the subject matter, allowing me to keep the form as well as content of these texts refractively networking between the volumes. As this network of texts was coming to completion, however, I wrote some brief introductory texts which took on a life of their own, a dense and wide-ranging *Manifesto*, and its more user-friendly *Introduction*, and this book is the result.

The wider networks of which this book is only a part, however, are not limited to the printed page. The ideas presented here are crystallizations of notions I have worked to produce by means of an extensive set of writings on a wide variety of topics, which are available on my website at http://networkologies. wordpress.com.

Brooklyn, NY
Spring 2014

Acknowledgments

Writing several volumes worth of interconnected books before publishing the first would never have been possible without the amazingly supportive and creative environment provided by the School of Liberal Arts and Sciences at Pratt Institute in Brooklyn, New York. My department chair Ira Livingston was an incredible mentor through the process of giving birth to a first book, and it was his encouragement to follow my passions freely that really gave me permission to pursue this fully. Dean Toni Oliviero took the risk of hiring such a young teacher, giving me the freedom to develop and publish as I chose. And my amazing colleagues have provided the ideal creative environment. Jonathan Beller and Ethan Spigland were perfect partners in serious intellectual and political games, I have learned so much from both of you. Gregg Horowitz, Lisabeth During, and Jeffrey Hogrefe, along with Jon, Ethan, and Ira, read parts of the manuscript and gave crucial feedback. And my other amazing colleagues, including Stephanie, Ann, Mendi, Uzma, Jennifer, Danny, Tracie, Suzie, Nelson, and Christian, along with Gloriana and Danielle, all the amazing students, and our new Dean Andrew Barnes and new Chair Maria Damon, have made Pratt a wonderful place to grow.

Many teachers and advisors were also a great inspiration. Emily Apter was an amazing dissertation advisor who had faith in me and was a crucial influence. Three additional mentors had a profound impact on the way I think: Eva Geulen taught me how to read, Kaja Silverman taught me how to see, and DorisAnn Markowitz taught me how to create. In addition, Richard Sieburth and José Esteban Muñoz were wonderful mentors and teachers. And I will never forget the amazing experience of studying in truly inspirational classes taught by Fred Moten, Avital Ronnell, Carolyn Dinshaw, Patrick Deer, Barbara Spackman, Rachel Newcombe, Robert Cohen, Lisa

Duggan, Michael Schultz, Max Pensky, Martin Dillon, Donald Weiss, Hubert Farnsworth, and Tom Carter. I also learned so much having the chance to study during summer 2008 at the Complex Systems Summer Program at the Santa Fe Institute in Santa Fe, New Mexico. On the editorial side, Paul Ennis, Liam Sprod, Julia Steinmetz, and above all Dave Kim and Zach Slanger went above and beyond the call of duty in providing detailed commentary on the manuscript, especially Paul and Julia early on, and Dave and Zach at later stages. Extensive feedback from Jason Frenkel and Aaron Hollander was also incredibly helpful at various points along the way. And many thanks to Tariq Goddard and Trevor Greenfield at Zer0 Books for being so flexible with deadlines.

Family and friends have been an incredible support. My friends who became academics, including Ronit Fainman, John Hartman, Daniel Just, Caitlin Benson-Allot, Thomas Philip, Jason Hoffman, Dave Kim, and Aaron Hollander never cease to inspire me. Special thanks to Sam Albright and Jonathan Root for helping to keep me sane during periods of hard work (and to Jon for doing the diagrams). Many other friends have been a wonderful source of support, learning, and joy, including Stan, Tuck, Craig, Kristin, Brent, Steph, Donn, Jess, Shane, Ian, Ray, Geoff, Paul, Adam, Lisa, Dayna, Shay, Ersin, Ralph Parilla, and all the amazing folks of RBN, including Gerrit, Meika, Alan, Sydney, Nan, Candice, Dana, Marshall, Sam, and Jen. To my family, thank you so much for everything!: Dad (with his amazing meteor protection abilities), Grandpa Frank (our rock), Mike, Matt, Joseph, Ricky, Ashley, Adam, Marcella, Steve, Maria, and Carl. My dear doggie, Puggle, was my constant companion for many long hours spent researching and writing. Mimi Spiro was a steadfast source of inspiration and caring. My Mom and Aunt Barbara, as always, are my center in this world.

Finally, I'd like to dedicate this book to my dear Grandma Netta, who passed away as it was nearing completion. You lived with this book project's development almost as much as I did. Your love for me knew no bounds, and you always wanted the best for me. I will never forget. The gift of love you gave me is something I will carry with me all my days, and try to learn from. I will always love you. My soul is with you always, and yours with mine.

Brooklyn, New York
Spring 2014

Part One

Introduction to a
Philosophy of Networks

Living in a Networked Age

"Everything is connected." "All is One." "The One in the Many, the Many in the One." In today's digital hypermodernity, these insights, found in many ancient traditions around the world, are often reduced to sound-bite mantras. And yet, defying the seeming linearity of time and history, these notions now seem to haunt us, uncannily, not merely from the past, but also from the future. For our world today really is more connected, and more so by the day.

While few would deny this, it also seems clear that this new connectedness is happening in a manner quite different from what many had predicted. In place of yesterday's futures, so many visions of a triumphant "end of history," or a smoothing out of differences in a world full of discrete atoms, binary switches, orderly grids, frictionless precision, synchronized simplicity, or tidy certainties, things have taken a turn for the strange. Today's world is full of distributed agencies and virtual potentials, rippling deconstructions and flash-point emergences, all eluding easy categorization or comprehension, at least by means of yesterday's models. The future is not what it used to be: it is much more unpredictable, dangerous, sly, and interesting.

Although all truly *is* becoming one, this new connectedness is far from unitary. Rather, it is fractal, multiplying in layers within layers of burgeoning complexity. We live in an age of radical differentiations, cascades and crashes, decentralized affiliations and baroque complexifications, all of which shatter as they recompose and destroy as they create. It is as if we woke up one day, and suddenly all the points in the world had burst into webs, all the straight lines into nets of wires, and all the planes and volumes revealed textured layerings of branchings within branchings. Nothing is what it seemed it would be.

While the Internet and its new virtual worlds on the Web

2

nevertheless function as epitome and guide, mirror and engine, even these often appear to be mere refractions of some new, deeper, and profoundly discomfiting logics. In place of the euphorias of the early computer age, so many hopes of a borderless, post-Cold War techno-utopia, our world now dances to the rhythms of neo-religiosities and digital protests, video-game wars and financial weapons of mass destruction, invisible labor and long distance oppression, all coordinated by new agencies which are always beyond reach, everywhere and anywhere but where they appear to be. As space contracts, distances only increase, filling in with firewalls against cyber-feints, security checkpoints and walls both virtual and concrete, even as wormholes seem to continually arise in front of ever more obscurely distributed agencies.

We need to try to understand what these new forms of inter-connectedness could come to mean, and on their own radically new terms. But where to start? If there is one word which brings together the multiform new logics which are so rapidly changing the structure of our world, a word which describes the ways in which everything is fracturing so as to reconnect more intensely, it is the term "network." Whatever is changing our world seems to be indicated by this term, even as it all seems to mutate by the minute. And so it seems almost a truism to say at this point what seems so obvious: ours is a networked age, and seemingly more so by the day.

What this could mean for us, however, is much more difficult to determine, for it is not even easy to say how we got here. While the Internet clearly was an essential catalyst which helped bring this all about, that which brought these changes to critical mass, it is also perhaps merely a symptom. For long before we began to link computers together the world was growing networked, knitting itself together by means of satellite commu-nications and television signals, flows of products and currencies, telephone wires and railroad tracks before this, even

3

if we would never have thought to call these changes networked at the time.[1] What is more, scientists are increasingly showing that the physical and biological world from which we evolved was already networked to the core.[2] Perhaps then we have only begun to see the ways in which the world was always already networked, as if waiting for us to remove the blinders of our more orderly, modernist inspired dreams. If so, the Internet itself could then simply be a messenger of things to come, or a strange sort of return home, even if one which clearly developed the networks in the world to both quantitatively and qualitatively new levels of possibility.

Whether or not the past was always already networked, or we are just learning to see this, it seems clear that the rules of the games which dominated humankind for millennia are changing in dramatic ways. With each passing year, space appears less like a grid, and time less like a linear progression, even as neither seems to be returning to the simple bordered terrains or cyclical seasonal patterns of old. Notions like before and after, cause and effect, ancient and modern all seem to shift relative to changes in the gravity of our new spatio-temporal intertwinings, with so many crystalline webs of potential pasts and plural futures continually reworking our positionality even if we stand still. Nettime and netspace are now distributed in webs which continually re-update, shimmering and flickering in relation to each other.[3] producing new landscapes which transform, deepen, and layer without necessarily progressing or pointing out a privileged direction or orienting trajectory. Compressing and decompressing, the spacetime of networks loops back into itself, creating new rhythms within and between its locations, shattering and recomposing what was solid into dynamic symmetries in fluid fabrics with new habits and structures all of their own. Futureshock turns to whiplash quite quickly in today's virtual kaleidoscopy, where morphing planes and crenellated surfaces seem to enjoy swallowing histories in their wake.

In such a world it is hard to even know who, never mind what, we are becoming. For we are increasingly composed of so many quasi-living distributed intelligences, meshes of data, images, and commodities, all of which seem to increasingly manipulate us according to their own sub- and supra-human desires, fears, hopes, and dreams. Assemblages of screens and avatars, interfaces and software platforms, digital communities and semi-anonymous agencies, we now find fibers and channels, flows and feedbacks, patterns and prostheses where we once thought there were human beings. And yet, within all this, all of our selves still seem to need to find some form of orientation, some way to gain a hold on the changes we clearly unleashed on the world, but which seem to be quickly redefining anything and everything in and between whatever, wherever, and whoever we thought we used to be.

No matter how things got this way, no matter what we thought the future would be, it seems clear that the time to understand networks, and what they can mean for us, is now. And there is definitely an urgency to this. For our world is increasingly shaken by crises which seem to be describable only in networked terms, from financial crashes to terrorist organizations and digitized militaries, to changes in modes of organizing protests and revolutions, to shifts in how we relate to our everyday work, leisure, and socialization. And this is only the start. For our networks are on the cusp of producing revolutions in bio- and nanotech, and when this comes about, they will truly have the power to rework the very foundations of the biological and physical worlds which made all this possible, and in ways which are likely to further synergize with our increasingly webbed hyper-virtual realities.

If we want to intervene in these processes, to partake in these new interweavings rather than simply be recreated by forces of our making but increasingly beyond our control, we need to begin to be able to think and act on these new terms. Static territories, rigid boundaries, linear trajectories, flat surfaces, and unitary individuals, all the basic components of the world of yesterday need to be recast. In order to truly deal with the challenges of our age, we will need to learn how to think, act, experiment, learn, value, and perhaps even dream networkedly. We need a new worldview: a philosophy of networks for our hyperconnected age.

•

Networks – and Philosophy?

But what exactly does the notion of a "network" even mean? Certainly the term is everywhere today. And yet, the meanings attached to this notion, at least in everyday speech, are far from clear. It is as if the term were designed to proliferate and slip away from us, to multiply and increase in intensity, functioning differently in ever more situations, moving from tired and hackneyed to surprisingly different and back again, giving rise to new possibilities in the circuits of flight in between. Hypervisible and so obvious as to be often taken for granted, networks have become such a part of the fabric of daily life that they are like the air our techno-bodies breathe, even as it is often unclear precisely what they are, or could be. Trying to pin down the essence of networking can be an experience of vertigo, of an oddly centerless centricity, as if the sense of networking is continually dematerializing and recrystallizing in ever shifting prisms of color which give us back reworked versions of where we used to be. Perhaps the trick then is to learn to ride the waves of networking first, and from there figure out what there is to be seen.

All of what I have been describing managed to manifest itself in the process of writing this book. Whenever people asked me what I was working on, I responded by saying a philosophy of networks, and was then almost always asked if this was some sort of study of the impact of social networking. That is, the idea that philosophy and networks could have anything in common seemed strange to most. But rather than something like a sociology of networks, this project aims to truly be a *philosophy* of networks, an attempt to think what networks and our networked age could come to mean in the widest possible sense. And so I would reply to my questioners by saying that while this project is not unrelated to technologies like the Internet or social networking, it is more about networks and networking as such, about how anything and everything we have ever experienced can be thought of as networked, and why anyone would want to view the world this way. My questioners then usually expressed a mixture of confusion and curiosity. When I pushed this, I found that while anyone I spoke to could give examples of networks all around them, few could really say exactly what a network itself might mean. This project finds one of its points of entry into the pressing social issues of our times in this productive ambiguity.

None of which is to say, however, that popular notions of networking are all there is on the subject, for in fact, the science and mathematics of networks have some rather precise notions of what it means to network, and this project will draw extensively upon these, expanding them so that they can be applied beyond the traditional domains of mathematics and science. Nevertheless, I found that as I began to rework scientific and mathematical notions of networking to make them more flexible, pushing them to their limits so that they could be applied to new types of situations, the terms would often mutate ever so slightly, or even fracture, until they gave rise to more branching networks of terms and concepts. Each time I thought I had finally managed to grasp what was really at stake with networks themselves, they seemed to slip away, as if trying to defy any attempt at grasping them conceptually. There was an unsettling multiplicity at work, one which I increasingly began to feel pertained to the very attempt to conceptualize networks, with implications for how networks are transforming the world around us, and what our potentials for networked futures could be.

And so, while what follows will draw extensively upon contemporary mathematics and science, and will be careful not to conflict with any of the findings in these fields, it will rework many of the often pre-networked aspects related to these. And it will do so in a way which also goes beyond the manner in which science and mathematics traditionally limit themselves to issues of quantity, such that it becomes possible to speak about how networks relate to issues of interpretation, value, culture, ethics, politics, and more. While the science and mathematics of networks will remain crucial sources, this will ultimately be a work of philosophy. But it will hardly be a traditional one, for it will also attempt to rethink what is meant by philosophy in light of networking.

Nevertheless, many seem to feel today that we are no longer living in a time in which philosophy can really say anything worthwhile at all, and certainly philosophy seems hardly relevant to most people in our world today. To most, philosophy seems to be something that specialists do in universities, far from the concerns of the everyday. But the general skepticism about philosophy today can be seen as the result of some very constricted notions about what it means to do philosophy, and the prevalence of these ideas not only in "mainstream" culture, but amongst those who "do" philosophy for a living. This lack of imagination limits not only philosophy, but also the role it plays in culture, even when it is most needed. For perhaps philosophy is simply what happens whenever we try to describe how the world looks to us as a whole, here and now,[4] in a way which can help us map our potentials for thought and action. Philosophy then would not need to try to be beyond time, place, and culture, but rather, speak from and to these, such that perhaps every culture engages in philosophy, even when it seems to be doing other things.

In this sense, the so-called "death of philosophy" in our world today can then be seen as an opportunity.[5] For it is only when past forms of thinking seem naïve or less relevant than before that we can begin to question anything and everything, including what we mean by thinking. Each age needs to reinvent philosophy, to learn to dream anew about what it might mean to think in regard to the challenges of the times, and hopefully, point towards ways to help make the world a slightly less oppressive place. And if philosophy is viewed as the manner in which we try to make sense of the big picture in regard to how it appears from here and now, then this would mean that since networks are changing our world they need to be considered a proper subject for philosophy.

That said, to think that it might be possible to truly philosophize about networks in the manner of the past, particularly when networked approaches to neuroscience and artificial intelligence present some radically new notions of precisely what is meant by thought and thinking, would be some creative imagineering indeed. Networked times call for networked means. This project therefore will not simply philosophize *about* networking, or apply traditional notions of what philosophy might mean to networking. Rather, it will work to rethink philosophy as networking, to produce a philosophy *of* networks, in all senses of these terms. For by reimagining everything in the world as forms of networking, it may become possible to get a sense of what networks have to show us, not only about science and technology, but about what our world and even ourselves could become. And in doing so, it may even be possible to return philosophy to something that can matter to everyone, as a lived practice beyond universities, more in sync with our contemporary and potential future forms of networking.[6]

This is the task that what I have come to call "the networkological project" sets for itself. What follows is a thought experiment. Its goal is to see if everything in the world, from matter to markets, organisms to molecules, brains to societies, languages to love, can be seen as composed of networks of networks. The hope is that this can help reframe some of the impasses that dominate our world today, so as to indicate pathways towards new and potentially better ways of navigating the challenges of our increasingly complex networked realities. Welcome to the world of networkologies.

Building on the Science
and Mathematics of Networks

The project to develop an entire worldview based on networks luckily does not have to start from scratch. During the second half of the twentieth century, the science and mathematics of networks, a major component of what is often called "complex systems science," began to revolutionize a variety of fields of study in a manner which continues today, and which can provide a starting point for this project. Developing from cybernetic, chaos, information, graph, and systems theories, complex systems approaches bring together a variety of research modalities. What unites them is the notion that in order to understand many of the more difficult and interesting aspects of our world, it is necessary to not only get a sense of how the parts of a system function individually as isolated units, but also in regard to how they interact with each other and their environments as wholes.[7] By showing how the intertwining of entities in dynamic webs can lead to effects which were not predictable from the distinct form of the parts involved, this more holistic approach has led to an ability to understand many phenomena in the world which often previously defied scientific modeling.

Complex systems science is a relational and network-oriented approach to scientific thinking. Opposed to various forms of "reductionism,"[8] complex systems research shows how modes of interaction between relatively simple parts can give rise to highly complex behaviors. For example, individual ants have limited brain capacity, yet colonies of ants can build massively complex dens, just as individual birds or fish can flock, molecules of water can form a whirlpool, or investors in a financial market can start following each other into a cycle of bubble and crash. Using models which do not isolate individuals from each other, but look at how they interact in systems, researchers have increasingly been able to simulate and better predict the behaviors of such systems, often using explicitly networked models. While the field began by modeling relatively simple systems, such as flocks of birds and ant colonies, these were only the beginning. Artificial neural networks, for example, have revolutionized artificial intelligence, giving rise to simulations which model the basic components of living brains and which, unlike more traditional forms of artificial intelligence, can learn, forget, associate, and even guess in ways shockingly similar to the thinking styles of highly developed organisms. Insights from this work are increasingly helping to guide the study of the human brain, as well as exerting a profound impact on what computation and intelligence have come to mean in a variety of fields.[9]

All of these developments have occurred, however, by means of software run on non-networked, binary, "serial" computers, like the type normally seen on desktops. And so, while the software simulates networks, it runs on non-networked hardware. Though the development of non-binary, "parallel," networked computer chips is still only in the realm of technological fantasy, and will likely have to wait for advances in genetic, nano, or quantum computing, software simulations have provided the first glimpses of what is likely to come, even as the Web's virtual networks continue to pave the way. Even with our limited hardware, however, much has already been accomplished simply by starting to think and model the world by means of networks. Network models have been used to map the Internet, better understand social networks, predict crashes in markets and electrical grids, simulate crowd behavior, and design roadways to decrease congestion.[10] All that was needed, in a sense, was a change in perspective.

Complex systems science has led the way in all this, and can be seen as a complement to the networked technologies and ways of thinking which made the Internet and related developments so powerful. Nevertheless, complex systems science alone does not provide a full worldview based on networks. For while various branches of research in science and technology have been revolutionized by network thinking, there is more to life than science, and these new approaches have only begun to impact the way the world is thought of beyond the quantitative. And yet, networks are changing nearly everything about our world, with ramifications for how we raise our children, study, communicate, organize politically and socially, and so much more. If we are increasingly becoming networks, we still are networks which love and hate, produce art and war, hope and even dream. Unless our attempts to understand our increasingly networked world goes beyond science, technology, and the quantitative, all we will ever do is produce measurements and models which lead to faster and bigger versions of the status quo.

To produce a philosophy of networks, it will therefore be necessary to intertwine the study of science and technology with concerns of meaning and value. While it may seem strange to do so, we may soon have no choice. For as mentioned earlier, as we increase our ability to rework the physical and biological fabrics of who and what we are as individuals and a species, as well as the physical, biological, and cultural contexts in which we evolve, the discussion of meanings and values in relation to science and technology will become impossible to avoid. All of which lends credence to what many historians and theorists of science have long argued, namely, that interpretation and value are always at work within scientific and mathematical practices, even if these are often difficult to see except from the perspective of a different culture, or in relation to the past.[11] And yet, even from here and now, it seems ever more clear that from the drive to profit in relation to industry, to the government's desires to shape social policy or gain advantage in wars, our society is permeated by attempts to control teaching and research, and in ways which have enormous impact upon the way these describe the world.

While many argue that these exceptions prove the need for freedom from bias, it seems naïve to think we will ever be in a situation in which those who pay the bills and establish the rules will not impact the form of our inquiries. The claim of freedom from bias is perhaps simply one of its more concerning forms, one which assumes a "common-sense" standard which tends to support whatever structure is currently dominant in society, and which attempts to close down the possibility of questioning before it even starts. Rather than eliminate values from research, in whatever field, perhaps we should try to relate to them in a more substantive way, by asking what sort of values we want to have, and why. Arguably a more honest approach, this would certainly also be less reductionist, more relational, and more networked. And as will become clear in what follows, such an approach is also in resonance with some of the more radical advances in twentieth century science, mathematics, social theory, and, in many ways, the structure of networks themselves.

The rise of network thinking, then, can be an opportunity in more senses than one. Since networks make it much more difficult to see the world in isolated and restricted ways, the growing networking of the sciences, not only with the world beyond the lab, but by means of complex systems science itself, indicates a potential opportunity to imagine new ways of thinking the relation between these. For only if we can find ways to talk about how power and money, interpretation and values, quantity and quality, and hopes and fears impact all modes of inquiry and practice can we get beyond the fantasy that we can ever be truly objective, or that we should at least strive for what is often simply another way of reinforcing the way things currently are. A more networked, relational approach would be to try to understand how our values always do this anyway, whether we admit this or not, and to try to question what sort of values we might want, and how this could help guide our practices towards better futures. The hope is that perhaps this can

help produce futures which are not merely efficient or complicated, but potentially liberating as well.

What is a Network? A Brief Primer

Before going further, however, it is worth saying a little more about networks themselves, beyond their applications. When most people think of networks today, they often think of social networking, or the Internet, or networks for mobile devices. Ask scientists or mathematicians, however, and they are likely to think of network diagrams, specialized pictures which describe how aspects of the world hold their parts together.[12] Nevertheless, these same scientists often refer to the aspects of the world being diagrammed as networks themselves, simply because they can be represented by networks. What could it mean, then, for something to be networked, whether as an aspect of the world being diagrammed, or as a diagram itself?

At its simplest, a network is any whole, composed of parts, distinguished from a background, and composed of other parts and wholes, layered into each other at multiple levels of scale. Anything which can be thought of in this way can be seen as a network, which is a general way of thinking about how things intertwine, interact, and hold together. For example, a tree in the park can be seen as a network of branches and roots. This network is distinguished from a background, which includes the soil in which it grows, the air around it, and the rest of the park, and all of these composed of more networks in turn. There are cells in the roots and branches, and these are also networks, just as the tree is part of the park as a whole, both of which can also be seen as networks.

While this is a relatively concrete example, even dispersed aspects of the environment, such as the air surrounding the tree, the soil in which it grows, or the clouds in the sky above it are all networks, which is to say, parts connected to others, distinguished from a ground, and layered at multiple levels of scale. Even more abstractly, all these networks appear to me, the one in the park observing them, even as I am also a network, composed of more networks. The manner in which I perceive the tree as a network is also itself a result of the way in which we network together in the mode of intertwining generally called "perception." Whether considered from "inside" or "outside" a given observer, it is all networks, all the way down, simply of differing sorts.

While it might seem simple to say that everything is composed of networks, the descriptive potentials of this approach manifest in the different types of networking, and how this impacts the way networks relate to each other. Any network can *diagram,* or represent, any other, though abstract ones tend to be particularly good at describing the ways other networks hold together, which is to say, the ways they network their parts. For example, a network of lines can be used to represent the structure of the branches of a tree, just as a network of points against a ground can be used to indicate the layout of trees in the forest as a whole, even if these points are only linked together as a network implicitly by the ground between them. In all these cases, when a network resembles aspects of one or more other networks in this manner, whether this is done intentionally by a human or not, it diagrams it.

Diagramming describes how networks deal with issues of representation, recasting these notions, as networks tend to do, in more relational form. For networks can both diagram and be diagrammed, represented and representing, functioning as what linguists generally call signifier and signified.[13] Unraveling the reductive ways in which representation has often been described in and beyond linguistic models in the past, networks provide more polymorphous ways of theorizing what has often previously been seen as rigidly dichotomous.

All of what is described above can be refined by means of terms drawn from the science and mathematics of networks.[14] From such a perspective, the parts connected in a network can be recast as *nodes*, which are joined together by links. Nodes and links are always surrounded by backgrounds, or *grounds*, which are aspects of the more general *ground* of which they are themselves parts. While grounds may appear unified, whenever they are examined more closely, they are always composed of more networks, which then reveal their own grounds in turn. Considered together, nodes, links, and grounds give rise to networks, even as each is ultimately composed of more networks in turn. The manner in which parts and wholes of networks contain each other gives rise to layers which are called *levels, or levels of scale*. Nodes, links, grounds, and levels are the primary *aspects* of networks in the world. In what follows, the concept of networks in their most abstract sense will be referred to as *the network diagram*, a concept composed of the sub-concepts, or *elements*, of node, link, ground, and level, all of which are abstractions from the networks which manifest in the world.

Beyond these basics, the networkological project will examine the manner in which the nodes, links, grounds, and levels are the products of various processes. From this perspective, nodes can therefore be seen as produced, maintained, and transformed by processes of *noding*, links by *linking*, grounds by *grounding*, levels by *leveling*, and networks by *networking*. For example, when a tree gives rise to buds, it produces nodes, and this is an example of noding. When people make friends at a party and exchange contact information, they create new links, an example of linking. An ocean serves as a medium, support, container, and context for the fish within it, and in this sense, the ocean can be seen as grounding the fish. A more abstract form of grounding can be seen in the way in which descriptions of the world tend to justify themselves in relation to others, such that the contexts provided by these justifications act as grounds for the ideas in question. Grounds are intimately related to how nodes and links change, for they relate these to processes beyond them, and vice-versa. Grounds, like levels, are in many ways trickier than nodes or links, for they are necessarily both inside and outside of the networks in question. Beyond noding, linking, and grounding, there is also leveling, the manner in which networks give rise to levels, such as when an embryo divides from a mass of cells into layers of skin, bones, nerves, muscles, etc. And leveling, in turn, is intimately related to notions of the emergence of networks from each other, such as the way in which an embryo can ultimately give rise to a living human being.

The temporary solidification of processes which gives rise to particular nodes, links, grounds, and levels is what many discourses have called a form of *reification*, a term which literally means "thing-ification" (from the Latin word *res*, for "thing").[15] Reification is necessary to produce and maintain networks, even if it can come to dominate, paralyze, and stultify their ability to grow and change when taken to extremes.

While some degree of reification is not only necessary but also essential to the formation, support, change, and development of any and all networks, the term reification will generally be used in what follows to describe what happens when reification itself reifies, which is to say, when it is taken to an extreme and becomes harmful and "over"-reifies.

Reification will also be used to describe the way in which relatively reified entities tend to appear solid and fixed, even if they are ultimately composed of networks from within, and are aspects of other networks from without, despite seeming appearances to the contrary. While not all reification is "over"-reification, because our world is so dominated by reification and its effect, it will often be the subject of networkological critique in what follows.

While not all of the more abstract uses of notions such as noding, linking, grounding, leveling, and reification are explicitly referred to in complex systems science in the senses described above, these notions are nevertheless implicit in the general outlook whereby these approaches describe the formation, maintenance, and transformation of nodes, links, grounds, and levels in the world. In all these cases, the notion of a network is simply drawn from what all networks have in common. Everything in the world can be seen as a network, and in this sense, to call anything in the world a network simply means to see it relationally, as a network composed of networks, linked to others, layered in levels, against a ground, and as an aspect of various processes and reifications. Networks are then, more than anything, a way of looking at the world, a shift in perspective, a lens which makes everything appear networkedly.

•

Complexity, Emergence, and Robustness

While there is a lot more in the details, that is it, that is the basic model. Applying this to a variety of situations, network thinking fundamentally reworks approaches to the world based on notions of reified entities, rigid binary distinctions, linear developments, monocausal explanations, and other less relational formations, and replaces these with dynamic polyform networked models which are able to do the same work, but without the limitations of these more traditional approaches. Some of the radical implications of this set of transformations, however, only become clear when networked models are extended to deal with issues of how networks change, how they can be used to redescribe aspects of our world beyond traditional forms, and the ways this impacts the production of values and interpretations in the process. To illustrate this set of concerns, it makes sense to return to the science of complex systems, essentially the science of applied network thinking.

Complex systems, often called complex adaptive systems, are generally described by researchers as those which are "more than the sum of their parts," for they tend to be difficult to predict from knowledge of their components.[16] They are also often described as "non-linear" systems, for it is difficult to tell what they will do next by means of simple, predictable, linear modes of extrapolation or mathematical modeling. For example, when a drain is opened under a pool of water, a vortex, also known as a whirlpool, will often result. This new form of organization, which in no way resembles that of the water molecules involved or the shape of the pool in which the water sits, nevertheless draws upon all of these in interaction to take the form it does. What is more, this form shifts and adapts to its environment, such that if an obstacle is introduced into the whirlpool, it will begin to swirl around it. But the precise way in which the vortex moves around an obstacle cannot be fully predicted in advance, for minor perturbations can lead to large scale changes.

All of this happens spontaneously, such that complex adaptive systems are also often described as "self-organizing," or "emergent."[17] According to complex systems science, self-organization is promoted by a particular set of conditions, which include: diverse components, distributed organization, meta-stability, and feedback between aspects and environment in a manner which is itself diverse, distributed, and meta-stable, thereby potentiating sync between aspects, the emerging whole, and environment. When all these conditions are met, not only will a system spontaneously self-organize to greater complexity, it will generally continue to do so, at least until one of these factors begins to fall out of sync with the others.

For example, in the case of a whirlpool, once a drain is opened in a pool of water, a stable source of energy is provided due to the pull of gravity. This pull acts unevenly on the water molecules, because it is refracted by the mild attractive and repulsive properties between the molecules, giving rise to diverse flows and currents which all compete to get down the drain first. As some flows begin to move down the drain, the increase in speed affects the way these forces act upon each other, with the pulls towards working together and those towards pushing apart coming into balance. Flows begin to modulate each other in feedback, not centrally, but each molecule and flow in relation to those around them, giving rise to distributed modes of organization in which no single molecule or flow predominates, but all contribute. The result is a form of balance and sync which manifests in the novel form of a whirlpool, which could not be predicted in advance from the shapes of the molecules or the container, even as it is influenced by these.

Whirlpools do not generally remain stable or develop much further, however, because they tend to run out of energy quickly, and the relative homogeneity of their parts makes it difficult for them to develop new forms of complexity which could work to maintain or grow the system beyond this. Complicating this is the fact that while a whirlpool is much more organized than a simple mass of water molecules, and hence indicates a jump in complexity, it also goes through energy much faster, and in fact, all complex systems require energy to maintain and potentially increase in complexity. Living systems, for example, eat, and they also produce wastes, and only a steady flow of energy, such as that of the sun, can maintain and grow complexity, as well as deal with wastes produced in the process. Without developing distinct new systems to find new sources of energy and take care of wastes, the system is limited in its ability to maintain itself or grow.

The manner in which complex systems relate to energy helps explain why complex systems are often referred to as *dissipative systems*, for they consume energy and turn it into waste, dissipating potential in order to produce ordered complexity. In the process, however, they produce new forms of complexity, which can then give rise to new potentials, some of which can work to address these concerns. And so, while humans eat and produce wastes at a staggering rate, we can also farm and build sanitation systems, not to mention build computers and write novels, all things whirlpools obviously cannot do.[18] What is more, complexity tends to be self-potentiating, giving rise to not only more quantity of complexity as it grows, but new qualities and intensities as well, all of which can then feed back into the process of complexification. While complex systems dissipate energetic potentials in their environments, they can give rise to whole new ways of being in the world which can enrich these environments in new ways in the process.

While complex systems describe one of the primary ways novelty enters the world, not all intricate aspects of the world are complex. Machines such as cars or laptops, while incredibly *complicated,* are not complex. These sorts of systems are only designed for specific purposes, do not come about in the world relatively spontaneously in the right conditions, are unable to adapt and change themselves in relation to their environments, and neither repair themselves nor grow, and hence, are relatively limited and rigid. While complicated systems are often very good at particular things, such as being strong or fast, they are often limited to very particular ways of relating to the world beyond them. They rarely surprise, and are simply not designed to produce novel ways of relating to the world, nor to adapt to changes or grow and evolve in the manner of organisms.

While complicated systems can be extremely powerful, it is this ability to develop in new and more intense ways, to adapt to changes and rework themselves, not only in terms of quantity but also of quality, which makes complex systems truly unique. When complex systems self-organize in ways which increase their complexity, whether in quantity or quality, this is what complex systems science calls *emergence*.[19] Emergence itself comes in many degrees and forms. A whirlpool is an example of the emergence of a simple physical complex adaptive system, if one which is relatively short-lived. Living organisms are more developed forms of emergence, and they can give rise to new forms of emergence in turn, such as learning and evolution, none of which could be predicted by an examination of the structure of any particular part of the organism or its brain, but only by the relational intertwining between these in particular sets of circumstances. Beyond physical and biological emergences, cultural advancements can also be seen as forms of emergence, from the flocking of birds to the development of language in humans, and all of these feed back into physical and biological emergences to potentiate them further.

While complex systems are dissipative of energy, they do not necessarily destroy the contexts which produce them, and in fact, most do not, or they would not be around for long. When complex systems grow and develop in sustainable relation to their environments, this is what complex systems science calls *robustness*.[20] While all systems ultimately steal energy and materials from their environment, such as the manner in which all life on Earth feeds off the sun, robust systems are those which are able to grow and develop in relation to their environment in the least destructive and maximally creative ways, establishing feedback relations with their environment so that they do not destroy the conditions for the emergence of themselves or their environments in the present or future.

Robustness is potentiated by the same factors as emergence, but applied not only to the system in question, but also its relations to its contexts and beyond the needs of the present moment. It can therefore be thought of as a meta-emergence which syncs up multiple emergences in and across the boundaries between entities, systems, levels of scale, time scales, and beyond. When systems are not only emergent but also robust, they emerge emergently in the future as well as the present. For example, evolutionary populations tend to be robust in relation to their environments, while whirlpools, which simply go through their energy supply and then dissolve, are not. Systems which are able to account for changes over time, such as the way evolution stores memory in DNA, or humans can remember and learn by means of their complex brains, tend to potentiate the emergence of robustness, even as other aspects of these systems may tend to favor short-term benefit over long-term development.

The valuation of robustness, or the sustainable emergence of complexity, is implicit in much of complex systems science, whether in the study of physical systems, living systems, or cultural systems such as economies. Complex systems science studies the ways in which order sustainably emerges from chaos, and describes strategies for promoting this to evolve systems, particularly human systems, towards more robust conditions of sustainable growth and development.

While the implicit valuation of robustness is at work in much of complex systems science, it will be the explicit ground of the ethics of the networkological project. That is, while complex systems science views robustness as simply the common-sense way to produce more and better forms of growth, the networkological project will work to develop this into a fully-fledged ethics. Based on the valuation of the sustainable emergence of complexity, or robust complexification in regard to ourselves and our contexts, the networkological project sees robustness as a notion that can help develop an ethical way of thinking about a wide variety of issues beyond the more traditional and often individualistic ethics less in sync with the needs of our rapidly mutating networked age.

The Brain as a Model for Philosophy: Artificial Neural Networks and Beyond

For the reasons described above, the valuation of the robust emergence of complexity will guide much of this project. And if robustness is to serve as a potential guide for values, that which can ground the meanings which ground actions and choices in the world, then the process of studying robust systems in the world can help us gain insights on how robustness tends to develop. From this it may be possible to glean potential strategies to help us network ourselves with our contexts more robustly now and in the future. Of all the robustly emergent systems in the world, however, one stands out. Even today, despite the rapid growth of the Web, the Internet is hardly the most complex, emergent, or robust network on the planet; this is still the massive complex of dynamic networks within each and every human brain. Learning about the brain can teach us valuable lessons about the emergence of robustness, and in ways which can help us imagine new ways to emerge in relation to our contexts, in and beyond the confines of our heads.

Nevertheless, up until recently, the brain was a mystery, its form baffling and its secrets beyond us. It was therefore often described as simply a place of residence for some ineffable spirit or soul. But today, advances in artificial intelligence and cognitive neuroscience have shown how the structure of the brain is in many ways that of a radically distributed complex network, one whose form is similar in many ways to that of the Internet, even if yet massively more developed.

All of which can help explain why, for me, this project crystallized when I learned about how artificial neural networks function. Artificial neural networks are, in many ways, the manner in which the principles of complex systems science manifest in the field of artificial intelligence, for they are simulations of networks of virtual nerve cells. These computer models have shown that a handful of wiring types can be used to link these simple units in ways which can give rise to the sorts of behaviors that form the basic building blocks of human-style intelligence. Artificial neural networks have shown themselves capable of remembering, recognizing, associating, deciding, categorizing, and feeding memories back into each other over time. What is most shocking, however, is that these networks are not programmed. Rather, they learn from experience, which is to say, they are taught, like infants. When overloaded with too much information, they forget and blur details, and when given incomplete information, they guess, and if they had enough opportunity to learn from enough prior experience, they tend to guess correctly. Research in artificial neural networks is increasingly influencing research in the cognitive neuro-sciences, with these two fields starting to feed back into one another.[21]

What makes artificial neural networks unique is their form. Unlike "serial" computers which make use of strings of binary switches, artificial neural networks are non-binary and networked in structure, and hence are often described as forms of "connectionist" or "soft" computing, in that they do not handle tasks in linear sequence, but rather, make use of many distributed agents working to solve a problem in "parallel." If you try to look at how they are "programmed," aside from the basics of how each simulated neuron works, there is no code, just a series of connections and flows of feedback between simulated neurons. Each node is therefore slightly distinct from those around it by means of the connections it links, which continue to "rewire" themselves as new inputs arrive, in a form similar to that of living brains. From there, artificial neural networks emerge on their own, for they are diverse, distributed, meta-stable, and promote multiple forms of feedback which have these qualities as well. Though the technology behind artificial neural networks is still in its infancy, the fundamental building blocks are all there, in many senses waiting for our hardware to catch up with what they can do at the realm of software, and produce networked chips which can rewire themselves on the fly, beyond our current network simulations on more static silicon.[22]

Despite the radicality of these developments, since they have yet to produce technologies which impact large groups of people directly, many have never heard of them. And so, while in many senses I have been working on the networkological project in one form or another for as long as I have been studying philosophy, during most of this time I did not realize that networks would end up becoming the means to articulate the new forms of emergent relationalism I was trying to produce. And this is perhaps hardly surprising, for to most people, even those who study philosophy, networks and philosophy are very different things, with seemingly very little in common. But after years of studying philosophy, and trying to articulate a new, relational, immanent, and increasingly emergent way of looking at the world, I discovered, to my surprise, that networked models in science and mathematics were working on tools that could help bring these concerns together.

Nevertheless, when I first learned how artificial neural networks function, it was like a revelation: all I had been trying to articulate in philosophy was right here, given simulated-yet-concrete form, right in front of me. For if even the most complex forms of human thought can be described as produced by means of networks, such that perhaps mind is simply what it feels like to be a network of this complexity from the inside, then perhaps everything in the world, down to its very fabric, can be seen as aspects of one fundamentally self-differing stuff which complex-ifies by means of networking. Needless to say, this led to years of research on my own to learn the necessary science and mathe-matics, with this project as the result.

Artificial neural networks can be a technology whose structure transforms the way we see the world, even though these simulations remain, at the time of the writing of this book, still a relatively obscure technology of which few philosophers, not to mention others, even know exist. But the reason why artificial neural networks can have such a profound impact on the way we see the world is not because of the new smart devices and even artificial minds to which they might lead. Rather, it is because they deconstruct, by means of their very form, some of the most widespread and persistent myths which have kept non-networked thinking firmly entrenched in many of our ways of looking at ourselves and our world.

For what artificial neural networks show, in their very existence, methods, and startling successes, is how even the most complex manifestations of our world, up to and including those of the human mind, can be seen as produced by networks. The very fact that any of this is possible nevertheless debunks some of the most long-standing myths of Western culture. What the new science of networks has shown then, and artificial neural networks in particular, is that the types of experience given rise to by the human brain can be produced from the networking of the stuff of the world with itself. What matters isn't what is networked, but how. Nothing less, and nothing more. This could possibly change the way we see almost everything.

Such a perspective is also increasingly supported by developments in contemporary neuroscience which are increasingly calling the traditional dualistic views of mind and body into question. Scientists are increasingly coming to the conclusion that what we call thought and consciousness does not arise in any one particular center in the brain, but rather, is the result of a play of shifting networks of synced pulsations within radically dispersed centers of the brain, and in a way which is fundamentally intertwined with the networks of the body in an indissociable way. Viewed as such, consciousness and our sense of who we are results from a dynamic and shifting network of syncing pulsations, layered within relatively more stable distributed nets of neural connections, which nevertheless continually rewire themselves as well in regard to continual flows of feedback from each other, our bodies, and our environment.[23]

What is more, advances in experimental robotics and "embodied cognition" seem to indicate that we should increasingly begin to think of the very physical structure of our bodies as a form of thinking, in that the brain relies on the structure of our tendons, bones, and muscles, honed by the "thought" process of evolution itself, to do most of what we might assume are the "calculations" which make coordinations between movements possible. In this sense, the brain could not think the same way it does without the body "thinking" with it. The same could be said in regard to emotions which, through the limbic system, modulate the general relations between brain and body by means of complex maps of bodily aspects present in the brain, allowing for feedback between brain and body in ways which impact global functioning in the form of moods and emotions. Thought is distributed beyond the brain, with the brain functioning as a relatively centerless network, with our sense of a self as just one more aspect of this, a dynamically emergent network effect amongst others.[24]

There are many reasons why such a radically immanent, relational, and networked perspective on the world is liberating from the reifying and hierarchical binary divisions and dualisms which have haunted Western philosophy and science for hundreds of years. For if mind and matter are radically different, as many have argued since the time of René Descartes, then it becomes difficult to say how mind and matter could influence each other, or how mind could arise from matter. If, however, mind is seen as some basic form of feeling present within any and all matter, then notions of "thought" or "mind" can be seen as what happens when matter complexifies the way it feels itself in relation to its world. Ideas would then be the way we feel our brains, feelings would be how we feel the way our brains feel their relations with our bodies, and sensations would be how we feel the way our brains feel our bodies. There is then no longer a need to believe in a firm split between mind and matter, nor to imagine all that makes humans or even life so special as being fundamentally different from the world itself, for what this indicates is that everything we need to understand the brain is inherent in the patterns whereby it folds its pulsating flesh. The need to posit something uniquely human, something which separates us fundamentally from the networks of the world, vanishes.

As terrifying as this might at first seem, it can also be seen as potentially liberating. It allows us to imagine that everything that makes humans so special might also exist, in simpler forms, in anything and everything. The world looks quite different from such a perspective, for rather than some ineffable or magical quality, "mind" can then be seen as simply what matter feels like from the inside. Since our brains are the most complex forms of dynamic matter we know, they have the most complex types of experience we know, but are not composed of stuff fundamentally different from that of the rest of the world. Viewed as such, the binary rifts which have dominated so much of the Western project would then find the capstone of their arch, the uniqueness of human experience, removed from its central position in our worldviews. There is no need to imagine an eternal "soul," nor some transcendent "God" needed to grant or guarantee this; it is all just networks of varying degrees of complexity feeling themselves from within and without. We demote ourselves, but in the process gain an entire world of gradations of complexifying networks of experience, and in place of a sense of radical jumps between matter and mind, mind and God, we have gradations of complexifications which allow us to see wonder everywhere and anywhere in differing degrees and forms, not merely in the traditional limited repositories.

Rather than mere materialism, the perspective opened up by

these developments allows us to see the world and everything in it as the result of complex networking. For if the potential for mind is simply the result of the networking of neurons, essentially living wires, and these are themselves the result of the dynamic networking of matter and energy, which are themselves networks of quantum events, then this means that the potential for human experience, and all we have ever felt or even dreamed, lies not in *what* things are, but in *how* they are intertwined. That is, what something is and what it can do is determined by how it networks, from molecule to emotion and thought and everything in between. If the human mind can be seen as produced by the networkings of matter, then so can anything else we have ever known. From such a perspective, every aspect of our world can then be seen as having infinite potential for emergence in and from itself, even if this can only ever be unleashed by means of complex robust networking.[25]

There are some surprising consequences of such a view, however. For we might then have to begin to wonder if non-living matters such as stones might in some way experience or "feel" the world around them as well, though this "feeling" would only be in a manner much more global and simple than that of the most basic organisms, and they would not "know" this, they would simply "be" this process of feeling. That is, an atom of hydrogen might be what a hydrogen-like way of feeling its contexts looks like, such that "being" hydrogen might be really, in a sense, a way of feeling the world "hydrogenly." Only animals with complex nervous systems, however, would be able to feel that they are feeling the world, and hence, would be able to become aware of this.

While it might seem odd to imagine molecules "feeling" things if they are not able to reflect on or be aware of this, this is just another way of describing how we already relate to them. We already say molecules are "attracted" to or "repulsed" by each other due to a variety of forces, and they even seem to make "decisions" in particular situations. When you break a stick over your knee, for example, the particular emergent breakages produce patterns which could hardly be predicted in advance, for they come from the complex interplay of a variety of micro-decisions, each the result of how any given aspect of that branch "feels" the impacts of the forces and stresses put on it by its environment. While these notions might at first seem odd, they are in fact not that far from how we already describe things; they simply extend this to the possibility that there could be some level of interiority at work within all matter, no matter how rudimentary.

While these notions might sound strange at first, they help solve a lot of problems which have made philosophers and scientists scratch their heads for centuries. For now there is no need to imagine how mind arises from matter, since the ability to "feel" is likely part of all matter, a capacity which increases not only quantitatively but also qualitatively as that matter increases in complexity, and particularly, as in the case of living entities like living organisms, this feeling begins to feed back onto itself, begins to feel itself feeling and to develop feelings about this, such as "caring" about its ability to continue to feel, and to potentially continue to do so at this level of complexity, or more, in the future. It is all networks and feedbacks between them, at many levels of scale. Since there is no reason why this might not be the case, nor any way we could prove or disprove this, at least anymore than we could prove or disprove the notion that other humans feel the same way we do, the reason for or against adopting such a position seems likely to be the worldview it can help produce, and the problems such an approach solves.

This all helps explain why scientists in artificial intelligence and neuroscience increasingly find the constraints imposed by the binary distinction between mind and matter unnecessary and untenable, and why they are starting to look for new paradigms. And so, scientists are once again beginning to see *panpsychism*, or the notion that everything in the world has something like "mind," even if in a very rudimentary way, as a viable scientific notion.[26] Despite the sound of the term, panpsychism is not in any way related to notions such as psychic powers, the paranormal, or anything like that. Rather, it is a philosophical term for the notion that, even in very simple form, all aspects of the universe "sense" or "experience" in some manner or another.

From such a perspective, a brain like ours has a complex way of feeling itself and the world simply because of the complex and dynamic form of its networked matter. Mind would then be simply what matter "feels" like from the inside. Such a worldview, famously articulated by Baruch Spinoza as a way to counter René Descartes' radical split between matter and mind, argues that mind and matter are simply two ways of looking at the same thing, with more complex matters having more complex minds, and mind being what matter "feels" like from the inside, from atoms to brains. Increasingly, scientists are coming to see this as a way of avoiding the need for a radical jump in nature which separates those aspects with mind from those without, and hence, as a way of getting around the impasses which arise from a binary and dualist approach to the study of brain and mind.

All the stuff of the world can then be seen as having the ability to feel, with thought and emotion (in the sense we know them) as the manner in which highly complex organisms do this. Computers seem to fail to think and feel like we do, but this would be not only due to their "serial" non-networked brain architectures, but also because they lack the complex networks of feedback which make humans reflect and feel their own processes of thinking, feeling, and acting in relation to their bodies. But any simple matter can become part of the complex thought and feeling of any system of which it becomes a part. And so, when we eat, the matter in our food becomes part of us, and gains the ability to think and feel, and when those parts breakdown, it loses this and returns to the world around us, even as our networks maintain thinking and feeling by recycling matters and energy to reproduce similar forms of networks within us, even if of continually different material components.

That which was formerly seen as transcendent of matter, such as life or consciousness, can therefore now be seen as immanent in matter, always already there, part of its potential, down to its very core. There is then no need to posit something like a "soul" or "spirit," for rather, these seem immanent to the very fabric of the world, even if this only ever seems to become apparent by means of complex networking. What makes some of this stuff able to come to feel its own ability to feel, to realize it experiences, to find the world meaningful, express values, and think is not then the result of some incomprehensible gap or leap within the stuff of the world, that is, unless this split is within the very stuff of the world itself, in every aspect, and in fact is that stuff itself. All that has previously been thought of as the "transcendent" aspects of our world can be seen as immanent within all matter, as a potential which emerges by means of the distributed, complex networking of the stuff of the world with itself, up to and including self-conscious thought, and potentially new forms of thinking and feeling which we have not yet even begun to dream.

Despite the often off-putting name, panpsychism, or the way in which relational, networked thinking relates to issues of mind and brain, matter and feeling, is an essential component of a networked worldview. Much of contemporary research at the forefront of artificial intelligence and cognitive neuroscience would make little sense without the holistic approach to questions of the relation of mind and matter it implies. As this project will work to show, there are many ramifications of this way of viewing the world, for not only does it mean that mind can now be seen differently, but in fact, that one of the most stubborn binary oppositions in the history of thought, one which served to anchor so many others, now can be recast. From this, it becomes possible to develop a worldview which is radically non-binary, fundamentally immanent, relational, distributively refractive, and emergently self-potentiating. While there will always be more restrictive aspects in our world, when recontextualized by means of such new models, they can hopefully no longer seem quite as inevitable or necessary. No longer supported by the human-centered exceptionalism of the split between mind and body, mind and matter, the single most important impediment to the development of a truly networked worldview falls away. The question then becomes what such a perspective on the world allows us to see, and how this might help us find better ways to deal with our world today.

Network Dynamics:
States, Processes, and Tendencies

Artificial neural networks, non-dualistic approaches to mind and matter, complex systems science, and the basic science and mathematics of networks provide many of the essential contexts for the networkological project as a whole. While most of what has been described so far has been adapted in a relatively straightforward manner from explicit or implicit aspects of contemporary complex systems science, the following sections will now describe in greater detail what a networked worldview looks like, moving beyond the traditional limitations of science and mathematics in the process. It will do this in ways which do not conflict with the findings of science, but which may often recontextualize or problematize some of the assumptions at work within these practices, while making it possible to link the insights of complex systems science with philosophy and social and cultural theory, economics and politics, in ways which have some potentially radical implications.

This section will work to say a little bit more about what networks are like in regard to dynamics and change. Building on the findings of a variety of disciplines in contemporary complex systems studies, the networkological project views all networks, even if they appear static, as ultimately dynamic at lower levels of scale, for they intertwine processes and reifications in ways which give rise to relatively stable networks, each of which is always a *pattern of balance, state, or symmetry* between change and stasis. Nodes, links, grounds, and levels are produced by the intertwining of processes in this manner, just as these are produced by other networks, and can give rise to others in turn. Processes of reification and *dereification, or dissolution,* exist in a continual game of balance, and either extreme can be dangerous to the survival and growth of any network.

All dynamic processes in networks are therefore expressions of the ways in which networks intertwine various forms of *potential*. Potential is always abstract until it unfolds into some form of *actualization*. For example, while the energy in sunlight can be seen as an abstract potential, the manner in which this can be used to help a plant grow on a given day would be a particular actualization of aspects of this potential, which could then be further actualized in turn. The more intensely networks contain one another, the more potential they have within them, even if they can only ever contain or release potential by networking with other networks.

Potential can be released to create change in the way networks relate to each other, and in ways which can maintain and develop the complexity of these networks if this potential is re-networked with them. For example, quantum phenomena wrap themselves into knots to give rise to various forces, and these forces intertwine to produce the various forms of matter and energy. These then intertwine with each other, giving rise to physical systems, organisms, and cultural systems around us. All of these are complexifications of potential by means of its networked intertwining in various forms of matter and energy, the simplest and most general forms of potential in our world. More complex forms of potential come about from the ways that matter and energy differentiate and intertwine in networks in relation to each other.

Those networks or aspects of networks which monopolize potential, and hence, have more control over other networks, are known as *hubs*. When a network has few hubs, and works to reduce the number of hubs in its surroundings, it is known as a *centralizing network*. Centralizing networks tend to be hierarchical and efficient, as well as rigid and limiting. These networks have a *reflective* form of organization, for they tend to unfold potentials so as to reproduce the content and form of their hubs in all their parts and wholes, and if possible, their inner and outer environments. This leads to a structure not unlike that of a hall of mirrors, with the hubs of the networks in question ultimately being all that is reflected. Like processes of reification and dereification, those of centralization and *decentralization* are determined relatively in relation to each other.

There are other types of networks, however, that exist between the extremes of centralization and decentralization, reifying and dereifying, and these are known as *distributed networks*. Because these networks tend to shift the composition of their parts and wholes in relation to a variety of influences, which impact each other in a spread out manner, they tend to not simply reflect the same form and content within and beyond them, but rather to coordinate a diverse if resonant set of contents and forms. While centralizing networks tend to exert control from the hubs to the periphery, and from the periphery to the rest of their contexts if possible, distributed networks modulate themselves and their relations to their contexts in a relatively decentralized manner. As such, they tend to resemble the structure of imperfect crystals rather than halls of mirrors, and so, the networkological project will also call distributed networks forms of *refractive* or *crystalline* modes of organization.[27]

Distributed networks are messier and less efficient than their more centralized counterparts, but are better able to adapt to change, both in regard to the world around them and from within themselves, for they have a more diverse set of resources at their disposal and have more flexible and responsive organizational structures. Centralizing networks tend to go into crisis at the slightest impurity or change in their environments, for their rigid modes of organization are easily destabilized by difference. In contrast, distributed networks can go into crisis when their contexts try to force them to begin to centralize, something which their divergent components and modes of organization do not easily allow. Conversely, they can also go into crisis if the dereifying and decentralizing tendencies within them get too strong, and begin to tear the network and its elements apart. Taken to its extreme, this can lead to the dissolution of the networks and elements involved.

Dissolution is always a possibility whenever networks change, but it also has potential rewards. When dissolution is only partial, it can actually be beneficial to the developments of networks in the area, for this is one of the ways in which *differentiation* comes about. When differentiation occurs in a relatively distributed manner, the minor differences in the local formations and modes of organization can give rise to the sorts of new and diverse networks which can provide the building blocks for new forms of networking in the future. When differentiation occurs in a manner which is overly controlled, however, it just gives rise to copies of the centralizing networks which produced them, and ultimately, just more of the same, often crowding out existing diversity and potentials in the process. Dissolution is not the only way novelty can arise, however, for networks can also differentiate due to sensitivity to local influences during the process of growth.

In all these cases, the form of a network, whether centralizing/reflective or distributed/refractive, as well as the many variations in between, are known as that network's *state, form, shape, mode of organization, or topology*.[28] Topologies have an enormous impact on how networks relate to other networks, and how they release and capture various potentials for change, growth, and action in the world. The reason for this is that the structure of networks determines the ways in which they control flows of potential within them at lower levels of scale, and in relation to their environments. In this sense, topologies are reifications and representations of the processes which give rise to them, even if they tend to feed back into these processes in turn, such that topologies tend to self-potentiate. That is, centralizing networks tend to become more centralized, and promote centralization in themselves in the world, unless something intervenes to halt this process, for they unfold potential in centralizing ways. Likewise, distributed networks tend towards more distributed states and the promotion of these in their environment, unless something stops this from happening, and the same can be seen in regard to networks in the process of dissolution. This helps to describe how states and processes can be seen as aspects of *tendencies*, even as these are ultimately aspects of each other within the general actualization of potential in a given system.

Many of the processes and states described above can therefore be seen as having corresponding tendencies. *Reifying and dereifying tendencies* are the simplest. Beyond these, *centralizing tendencies* are those which increase the organization and rigidity of networks, and describe the manner in which reifying tendencies manifest in the form of networks themselves. Taken to the extreme, these tend towards the creation of hyper-organized and relatively segregated islands which often destroy any links between themselves and the wider world. When centralizing tendencies cannot completely cut off relation to the wider world, they tend to try to manage the situation by reproducing copies of themselves or their structure, thereby channeling change into the least threatening manner possible, giving rise to *cancerous tendencies*. *Decentralizing tendencies*, the organizational manifestation of dereifying tendencies, loosen the organization and rigidity of networks in a manner which, if taken to the extreme, will dissolve networks into their contexts, while cancerous networks will tend to swallow them, crashing the system as a whole. While centralizing, decentralizing, and cancerous tendencies are destructive if they dominate any network fully, these networks tend to disappear rather quickly, for they describe unsustainable ways of relating to themselves and the wider world.

When centralizing and decentralizing tendencies reach a point of balance, in regard to both internal and external contexts, the result is refractive, or distributed network topologies, often known as "small world" networks in complex systems science.[29] Any tendency which brings a network back to a more distributed state from one which is moving towards a centralizing or decentralizing extreme can then be thought of as a *distributing, or distributed tendency*. Distributing tendencies do not exclude centralizing organization, decentralizing differentiation, change, or growth, but work to integrate these in dynamic patterns of adaptation to changing circumstances. In this sense, distributing tendencies describe the manner in which order emerges in the world in the most sustainable and least overall destructive form. Much of what follows will concentrate on the differences between centralizing and distributed networks and tendencies, and those factors which give rise to these in various networks in the world.

One of the ramifications of the differences between centralizing and distributed networks can be seen in the ways in which they change. Centralizing networks, whether conservative or cancerous, tend to change by dipping into more distributed or decentralizing states, just as distributed networks tend to temporarily loosen to allow more decentralizing states, such as those which give rise to differentiations which can then feed back into new and different forms of networking. Whenever a network dips into a more disorganized, decentralized state, it leaves the safety of a *stable, or equilibrium state*. If the network continues on this path, it could end up in an *unstable, or chaotic state*, a state which is often erratic and unpredictable, and if continued, could lead to a state of differentiation, or even dissolution.

In between stability and instability, however, and at the upper bound of a system's ability to adapt to changes in its contexts, is a state which complex systems researchers call a *meta-stable state, or meta-stability*, which is often described as what happens when a system functions "at the edge of chaos."[30] If stability is conservative and instability dangerous, meta-stability is the manner in which networks grow and develop in the most sustainable way. Distributed states and tendencies are those organized around maximum meta-stability, for they are oriented towards a balanced relation to a changing world which maximizes growth and the development of greater complexity which could help it adapt to changes in the future. In contrast to this flexible relation to the environment, centralizing networks aim for maximum stability, and are oriented towards making their environments change in ways which support their ability to change as little as possible.

It should not be thought that networks only take on one form or topology rather than another. Rather, they will often shift between differing intertwinings, layerings, and combinations of these tendencies and states, balancing them off each other in a variety of ways, and these impact not only how they change but also how they grow. While it may be tempting to romanticize decentralizing tendencies for their own sake, there are times in which the maintenance and growth of complexity in a network requires greater centralization. For example, during times of enormous scarcity and relative stability, centralizing topologies may be necessary for survival of a network as a whole. But in times of relative plenty yet full of change, greater decentralization and more distributed modes of organization are necessary to allow for adaptation, and to prevent the collapses or tendency to be surprised by changing circumstances which overcentralization tends to produce. Distributed networks and tendencies make use of all of these to maintain a dynamically balanced relation between aspects and their environments.

If networks are to adapt to the world around them, they need to be able to change. The manner in which systems regulate their own functioning, whether towards distributed ends or otherwise, comes about when they take some of the outputs as inputs so as to be able to adjust their behavior according to changing conditions. This is known as *reentry, reflexivity, recursion, modulation, or feedback*, which describes not only how processes and states give rise to tendencies, but how they can also regulate their own actions in regard to changing circumstances.[31] For example, a thermostat, often formed by a coil of metal which expands to shut off the heat when it hits a preset level, can regulate the temperature of a house by allowing itself to be influenced by the heat it helps produce. More complexly, animals will often observe the impact of their behaviors so as to learn from their mistakes, a process of feedback of outputs to inputs in a living system.

Feedback and modulation can take many forms, and as with reification and dereification, centralization and decentralization, both too much and too little feedback can be detrimental to the ability of networks to grow and change. When networks do not engage in feedback, they cut themselves off from the world around them, and are unable to adapt and change. But when feedback overwhelms the inputs coming from the outside world, a system can cut itself off as well, and even overload. For example, when a microphone nears its own speaker system, the sound coming from the speakers can drown out the speaker, and even blow out the whole system. Likewise, if a person worries too much about what other people think about them, they will often scrutinize their own words and actions so much that their worries about how these will be seen by others will lead to an overall anxiety which makes it nearly impossible to act. Even a thermostat can melt or freeze, and hence cease to function. While these are radically different types of systems, they all engage in feedback to modulate their behavior. Since feedback is, like any other tendency, one which tends to self-potentiate, it often makes sense to use feedback to modulate feedback.

Any of the tendencies, processes, and states described above, with the exception of those which tend towards balance, can be dangerous if taken to the extreme. Those systems value stability above all else, and try to ward off all growth if possible, because of the instabilities this can bring, and prefer if possible to maintain a steady, equilibrium state. When such systems do grow, they tend to do so in ways which either use growth to defend against change from within, or in ways which try to overwhelm whatever is not like it, from within or without. In this sense, there are two types of centralizing networks. The first are *stable, conservative, paranoid, or defensive networks.* These networks tend to change and grow only haltingly, with great difficulty, and largely in the buildup of defensive structures designed to protect them from the need to change in more funda-mental ways. Most conservative networks in the world which are able to exist for extended periods of time are of this less extreme type.

There are other types of centralizing networks, however, which are able to grow fluidly, and even absorb many forms of change from both internal and external environments. They use the growth which this allows to defend against having to change in more fundamental ways, instead of reinvesting their growth towards defense, using some limited forms of distributedness towards ultimately centralizing ends. As such, they do not tend towards rigidity and disconnection, but rather, towards unchecked absorption and expansion. These are *cancerous networks.*[32] While these systems can often tolerate high levels of superficial diversity, this is only to the extent to which these feed back into the reproduction of one ultimately centralizing logic. The result tends to be a crisis of feedback which can ultimately lead to an overload and crash of the network and its environment, for its logic is to turn everything around it into fuel for growth, to the point where it can often destroy the very aspects of its contexts which support that growth in the first place.

Evolution of complexity and life as we know it seems to primarily arise because of relatively distributed modes of organization, for only relatively *distributed networks* tend to be able to adapt and change while growing and developing sustainably in relation to their environments. That said, within distributedness, these tendencies manifest as well, if to a lesser degree, such that there are centralizing, cancerous, decentralizing, and distributed forms of distributedness, all of which describe those which exist in the physical, biological, and cultural worlds we know. Because the underlying tendencies and structures are self-potentiating, however, those which are not distributed, and hence, not continually adapting to changing circumstances, can become limiting or dangerous in regard to the long-term survival and growth of the networks in question. Distributedness can therefore be seen as the continual attempt to rework itself in changing situations so as to steer clear of the three primary pitfalls of overcentralization, overdecentralization, and hybrid cancerous formations, as well as the various forms of feedback crises which can tend to potentiate these in a number of ways.

There are many ways these insights, derived from the way the science of networks deals with physical, living, and technological networks, can be applied to ethical, political, and other cultural domains. In a manner oddly similar to Sigmund Freud's metaphorical notions of a "life" and a "death" drive at work in all matter, or "difference" and "repetition" in the work of Gilles Deleuze, complex systems science has shown that the tendencies to centralization and decentralization, as well as their aspects and corollaries, need to find balance in distributed formations in order for there to be sustainable growth and development.[33] This seems to apply not only to material energetic systems, but living and cultural systems as well, from organisms to economies, for these are all structures in which the extreme tendencies described above can become limiting or even dangerous if not balanced. Reworking Freud and building upon Deleuze, it may then be possible to speak of a tendency towards life, which takes the form of distributedness, and which manifests within all matter, life, and culture. Likewise, it is also possible to speak of a tendency towards death as that which shows up in various forms in radically decentralizing, centralizing, or cancerous tendencies. Distributedness in all its manifestations is that which seems to lead to life, as well as its fullness, growth, and evolution, not only in regard to living systems, but also networked systems of various sorts in the world, with many potential ramifications in science and beyond.

Networkological Description:
Immanence, Relation, Refraction,
Emergence, and Robustness

The networkological project will view all we experience as due to the robust emergence of complexity. In this manner, it will rework and extend the perspectives articulated by complex systems science to domains beyond the sciences, in the manner sketched above. Such an approach has much in common with the work of relationally oriented philosophers of the past, such as Henri Bergson, Gilbert Simondon, or Gilles Deleuze. These theorists value the sustainable development of creativity, similar to the valuation of robust emergence of complexity in complex systems science, and in a manner which is fundamentally anti-reductive, and often even draws upon early work in complex systems theories. While these philosophers wrote before the rise of the Internet, and were unaware of developments in artificial neural networks, their work guides this project in a wide variety of ways.[34] From the potential synergies between complex systems science, philosophies of relation and radical creativity of the past, and the unique demands of our times, this project will construct its view of the world.

Four networkological principles will help guide and structure this process. Abstracted from the sources described above, as well as the potentials for networked description in general, these principles will guide the construction of what follows, much of which is designed to help network around many of the impasses which have dominated a number of diverse fields of inquiry and practice. Each principle will now be addressed in turn, even though the reasoning behind these will largely only become clear in the materials addressed at greater length in the project as a whole.

According to the networkological *principle of emergence*,

everything in the world can be seen as the result of the robust emergence of complexity, which comes about by means of the networked unfolding of potential. From such a perspective, the very fabric of the world is fundamentally emergent. Potential and actual, energy and matter, each are aspects of each other, and arise from the emergence of complexity out of the fundamental stuff of the world, which is emergence itself, the potential which actualizes itself to give rise to the world we experience. When reified, emergence gives rise to actualized complexity in the form of matter, even as dynamic complexity in the form of moving matter gives rise to energy, thereby allowing the potential for the active emergence of new forms of complexity and emergence in turn.[35] In conditions of diversity, distributedness, meta-stability, and feedback leading to the potential for sync, complexity complexifies, which is to say, it emerges, and it does this spontaneously, and in a manner which tends to self-potentiate further emergence. Back to the origins of our universe, emergence did what it has always done, which is to say, emerged from itself robustly, giving rise to matter and energy, space and time, self-differing and renetworking, and all we have ever experienced is a result and aspect of this, echoing it ever differently. As this project will work to show, everything in the world can be seen, directly or indirectly, as the product of the emergence of complexity, and its continuing emergence in ever new forms, in a manner which can be described by means of complex networking.

In regard to the *principle of relation*, the stuff of the world and all its networks are seen as fundamentally relational in nature, for everything is ultimately the result of the complex networking of its aspects with each other. From such a perspective, nothing is ever truly isolated from others, and anything is only sensible and valuable in regard to that which it is related, which is ultimately the contexts and processes of the networks around it, up to and including that of the emergence of emergence itself. While reification is a part of the emergence of any aspect of the world, as well as any attempt to understand or evaluate it, these are only ever aspects of the contexts and processes which brought them about. And so, reified aspects of the world which do not work to sync with others, or which work to absorb others so they do not have to, ultimately work to decomplexify themselves and their contexts in the long run. Meaning and value are therefore only produced relationally, in regard to the more encompassing networks of emergence of which they are aspects, rather than in terms of reified perspectives liable to lose sync with the more encompassing conditions of emergence going on around them.

The *principle of refraction* views the emergence of complexity as fundamentally refractive, which is to say, distributed. Centralizing logics of reflection, and the reifications of which they are dynamic outgrowths, are only ever aspects of refractive modalities. While reflective, centralizing modalities seem to always attempt to turn to their own ends, this only ever happens in ways which, in the long run, inhibit or destroy robustness, and hence run counter to the emergence of complexity which has been the rule rather than the exception in the history of our world. Refractive networks are fundamentally distributed, continually reworking the relations between parts and wholes in ways which do not merely reflect aspects of the hubs to the parts, but give rise to structures in which parts and wholes fundamentally exceed each other.

Finally, according to the *principle of immanence*, the world is seen as composed of one fundamental stuff, such that matter and energy, matter and mind, space and time, subject and object, are all aspects of emergence itself, that which gave rise to and continues to give rise to these. Anywhere and everywhere, the stuff of experience itself, emergence is that of which all experience is an aspect, and which exceeds any and all aspects thereof. The *matrix* of the world of experience, emergence is beyond any "one," it is one-"and," which this project will describe by means of the notion of *oneand, or the oneand*, for as the matrix of experience it exceeds any attempt to reduce it to one of anything, in that any one of anything always has the potential to emerge in relation to the emergence around it. Such a perspective only makes sense in a changing world, however, if emergence is fundamentally able to differ from itself, which is to say, that it has the potential for radical difference immanent within it. Emergence is this differencing, that which differentiates and then renetworks back with itself, and continues to do this, giving rise to any and all we experience, and the potential for yet more. The potential for anything and everything we have ever dreamed of is always only ever here and now, right in front of us, in the very fabric of the world, even if this can only ever be unleashed by means of the way things network with each other.

Bringing this all together, each of these four principles is ultimately an aspect of what this project will call the *valuation of robustness*. As described earlier, robustness is emergence which is able to emerge from itself not only in the present, but the future as well, for it is the sustainable emergence of complexity, emergence which is able to feedback into itself in complexly emergent ways. In this sense, robustness is the most complex and most emergent form of emergence. The valuation of robustness grounds the networkological project in a wide variety of ways, and all other aspects of this project, including the four networko- logical principles, flow from this as its aspects.

In addition, each of the networkological principles roughly corresponds to one element of network diagrams, with the principle of immanence corresponding to nodes, the principle of relation to links, the principle of refraction to grounds, and the principle of emergence to levels. The valuation of robustness corresponds then to the way in which levels open onto processes of emergence, which ultimately are at their most emergent when they are robust. In this sense, all networkological principles, as well as elements of network diagrams, can be seen as refractions of each other in regard to the valuation of robustness, for all these only make sense in relation to the ways in which they refract the world around themselves in relation to each other.

As this project will show, to view the world as networked, which is to say, as composed of nodes, links, grounds, and levels, is to see it as refracting the principles and valuation described above, and vice-versa. The mode of description which arises from this will be called *diagramming*, and the complex conceptual network which describes this in its most abstract form is what will be called the *concept of the network diagram*. Composed of the sub-concepts of node, link, ground, and level, and opening on to the emergences of which these are all aspects, the network diagram is both an abstraction from and a guide to the production of further robust networks in the world.

Everything in the networkological project will follow from the ramifications extracted from the concept of the network diagram, the networkological principles, and the valuation of robustness, which are ultimately refractions of each other. In many senses, this project is simply an endeavor to see what the world would look like if redescribed by means of networks in regard to these notions, even if ultimately these are simply the means which would allow for the world to be redescribed in terms of networking in the first place. Ultimately, however, this project as a whole is grounded, which is to say, finds its significant context and reason for being, in its valuation of and commitment to robustness. This means that not only does the networkological project value whatever promotes the robust emergence of complexity in the world, but this is only itself valuable, according to its own values, to the extent to which it can help do the same.

Networkological modes of description diagram the world in regard to a valuation of robustness, and only make sense from this perspective. The descriptive principles articulated above, as well as the general orientation of complex systems science, not only imply this valuation, but only make sense in regard to it, and network ethics, politics, aesthetics, and more all flow from this, even as robustness is itself only an abstraction from networks in the world itself.

Network Economies:
Networked Models of Value, Meaning, and Experience

Some of the ramifications of this way of describing the world in regard to the principles of the networkological project and its commitment to robustness can become apparent through the way in which this project describes how networks process potential, and how this leads to an account of value, meaning, and experience. While some of the rest of this section may seem untraditional, these notions follow from what has been described above, and articulate in condensed form some of the ways in which this project will work to link these principles, from complex systems science to philosophies of emergence and beyond, in order to address a number of cultural issues.

Whenever potential is unfolded into action, whether in the form of moving matter which conveys energy in physical systems, chemical energy stored in adenosine triphosphate (ATP) in living organisms, or the ways in which humans invest labor or thought in matters to give rise to various cultural qualities, the matters which a system uses to organize its relation to potential can be seen as functioning, in relation to the way the system modulates itself from within and without, as a form of *currency*. From such a perspective, food and status can be seen as forms of currency as much as money or electricity. All of these produce potential in relation to particular systems, which make use of and, in this sense, value these, if in each case differently. When currencies (in whatever form) are stored or invested in that which works to give rise to more currencies, these can then be seen as forms of *capital*, and so, not only can factories be seen as capital, but also muscle, and even matter, if each in regard to the systems in question. Each of these forms of capital, which can also be thought of as *capitals* in that, like capitals of nations, they tend to self-potentiate their own emergence, can then be put to work at higher levels of scale to produce more currencies, as well as the various forms of complexity and emergence to which these can give rise.[36]

When networks are analyzed in regard to how they relate to currencies, they are known as *economies*, and as such, a car engine, a tree, a dog, or elections can be seen as economies, even if of radically different sorts and in relation to different capitals. Some economies exist to produce particular things, such as the ways in which car engines produce motion, but most economies, such as organisms and other complex systems, produce primarily themselves, and other things only secondarily, and for this reason are often known as autopoeitic, or self-producing systems.[37] Systems act, even if only to perpetuate themselves, by unfolding potential in the form of currency at one level of scale into action at another level of scale. In this sense, actions represent expenditures of currency and hence potential, such that the actions which an economy takes are *valuations* which indicate those aspects of the world which the system *values*. A system values what it does in a particular context, the manner in which it expends its currencies and forms of capital, and as such, what it does can be used to understand what it values. Value can thereby be attributed to processes, modes of relating, qualities, and things to the extent to which systems perform actions in relation to these in particular contexts.

A stone, for example, unfolds its quantum potentials, a continual movement of particle-forces which manifest as energetic currencies of moving matter-energies in a manner which perpetuates its molecular form.[38] In doing so, it acts to minimize its loss of energy in the way it interacts with its environment.[39] From the perspective described above, it is therefore possible to say that maintaining its form with a minimum loss of energy, and hence, maintaining its complexity, is what a stone values, even if this is always in relation to the economies of which it is a part, and the processes which brought these about. A stone is, of course, ultimately a very limited sort of economy, for such a static and rigid mode of organization can only continue in rather stable conditions, and is unlikely to be able to adapt if the world changes around it, at least not in ways which are able to maintain or promote the growth of its complexity. In situations of surplus flows of energy, and in regard to the conditions described by complex systems science, systems tend to complexify on their own, thereby giving rise to more complex forms of valuation in the process. Living organisms value various nutrients, and each of these can be seen as functioning as a currency in regard to particular economies at work within the more general economy of the organism. In this sense, a human organism is a complex meta-economy, one which intertwines economies of water, oxygen, minerals, and other currencies within it.

Systems nevertheless only have limited degrees of ability to change what they value, even if this increases with their degree of complexity. Stones, for example, seem to have little to no ability to act, and hence value, differently. Simple organisms tend to value whatever they are programmed to by evolution, and this tends to be whatever the organism's instincts tell it will likely further the maintenance and growth of its complexity. But since instincts are hard to change, in that they are often hard-wired into the form of the animal's body and brain, this leaves these organisms vulnerable to changing environments, and limited in their ability to explore or create new ones. As organisms develop in complexity, however, so does their ability to plan and adapt, with humans and their various cultural economies, from gestures to language and culture in the widest possible senses, as so many supplemental levels of complexification of this process. Diversification and feedback within processes of continual adaptation to inner and outer changes leads to cultural systems in human societies valuing many different aspects of their worlds, including degrees, positions, prestige, time, skills, commodities, property, or labor, and all of these regulate the values of each other by means of various forms of exchange and interdependency. Money is thus only one particularly abstract and limited type of currency within human social systems.

Because currencies traverse the boundaries and levels of scale of economies, they are not only what powers economies, but the way in which they feed back so as to produce sync in regard to their environments as well, for not only do they represent what a system values outside of itself, but potentially within itself as well. When systems are complex enough to use multiple currencies, they can use these to regulate each other, and when they do this, these function as *meta-currencies*. When a single currency regulates the ways in which others evaluate the values of currencies and actions in a system as a whole, it tends to represent the value of value in the system as such, and this is known as a *hypercurrency.* Money in social systems and ATP in living organisms are examples of hypercurrencies.[40] The relation between meta- and hypercurrencies is usually one which changes in regard to varying degrees of centralization and distributedness, for centralizing networks tend to employ hypercurrencies to keep all its functions tightly regulated, while more distributed networks tend to make use of a greater variety of meta-currencies. The human body, for example, while it makes use of ATP to move energy around, also makes use of a number of other meta-currencies, such as hormones and electro-chemical impulses, to regulate its various functions. While ATP is a hypercurrency of sorts, it is a weak one at best, and this is precisely what allows it to foster robustness rather than hinder it.

The danger inherent to hypercurrencies is that as a system comes to value only one currency over others, it increasingly tends to drain everything else of value, shifting value from quality to quantity, allowing the distributedness of its relation to sub-currencies, economies, ways of relating, and modes of acting to cease functioning. This can quickly lead to a cancerous feedback loop which can crash the system and even that of its contexts. For this reason, most systems use hypercurrencies and meta-currencies in ways which are relatively distributed, so as to regulate the disbursement of investments of capital and currency into various actions and projects in ways which meta-stably feed back into the systems of production of value of which they are a part. However, if a system begins to value the production of its own hypercurrency for itself, which is to say, reproduction for its own sake, it can become cancerous, resulting in a self-perpetuating feedback loop which can undermine not only the long-term robustness of the system itself, its ability to produce qualitative and quantitative abundance, but also the viability of the very systems which are around it.

Economies do not only produce and express values, but also *meanings*. Meanings are the solidification and expression of values, which are themselves solidifications of processes of valuation, into patterns that can lead to interpretations of particular aspects of a system or its contexts in regard to those contexts. Simple systems, such as sub-atomic particles, exist at the cusp of meaning and value, matter and energy, expression and incarnation. But more complex systems produce layers within themselves which intertwine processes of valuation with many possible forms of action and interpretation in regard to varied situations. The meaning of any particular aspect of the world can then be seen as its position in relation to the patterns at work in the things, qualities, modes of relating, and actions and processes involved, even as each is in turn an expression of the values of the systems which produced these.

For example, the meaning of one animal to another, as food or threat, depends on the ways in which it was evolved to interpret aspects of the world in regard to its value for its own life, even as it was developed in a way that has a particular set of meanings in regard to the values expressed by the actions of the evolutionary processes which gave rise to it. More complex organisms have more freedom in this, such that the meaning of water for a plant is determined by the structure of the plant, while a human can view water as something to drink, as scientific evidence, or as inspiration for a work of art. This is because humans have more potential systems of valuation at their disposal, which can then be used to select various ways of interpreting experiences, thereby giving rise to meanings.

Living organisms continually read the world by means of perception, write by means of action, and translate by means of these, producing meanings which express their values. Simpler economies do this in simpler ways.[41] A molecule reads the world around it, and its reactions are interpretations of these meanings, such that its very form can be seen as its interpretation, both reading and writing, of both its internal and external contexts, the result of balances between economies of energy within and beyond it. The ways in which a molecule transforms or does not are then the ways in which it and those systems around it unfold their potentials, giving rise to interpretable meanings in the process, which can be read by whatever is around.

As with value, meaning is determined retroactively, in regard to how a system reads or writes something, which is ultimately expressed by actions which express its values. And so, the meaning of water for a human can change, depending on what it values at a particular moment in regard to its many potential networks of hierarchies of value, while a plant has only as many ways of reading water as the values incarnated in its simple structures and economies allow. Humans have more flexible brains and bodies, and hence, more ways of reading and valuing at their disposal. That said, there are limits to the flexibility of human modes of interpretation and value. Some systems of valuation support others, such that without water to drink, water for inspiration or scientific evidence will soon cease to matter to any human in such a situation. Likewise, meaning and value are always relationally constructed, and so reading or evaluating aspects of the world in a particular way, even if theoretically possible, may end up producing a long-term lack of sync between networks if contexts are not taken into account.

These issues only intensify in regard to the cultural economies produced by humans. Languages are complex economies which continually interpret aspects of each other and the world around them, expressing the values of the various humans and situations which have given rise to them. Words such as "God" or "truth " are grounding terms which exchange at great value, regulating the meanings of other terms as near meta-currencies, while words like "I" or "is" function as fully-fledged meta-metacurrencies in regard to their contexts, for they express in their meaning the structuring values of their systems as a whole. Any system's grammar expresses not only its primary meanings, but those aspects of its orientation to the world and itself which are its primary values as well.

Mathematics can be seen as a particular form of sub-language, one which makes use of both words and pictures to interpret the world in particular ways, which in turn describe ways of relating to the world valued by humans. From such a perspective, then, human financial economies, currencies, and forms of capital are only particularly limited and limiting notions of what economies are and can be, for ultimately every-thing in the world can be seen as a form of economy. Likewise, languages are only a particularly developed form whereby meaning manifests in the world, for everything can also be seen as a language. Each presents a particular networked lens on the world, letting us see various aspects of the world in turn.

In and beyond this, however, human economies, beyond financial ones, have led us to project our meanings into the world in a variety of forms. External memory storage, or *wideware*, describes the ways in which we write our meanings upon the world, in forms such as gestures, tools, and languages, and indicates the ways we have altered our environments in meaningful ways according to what we value.[42] As a result, humans have progressed beyond the physical evolution of complex systems and the biological evolution of life, to the point at which our cultural products feedback into our evolution as well. We build cars and computers, each of which has particular meanings to us in particular situations, and expresses particular values.

All meanings and values only find meaning and value within the context of particular networks of experience. Each experiencer in the world always already finds itself in a world full of meanings and values, which arise because of the processes and contexts which gave rise to these experiencers in the first place. We always experience a world full of meanings and values, a world carved into slices which demand our attention and interpretation in regard to our needs and desires, our investment of currencies in regard to how we read the potentials for action around us. While humans do this in particularly complex ways, even simple physical matter interprets the world in ways which unfold potentials, and there is no reason not to suppose that even quantum particles might in some sense "feel" the world of fields in which they find themselves, even if they are not able to represent this to themselves, and hence "know" this in the ways which humans and other complex animals do. Nevertheless, we have no way of knowing if other humans experience either, but they do act and interpret, even as the simplest matters do, allowing us to interpret the meanings and values they express in terms of our own, which only ever manifest by means of our networks of experience.

Within this, each network is an economy, a language, and a world of experience of its own, nested in networks of others, and at potentially and infinitely practical levels of scale. Each tends to act in ways which perpetuate what it values in particular fields of meaning, based on how it reads its experiences in relation to its attempt to further its values in the world by means of its action. As deployments of currencies in some actions over others, these actions are meaningful valuations which value some meanings over others. The results are processes, ways of relating, qualities, and things, with these feeding back into other systems of valuation, meaning, and experiencing in turn, all in relation to the more encompassing processes which brought these about in the first place.

There are many ways in which the insights of complex systems provide lessons which can help us imagine more robust ways of dealing with our physical, living, and cultural worlds, including human financial economies. Finding the ethical, political, and social ramifications of these ideas, in regard to experience, meaning, and value, and towards the goal of promoting robustness, is one of the primary goals of this project. But before turning to these concerns, it is important to discuss the ways in which value, meaning, and experience relate to processes of sync, which can tie these all into issues of thinking and, ultimately, philosophy as well.

Sync:
Understanding, Knowledge, and Thinking

As a panpsychist view of the world, the networkological project views all matter as having the ability to feel. Simple matters feel the world simply, and only complex matters, such as those which have brains, seem to be able to feel themselves feeling, which is to say, to be conscious that they are experiencers. While ultimately we cannot know if even the person next to us thinks, indirect evidence seems to imply this is the case. The same can be said, from a panpsychist position, about the ability of all matter to "feel," with complex matters feeling the most complexly, and with what we generally call "thought" as the most complex manner in which this occurs in the world we know.

The networkological project will build on its account of experience, meaning, and value, briefly sketched above, so as to develop a broadly panpsychist account of thought and thinking. It will do so by drawing upon artificial neural networks and contemporary cognitive neuroscience, which have developed a new, networked image of what it means to think.[43] As many developments in these fields have come to show, thought is perhaps best described by the manner in which various aspects of the pathways in a neural network, simulated or otherwise, come into sync with each other. Perception can then be seen as the ways in which aspects of a brain's networks come into sync with those in sense organs, just as actions occur when aspects of a brain's perceptual and coordinating networks come into sync with those in motor cortexes and nerves.[44]

Thought then perhaps should not be seen as having a form which is linguistic, linear, binary, or computational in any tradi-tional sense, notions which were in fact dominant until relatively recently. Rather, it increasingly seems that thought, even in its most complex humans forms, is most likely to be the product of resonant coupling between aspects of complex dynamic systems such as the brain and various aspects of our bodies and world. While the brain presents the most complex form of thought we know, less complex forms of thought can be seen in the way simpler matters come into sync. Experience, interpretation, and valuation can then all be seen as simple forms of thinking. And as such, all formed matter can be seen as forms of memory, that which writes upon itself and other aspects of the world the traces of so many physical, biological, and cultural processes which then serve to potentiate others in the process.

Sync, or the manner in which aspects of the world work together in a way which maintains or develops complexity, can then be seen as one of the primary aspects of the process of thought itself. Sync is not sameness, nor is it necessarily hierarchical nor centrally controlled. Radically diverse entities can be in sync if they can find ways to work together, and if they can modulate each other in a distributed manner so as to produce effects in excess of the sum of their parts. Trying to come into sync is in fact one of the primary ways in which entities modify themselves in relation to others, for sync is the pathway to all the benefits which the emergence of new forms of complexity can provide. Humans learning to work together in a society, animal symbiosis, or molecules shifting their relational configurations to bond with each other, these are all examples of sync at differing levels of complexity. Complexity that emerges towards robustness is in fact nothing other than this, and the robust emergence of complexity in this manner describes a process of problem-solving which is the basis of more complex forms of thought.

From such a perspective, and building on emergent and embodied cognition theory,[45] this project will therefore see *knowledge* as the manner in which the potential for sync is reified and stored in memory in the form of matter, and *understanding* as what happens when knowledge is put to use to produce more sync. The body of a fish, for example, "understands" the form of water as a result of the "knowledge" stored in memory in its DNA, which can lead to the production of gills. But these gills understand air much less than water, because they do not know how to deal with air, and only by evolving lungs, a new form of knowledge, would this sort of understanding be possible. The same could be said of human artifacts, such as chairs, which know how to "understand" the shape of our bodies, because they remember the way we are shaped in their physical form. The "knowledge" stored in the physical form of a chair is then what allows it to "know" how to deal with our bodies, or to "understand" them, even if knowledge is ultimately static and know-how or understanding is relational and dynamic.

In a similar sense, the brains of organisms record memories of the world of experience, giving rise to meaningful traces within evaluative economies. Complex memory systems, such as the DNA and brains of organisms, store the knowledge which make complex forms of understanding possible, even if these knowledge banks only make sense within the dynamic economies of understanding which read and write in relation to them. The most complex forms of understanding, then, are the types of thought seen in human brains, those forms of intertwining of knowledge and understanding which allow an organism to reflect on its actions so as to be able to modify them in relation to changes in the environment. Learning is an example of *meta-understanding*, the attempt to understand the knowledge and/or understanding at one level of complexity, taking into account their limitations, and working to emerge in, with, and through them at more complex levels of scale.

In all these forms, *thinking* is the manner in which emergence comes into sync with itself so as to potentiate its emergence from itself as robustness. Thinking and the sync it embodies are not allied with sameness, but rather, they need, support, and give rise to the differentiation and change on all sides which is often needed to bring about new forms of sync. While thinking may reify, it has then ceased to truly be thinking, for thinking which continues as true thinking is always rethinking, changing, and emerging towards more robust forms of thinking. While most of the factors which potentiate robustness can destroy it if they fall out of sync with the others, thinking is this very sync, the differentiating and working together of diverse aspects in and beyond reifications and divisions. In this sense, thinking, emergence, and robustness are varying aspects of a perpetually differing same. In relation to experiencing, interpretation, and evaluation, thinking provides yet one more lens whereby to understand networks and to attempt to come into sync with them, with experiencing as the most restricted, and thinking the most robustly networked.

In its simplest form, thinking is knowledge stored in the form of an entity, a reification of sync, whether in the form of a physical body or patterns of memory stored in a human brain. Despite its limitations, knowledge is highly valued in contemporary society. A more complex form of thinking can be found in understanding, which is the dynamic "know how" which only emerges relationally between entities in sync. Meta-understanding comes about when systems work to understand their forms of sync so as to emerge from them towards greater complexity, with learning and meta-learning as examples of these. The most complex forms of thinking occur, however, when a system attempts to come into sync with the processes whose thinking it is, the contexts whose sync its own modes of thinking embody, and to develop meta-understanding towards greater robustness in, with, and through these. For humans, this would be to attempt to come into sync with our own physical, biological, and cultural evolutions, to think with, in, and through these towards more robust futures. This would require that we begin to understand how the limitations of our very modes of thinking in the present are the result of our evolution, and to begin to question how this might limit the ways in which we currently think about the way we experience, interpret, and evaluate aspects of our world.

.

Evolving Robustness:
From Evolution to Liberation

If thinking is the manner in which aspects of a network come into sync with one another in a way which potentiates robustness, then the attempt to think our relation to the world around us would entail an attempt to emerge robustly from the current forms of sync we have with the world, ourselves, and the relation between these. In order to do this, however, we need to understand how our current forms of sync, including the ways in which we experience, interpret, value, and think in the present, are the products of the contexts and processes of our emergence, which is to say, the processes of evolution which gave rise to us. For rather than reify human forms of thinking, valuing, interpreting, and experiencing, we need to understand them in context if we are to understand how to better emerge from them.

The human ability to value anything ultimately only makes sense in regard to the evolution of robustness, for humans only value because they were evolved to do so, and to do so in ways which are in sync with our evolution. And the evolution of life, as a distributed valuing economy, values robustness, which is to say, sustainable development of complexity, even if it has so far only been able to produce organisms which value what they believe will lead to the maintenance and growth of their complexity. There is a gap, in this sense, between what evolution values and what the organisms it produces value. Human evolution has emerged in this gap, and in this sense, our own value systems only make sense in regard to the values at work in the evolutionary processes of which they are not only the result, but also aspects. And if our values are the result, and in fact, a part of those of evolution, then the same is true with our experiences, our ways of interpreting the world, and our ways of thinking. All of these are the result of evolution, and aspects of its attempt, by means of us and beyond us, to experience, interpret, value, and think itself in relation to its world.

All thought and thinking comes about in the ways in which a diverse and often dispersed set of entities come into sync with each other and their world so as to emerge more robustly. Those which do not do this robustly often thrive in the short-term, but not much further beyond this. When viewed in this way, however, it is possible to see evolutionary populations as "thinking" as much as the wideware systems, or *"plexes,"* networks of tools, gestures, and signs, with which humans surround ourselves, for all these plexes grow, develop, and in fact think "as if" they were alive, even if they are ultimately quasi-living networks which come to evolve only by means of the life of living organisms. If wideware helps us evolve from feedback with external memory, evolution develops us in regard to our internal memory, stored in our DNA. Both forms of quasi-living networks think, even if they require living organisms, in this case, humans, to do so.

In this sense, evolution can be seen as the manner in which we think ourselves beyond ourselves. That is, evolution is an external brain with internal memory storage which thinks us into existence from simpler forms of ourselves, and in relation to the external wideware brains with external memory storage we have developed which have come to feedback into this process. And if evolution is the core brain of our ever complexifying collection of external wideware brains, so many collective intelligences of which we are masters and mastered, results and producers, then the environment which sculpts our evolution, and which increasingly we sculpt by means of wideware such as our tools and computers, is our external body. We do not have a single brain or body, but networks of them, with "our own individual" bodies and brains as nodes within larger networks of brains and bodies, experiences, interpretations, evaluations, and processes of thinking of which we are only ever aspects. What is more, even beyond this, our evolution, bodies, and brains are themselves also in a sense part of the manner in which the world comes to experience, interpret, value, and think itself. By means of evolution, then, we and the world think each other, in and through each other, and, potentially, beyond.

From such a perspective, all of human culture and development, including our self-consciousness, needs to be seen as aspects of this process whereby evolution has been trying to think in and through us in this manner. And there is no question that consciousness and self-consciousness have been adaptive for humans, for they are the result of and have potentiated our relation to our wideware, in ways which have made ever more complex forms of planning possible. As a result, we have increasingly come to alter our environments, in ways which have begun to feedback into not only our own process of evolution, but that of life on Earth and the planet itself as well. In the process of this development, humans have come to have a much wider grasp of the world around them, learning about the history of the universe and its physical evolution, as well as the manner in which its products spontaneously complexify under the right conditions. We have even come to understand the evolution of life, and the manner in which its actions value the evolution of robustness in its populations of organisms.

If we were to extrapolate from this, it would seem as if evolution were trying to evolve its organisms towards the self-conscious valuation of the evolution of robustness in themselves and their world. To self-consciously value the evolution of robustness in ourselves and our world would in fact be a turning point in the history of evolution of life, for it would be the first time in which its own organisms, the neurons in its collective brain, came into sync with it. Such a form of sync would be that in which our brains and that of evolution were in sync, not in the sense of being the same or similar, but in our robust emergence from all we experience, mean, value, and think. This is similar to the manner in which, when humans think, populations of neurons come into sync with aspects of the wider world in ways which sync with other aspects of the brain and ultimately the organism itself, as the process whereby perception is extended into action by means of its processing in thinking which emerges in the process.[46]

Such a process could not come about, however, in a way which is top-down, imposed, or not truly desired by those involved, all of which would ultimately sabotage that which it aims to bring about, as the history of utopian projects has shown. It is for these reasons that this project advocates the development of those factors which promote the spontaneous and sustainable emergence of robust forms of complexity. From what the study of robust systems in physical, biological, and cultural worlds seems to indicate, these factors include diversity and differing to the maximum degree possible without destroying ourselves, and meta-stable conditions which keep us on our toes yet with a safety-net to make risk taking by all creative rather than threatening. These factors also include the maximum sustainable degree of distributedness of potential and refractive modes of organization, as well as various forms of feedback between any and all, to whatever degree is sustainable. Such a process would require a continual questioning of the values of our meanings, the meanings of our values, and the modes of thinking and acting needed to bring these about, not only in regard to our environments, but also ourselves. And it would require an understanding of the contexts and processes which brought about our current modes of experience, meaning, valuation, and thinking, so as to think the process of robust emergence from these in relation to the environmental and evolutionary processes which continue to feedback into our processes of giving rise to these.

Nevertheless, even if we as a culture and even as a species decided we all wanted this, as we currently exist, there is no way this would ever be possible. For we have been programmed by our evolution not to allow us to want this, and to sabotage ourselves even if we decide that we do. The reason for this is that we have been sculpted by evolution to value our complexity and emergence, and for most of human evolution, this has meant escaping predators and killing them if possible. And while humans eventually evolved beyond this, and even managed to consistently feed ourselves, at no point did we cease to need to be paranoid and aggressive. For we remained stuck in a feedback loop, with the paranoid and aggressive tendencies wired into our very biology, the "reptile brain" of "fight or flight" in our cortico-adrenal systems, and this made us and kept us paranoid and aggressive in relation to each other.[47] Despite our massive abilities, our history is one of war and induced famine, poor planning and calculated aggression, and even to this day, it remains at least semi-adaptive to be paranoid and aggressive in relation to other humans, because ultimately, we prey upon each other. While perhaps today we often do this in a less direct manner than we used to, we continue to develop social institutions which do this for us in ever more indirect but nevertheless brutal ways.

It would therefore be suicidal to remove our paranoid tendencies instantly, even if this were possible, for those who did would be quickly destroyed by those who did not. Rather, we have to do the hard work of thinking our ways out of these, as a species. Right now, we are stuck in a feedback loop in which it makes sense to fear each other because of how aggressive our paranoia makes us, and yet, only increased modes of cooperation, which would require we all adapt, could make this cease to be the case.[48] And so, we have transported the "flight or fight" instincts from our early evolution, hardly modified, into our technological hypermodernity. Hence, we build incredible devices, massive virtual reality nets, yet so often use them to kill and oppress each other, rather than to imagine our collective liberation. We need to find ways to unlearn the defensive strategies which were so useful early in our evolution, but which now not only limit us, but, as our technology gets more powerful, also threaten us and all life on the planet. The prospect of a humanity able to alter its own genome or produce nano-tech before it begins to truly think its own evolutionary limitations, and how to begin to overcome these, is terrifying indeed.

All of which is to say that now is the time to think the values of our meanings, the meanings of our values, how the limitations of our ways of thinking, valuing, interpreting, and experiencing result from the contexts and processes which brought them about, and how we might begin to think of ways to change this towards more robust futures. Certainly top-down attempts to "make" people more egalitarian have failed radically and violently in the past. And so, fostering all aspects of the world which give rise to robust forms of meta-stability, feedback, difference, and distributedness so as to help potentiate the thinking of the bottom-up, spontaneous emergence of robust complexity is what this project seeks to give rise to in the world. This is not to rule out interventions at the level of governments or other large-scale organizations, but unless these changes arise from pressure from below as well, they will only ever be one-sided. For real change to be sustainable in the future, it needs to be diverse, distributed, meta-stable, and in multiform feedback leading to sync, or it simply will not be complexly robust enough to stand the test of time.

The time has come to liberate and heal ourselves from the traumatic history of our own evolution, and ultimately, from ourselves. In order to do this, however, we need to begin to think who we are and have been, and how this limits our ability to even imagine who we might want to become. For our world as it is now is full of paranoid and cancerous structures which keep us far from robustness, and result in the pain and suffering which only occurs when there is a destruction of complexity, and hence, of potential. This project is an attempt to help begin this process of thinking, one which must of course adapt to the changes at work in the world and in ourselves in the process, but which also must necessarily begin where we are, here and now.

Beyond the So-Called
"Death of Philosophy"

One of the primary aims of this project is to imagine what it might mean for philosophy to connect to culture at large again. This would not mean to dispense with difficult arguments or specialized terms, but to also speak directly to issues relevant to the crises of the age, and to show why and how these aspects need each other for philosophy to truly be philosophy, and for culture to see the potential ways in which philosophy can actually bring about needed change in regard to vital issues. Surely philosophy has done this before, and can do this again. Few times seem to need new paradigms as much as ours, as technology is providing us with so many new and confusing changes but very little in the way of a sense of what a more encompassing frame to help describe new interpretations and values, not to mention ways to think about thinking and experiencing, might look like. If we are to truly begin to act upon our networked age rather than merely be acted upon by it, we need the sort of insights that new philosophies can provide. While the need for a project like this might seem obvious, for all the reasons described above, it was nevertheless not long ago that such a project would seem hardly desirable or even possible. Understanding why this might be can help contextualize the ways in which this project differentiates itself from others in the present and recent past.

In the decades following World War II, after the initial optimism of the "return" of some sort of "progress" during "structuralist" philosophies of the 1950's, a wave of skepticism came about whereby many believed philosophy, or at least philosophy that could say something meaningful about the world beyond itself, was dead. Philosophy essentially dissolved itself and its relation to the world, if in a way that preserved its ability to go in circles within universities. Dominated by the partisan bickerings left in the wake of various forms of a "linguistic turn," philosophy was largely converted into arcane language-games which hardly attempted to impact the wider world.

The general consensus seemed, if not in theory then in practice, that since philosophy was always articulated in language, it could ultimately only talk in circles about language, and little more.[49] Any attempt to talk meaningfully about the world, or to try to change the world, to the extent that it used language to talk about more than itself, was naïve at best, deluded and even dangerous at worst. And so, philosophy talked itself into a very verbose silence, and largely sealed itself up within universities, as much a hall of mirrors as the post-modern culture which increasingly dominated the world around it.

This silencing of philosophy which occurred mid-century, and in many senses remains with us in one form or another to this day, seems to have paralleled a larger silencing of hope in the wider world during this time. For the twentieth century has been one of the deconstruction of all certainties, a period of incredible violence and unbelievable horrors inflicted by humans upon each other. Perhaps it is hardly surprising then that so many discourses also had crises in their ability to make meaning of the world around them at this time. Many worldviews deconstructed their foundations, without putting anything new or more solid in their place. This can be seen in a wide variety of fields, the pervasiveness of which is often obscured by the manner in which universities force researchers to overspecialize in relatively reified disciplines. Philosophy was in this sense hardly unique, simply one more discipline professionalized by the ways in which capitalism attempted to make sure it was harmlessly absorbed into the expanding industry of the educational-university complex.

And yet, when one goes beyond the blinders of any particular discipline it becomes evident that this century has witnessed a breakdown of certainty in nearly every field of human inquiry: not only the "linguistic turn" in philosophy, but the development of "uncertainty" in physics, "incompleteness" in mathematics, the abolition of the gold-standard and rise of "fictitious capital" in economics, the "end of history" and the "society of the spectacle" in cultural theory, "participant observation" throughout the social sciences, post-colonial critique and the end of "grand narratives" in history, modernist and post-modernist reflexivity in art, and much, much more. During this time, many argued that any attempt to theorize larger contexts, often called "totalization" by critics,[50] was something to be studiously avoided. At best, all one could analyze was fragments; resistance could only ever be minor and local. As a result even the most optimistic today seem to feel that, after this violent century and its shattering of certainties, there is no way to simply go back to the way things were without at least taking such crises of foundations into account in one form or another.[51] And yet, few have proposed ways to do this.

The "death of philosophy" during the late-twentieth century can then be seen as one aspect of a more general crisis of meaning during this time. The massive social changes of the twentieth century deconstructed most human paradigms and worldviews of previous eras in their wake, if in varying forms and speeds in different locations, generally without putting anything new in place. All of which feeds into a world in which the only value is to buy some more products, watch some more images, and increase wealth and power in one's own limited domain, simply because no one has been able to come up with an alternative.

And yet, this is hardly the first time deconstructions of traditional meaning-making paradigms have happened. In fact, history is full of examples of radical changes which led people to question their ways of describing the world around them, as well as a series of relatively consistent options for how to deal with this. Building upon the work of theorists such as Thomas Kuhn in science, Ernesto Laclau in politics, Jacques Lacan in psychology, Douglas Hofstadter in systems theory, and Jean-François Lyotard in cultural theory, it is possible to develop a relational account of crises of this sort, one which can help describe potential options and ways forward which can sync up with the wider goals of this project.[52]

From such a perspective, when a crisis in certainty strikes a cultural paradigm, one potential response is a *fanatical* belief in traditional forms of certainty, despite the inability of the traditional ways to coherently explain new realities. Then there is relativist *skepticism*, which eschews hopes of having anything to believe in, or any ability to produce meaning beyond the immediate. In practice, however, these are often combined, giving rise to *cynicism*, or a general skepticism combined with an often inconsistent use of the new and traditional when convenient. With ultimately little more to bring it all together than pragmatism at best, or the use of brute force to produce realities by means of a *realpolitik* of "might makes right" at worst, cynicism combines the incoherence of fanaticism with the incompletion of skepticism. The result is an inconsistency which favors atomization in the service of cancerous reproduction, just as fanaticism favors incomplete conservative centralization, and skepticism favors incoherent decentralizing dissolution.

All of these normally give way, however, when a new paradigm arrives, one which can once again capture belief. Nevertheless, the potential for the world to deconstruct cultural certainties always remains. Skeptical arguments are never new, they always exist within a culture, and date back, in many cultures across the globe, to ancient times.[53] During times of relative security, skeptical arguments are usually seen as little more than interesting paradoxes, or seductively dangerous games at worst. But when traditional forms of description seem unable to describe conditions in a changing world, people start to take skeptical arguments more seriously, and use them to decon-struct the meanings which have been taken for granted up to that point. This leads either to a pessimistic embrace of the incoherence of self-deconstructing skepticism, the defensive strategies of fanatical traditionalist incompletion, or various forms of cynical inconsistency. And this remains the case until a new way of describing the world arrives which can account for the old world as well as the new changes which disturbed old meanings and practices.

Such a perspective on crises of meaning and values is in sync with the notions of feedback described earlier. The questioning of certainties, in terms of meanings and values, is the manner in which cultures adapt to a changing world, and as such, these sorts of crises should be seen as the cultural manifestations of the ways in which systems attempt to change by means of feedback. Self-reference, or feedback, is always an attempt to bring a system's ways of acting and interpreting into line with its funda-mental values. For values are that which anchor, by means of patterns in the dynamics of the system, the meanings and actions at one level of scale into those values which determine why that level is constructed in one way rather than another. In physical or living systems, each mutation or modification is an attempt to pose a new answer to the question of how to survive, thrive, or continue and grow in the world, and feedback is an attempt to regulate aspects of that process so its tendencies do not lead to excesses which could sabotage the process. In cultural systems, a similar process comes about when a society begins to question the values of its cultural paradigms. Uncertainty in physics, reflexivity in art, incompleteness in mathematics, deconstruction in cultural theory, and the "linguistic turn" in philosophy, all these foundations crises in varied discourses during the twentieth century can be seen as the result of the attempts to reflect on whether our traditions are still meaningful to us in radically changing circumstances. They are attempts to question the values of our meanings and the meanings of our values in a rapidly mutating world.

Vertigo can set in quickly, and in regard to this a culture needs to guard against the euphoric embrace of the new for its own sake, the fascination with the dissolution of the old, or a desire to hold on to whatever one can in a world seemingly gone mad. For fanaticism, skepticism, and cynicism are simply the manner in which centralization, decentralization, and cancerous modes of organization manifest in regard to meanings and values during states of crisis in cultural paradigms, and each of these pathways is ultimately destructive. Centralization manifests as conservative paranoia, which can be seen in the various fanaticisms in the world today. Decentralization manifests as skepticism, such as that present in the deconstruction of all certainties and the reduction of philosophy to language games. Finally, there is cynicism, which manifests in the inconsistency and disavowal of capitalist postmodernities. All three of these options represent what happens when feedback ceases to modulate growth in relation to a changing world, but rather, works to defend against it. Fanaticism grows in frenzy and paranoia the more it feels out of sync with a changing world, skepticism becomes enamored of the impossibility of meaning and value, and cynicism puts deconstruction in the service of atomized growth of "might-makes-right" in a manner which is as unsustainable as it is dangerous for all involved. All refuse to try to understand the changes and produce new meanings and values which can help process these changes into pathways towards greater robustness.

Such crises, so long as they do not lead to dissolution, are nevertheless always an opportunity to develop more robust forms of complexity at the level of the system as a whole. Crises allow us to ask ourselves what values and meanings we might want for ourselves, and how this might relate to the larger contexts and processes in our changing world as a whole. This is an opportunity to recalibrate, and the rise of fanaticism, skepticism, and cynicism should be seen as evidence of the need for this. Rather than resort to strategies of defense, however, what is needed is to examine what changes in the world have caused these crises, and what this might mean in regard to the more encompassing contexts and processes within which these are situated. For the only way to modulate feedback gone haywire is to take it beyond itself, to work to bring it into sync with the forms of feedback at work in the wider contexts which brought about a crisis in the first place.

In this sense, it is only if we look to the contexts beyond our immediate cultural contexts that we can begin to formulate values and meanings which can help us orient in regard to the changes in our contemporary world. That is, we need to ask ourselves, in light of the larger physical, biological, and cultural processes which brought us to where we are, what helped to bring about the best of all we see? And how can we use this to help guide the development of means of interpretation and evaluation which bring these into sync with the new realities we face? From such a perspective, if we look at our world, those things which help produce the best aspects of all we see seem to share one trait, abstracted from them all, which is a process of creation which is never satisfied with any particular form thereof, but rather, always works to give rise to a creation not merely of more quantity, but also of more intensity and different types of qualities, both in itself and its contexts. Such a form of creation gives rise to more and different qualities not only in the present, but also in the future, as a sustainable complexity that works to maintain its ability to create in relation to the world around it.

If we look at our world, it is this, the process of the robust emergence of complexity, which has given rise to the best in our world, and can serve as a standard to help us develop means of interpreting and evaluating aspects of our new and changing world. The robust emergence of complexity is the essence of life, love, value, and the key to helping us go beyond the limitations which describe our current ways of networking. In this sense, robustness can be seen as the potential source of all values, that which modulates feedback in physical, biological, and cultural worlds, and that which can be a guide for creating new values and meanings in a rapidly recreating world, if we let it. The sustainable emergence of complexity for us and our contexts can be an ethic which can help us emerge from the deconstructive crises of the second half of the previous century, and adapt to our rapidly networking world in a manner which is robustly networked itself. And it can be a pathway beyond the fanaticism, skepticism, and cynicism which dominate our contemporary age, a guidepost for the development of new ways of networking.

A philosophy of the robust emergence of complexity is one which values creation for its own sake, in and beyond any particular creation to which this gives rise, to the extent to which it can potentiate more robustly emergent forms of creation. Skeptical of its own creations as much as it is of a relativist skepticism or cynical belief in "whatever works makes right," a philosophy of radical creation is one which is most itself when it changes in a way which can give rise to more creation in the world, in and beyond its own creations. In this sense, rather than reflect its values, top-down, to its aspects, it works to refract itself and its contexts in each other ever more robustly.

As such, this project will not pretend to have pure or axiomatic foundations, or the fantasies of certainty which often accompany these.[54] For beyond axioms which divide the world into that of which we can be certain, and that to which we need pay no attention, the "Oz" and "the man behind the curtain" of all attempts at proof, we have to realize that proof and certainty are games which are limited and limiting. There are no suppositionless, pure vantage points from which we could give ourselves a secure foundation. For any attempt at thinking always starts from where we find ourselves, *in medias res*. We are always already thinking in our older forms of thought, produced by a world which precedes us, thereby situating us within perspectives, meanings, and values.

And so, this philosophy will not start with simplistic definitions, nor rigid declarations of method. Instead, it will get inside previous ways of describing the world, and slowly unravel them from within. But it will not do this to simply deconstruct prior models and give us nothing in return. This only leaves us to go back to these ways of describing the world afterwards, with simply less certainty than before, or at best some vague hope that this will lead to inspiration for something new. Rather than embrace the nihilism of a pure deconstruction, this project will turn this on its head, taking a page from the creativity of cynicism, but without the myopia in regard to the bigger picture. Unweaving common sense as well as traditional philosophical and scientific ways of explaining things, it will reweave these in peculiar meta-stable ways which ride the boundary between fanatical certainty, deconstructive skepticism, and cynical opportunism.

Embracing whatever gives rise to more potential for sustainable creativity, only a commitment to robustness in relation to the world will guide this project. By redescribing whatever it touches in relation to this commitment, this project will give rise to a continually mutating, complex, meta-stable conceptual structure which refracts its ordering principles in relation to its contexts so as to continually emerge itself in the process.

Networkological Critique:
Networks Beyond Overreification
and Cancerous Reproduction

The networkological project is based on the principles of emergence, relation, refraction, and immanence, along with the valuation of robustness. Nevertheless, this project also articulates itself and these notions in regard to what it is not. For all the reasons described in the preceding sections, and in regard to its commitment to robust emergence, the networkological project views overreification in thought and action as the greatest threat to robustness in our world today. Whether in traditional, paranoid conservative forms, or more wily neo-conservative cancerous modalities, centralization dominates our world today, even as decentralization only ever seems to liquidate in order to serve reifying, and hence ultimately centralizing, ends. Cynicism and fanaticism are the order of the day, and this only ever alternates with skepticism to help these reconsolidate. Many continually shift between these positions as needed. Oscillation between naked territorialism and disavowed neo-territorialism in liberal and market-oriented garb describe much of the contemporary situation, with many on both sides skeptical of any alternative.

The time has come to have faith in creation again, to channel deconstructive energies to reconstructive ends, but in a distributed manner which values robustness for any and all rather than profit or control for the few. While reconstruction does need deconstruction, it must always guard against fetishizing the deconstructive moment for its own sake, as well as the feedback crises this tends to create, similar in form to those of cancerous growth. Keeping the pitfalls of runaway growth and destruction in mind, this project will work to deconstruct overreifications so as to loosen the hold they have upon our world. For given the right conditions, robust emergence tends to happen spontaneously, even though the forces of control in our world are not likely to allow that to happen so easily. And so, while it is essential to help imagine new structures which can arise in and around the margins of the conservative and paranoid aspects of our world, this needs to be combined with deconstruction and critique.

Overreifying, non-relational, reductionist, and reflective modalities have been used to structure a wide variety of violences throughout history, whether in traditional conservative forms, such as racisms or xenophobias, organized around a particular content such as the nation, or in neo-conservative cancerous modalities which organize themselves around a form, such as the abstract value of money. Such reflective modalities turn all deconstruction into reconsolidation of the status-quo, either defensively in terms of traditional conservatism, or in the defensiveness of unlimited growth of the same, as in cancerous forms. It is time we began to see both traditional conservatisms and cancerous neo-conservatisms as two sides of the same, which is to say, as threats to the generation of the sort of growth which makes growth worth striving for. This requires, however, that we begin to see the more subtle ways in which conservative and cancerous modalities often structure aspects of the world which we have come to see as the foundations of our own freedoms, such as atomistic notions of individuality or the "freedom" of the market. We also need to guard against the possibility that deconstructions of these can then be used to bring about ultimately centralizing ends.

The time has come to want more, to imagine a more relational and less atomistic future, one with fewer attempts to recuperate all activity for superficial notions of efficiency and value production which sacrifice long-term robustness for short-term fixes for the few that can get them. For too long have we pitted individuals against each other and their contexts in binary battles of me vs. world, subject vs. object, mind vs. body, us vs. them. For too long have we imagined individuals as billiard balls, colliding in imaginary fields, cut off from the complex systems of feedback that make the world so surprising, so creative, and so dangerous. For too long have we framed history in isolated linear historical narratives, screening out the complex feedbacks which give rise to change between the folds of our often monocausal attempts at explanation. For too long have we seen actions taking place on groundless fields of interaction outside time, place, history, or value, in relation to transcendent foundations and otherworldly goals reified and isolated from connection to this world. Pain and suffering are here and now, even as the gap between rich and poor, powerful and powerless, only grows. Reifying discourses and structures, whether in conservative or cancerous form, have only ever served to increase this, to consolidate power in the hands of the few, and to perpetuate institutions which keep the majority disenfranchised. While critique can only do so much, it can help loosen the seeming naturalness of these approaches, and question the need for the institutions they produce.

Drawing inspiration from critiques of reification found in other worldviews, such as the Marxist critique of "commodity fetishism," constructivist and process-oriented approaches to scientific or philosophical reductionisms, Buddhist attempts to liberate desire from craving, Sufi critiques of binding, Whitehead's notion of the "fallacy of misplaced concreteness," or Hegel or Spinoza's attack on "picture-thinking," this project will work to extend, intertwine, and radicalize these in various ways.[55] In place of atomistic, binary, dualist, linearized, and otherwise non-relational approaches to the world which rigidly emphasize disconnection, purity, resistance to change, boundary protection, hierarchy, or centralization, the networkological project will emphasize refraction over reflection. The world can be much more, and always has been, no matter how hard we have tried to make it more stable, secure, and ultimately, less interesting, less multiform, less diverse, less creative, and less robust. Critique needs to open up the sense of possibility right in front of us, debunking the myths that there is no alternative, that banks awash in cash, fictitious or otherwise, are broke, that things will be different after this next round of manufactured crises are over, so many tales of smoke and mirrors which keep systems of injustice in place.

We know the world can and should be different. The potential for growth, development, and freedom, it is all right here and now, we do not need to look to some impossible elsewhere, it is all in how things network with others. Value and meaning are produced relationally, and if people change the way they act, values and meanings will change as well. The economy cannot be broke, since the economy is just the networks which produce it, so if it is broke, this is the result of distortion and theft, and shows a need to call for a change to the organizational structures that make this possible. But this means that we need to critique our own participation in these processes, our own desires to accumulate. We do not need their products, we need a more just society, one which values labor and hard work, and lets no one starve or go without medical care or education. We need to be skeptical of constantly produced crises against imaginary enemies which are only ever designed to make us re-reify, and help keep the masses occupied while those at the top reap the gains. We need to opt out, stop consuming, start producing new networks for new ways of living, outside and around the systems that continually attempt to addict us for their own ends. We need to start outnetworking the systems of domination, as some at the margins have already begun to do on their own. But the more people see this as a possibility, the more potential there is to actually bring about substantive change.

Networks can help provide tools to imagine ways of getting around centralizing systems, but real change must always start locally. Few things are more local than our very selves and the networks we support, all of which can help explain why this project places such an emphasis on deconstructing the exceptionalism of the self. While there are many forms which reifying logics take in the world, the isolated individual human self, perhaps the most crucial fiction of the capitalist "West," provides the means whereby so many other reifying logics anchor themselves into human thought and action in a particularly fundamental way. While in some sense we all know that we are not truly islands, but rather, products of our psychology, culture, history, language, biology, and physics, we often act as if we did not realize this were the case. Despite our often intellectualized protestations to the contrary, the fantasy of reified individuality still remains operative. For up until recently, this received support from the notion that the structure of the brain was unfathomable, a mystery of mysteries, and hence, that the only possible explanation for the human mind was something ineffable and transcendent, a "soul" or something like this. From such a perspective, the human mind is cast as an exception to all the rules of the physical world. Notions such as the "human soul" or its various avatars can then serve as a knot whereby to anchor a wide variety of other logics of exceptionalism, so that they seem natural and necessary.

History is full of the consequences of this type of thinking and its analogs. For as soon as the human mind or soul is seen as the unique source of all value in the world, materiality is denigrated, and this denigration is then projected outwards. People start arguing why others are less than "fully human," and can be treated as means for their uniquely important needs. The horrors of slavery and colonialism, as well as the oppressions of various social groups due to religion, race, gender, sexuality, disability, wealth, lack of citizenship, etc., all these arise from a series of resonant logics of exceptionalism put into reverse. Exceptionalist logics which value the human, a particular nation, race, religion, or social formation (i.e.: the market), all these paranoid funda-mentalisms are radical dangers to what makes life worth living. For they tend to be justified by mechanics which are structurally similar to those which, throughout history, argued that various aspects of society and the world were not worthy of being valued, and others were so valuable as to be beyond value.

The notion that a king is the head of a sovereign nation, that a father is the unquestioned head of a household, that God is radically distinct from the world yet organizes it, that a better world or "heaven" is elsewhere and only for those who follow one creed, that "logical" systems are founded on pure axioms, that humans are "rational actors" who maximize utility, that everyone in society starts from a level playing field of pure competition, that observation in science or journalism can or should be unbiased, that history is progressive, that nations have a destiny, that binary approaches to gender, race, sexuality, species, or whatever else find justification in the world, that the environment or animals are there purely for use by humans - all of these ways of looking at the world operate by means of rigid, binary, exceptionalist logics whose consequences are violence and the limitation of robustness for any but a select few, and even then, for the most part, only in the short-term.

All of these exceptionalist logics found a strong center of resonance in the fact that, up until now, it seemed impossible to imagine that the human mind was anything other than a funda-mental gap, exception, and island in the fabric of the universe. Loosening the strands of the knot of human exceptionalism is therefore one of the primary tasks this project sets for itself. Once the human being is seen as not made of a fundamentally different sort of stuff from the world around it, we are able to think about value differently. Then either nothing is radically different and special in the world, the perspective of vulgar materialism, which is both depressing and hardly believable, or the human mind is simply the most complex form of what is valuable in everything and anything.

The relevant question then becomes which aspects of the world give rise to what is worth valuing, whether human or otherwise. We are thereby forced to think about why we value what we value, rather than relying on rigid certainties which are easily manipulated by those who acquire enough power to impact the continual redefinition of key terms such as "humanity" or "the soul" to fit their needs of the moment. This is not to say that the simple realization that artificial neural networks deconstruct the mind-matter boundary can change millennia of violent thinking. Our limbic systems are programmed into us by evolution to make changing this very difficult. But if we begin to see less of a need to view the world as centered around ourselves as atomized agents, we might begin to wonder if perhaps the very fabric of the world itself might be, in a sense, "holy," with each and any aspect of it as having the potential to radically emerge in the right networked contexts, and to wonder what this might mean.

A relational approach to meaning and value, such as that advocated by this project, makes it much more difficult to perform reifying operations without taking into account the wider contexts which make these possible. Networkologically speaking, meaning and value are always relational, for meaning and value must always account for the relation of any aspect to the larger contexts which always and necessarily exceed any local determinations or reifications thereof. We were never simply atomized agents acting according to rigid logics and linear narratives in simplified fields, nor is there anything in the world like this. These idealizing fantasies are dangerous, and have very real effects. Purity, and the rigid postures of body and mind that go with this, as well as the more subtly cancerous flows which nevertheless still feed the accumulation of surplus potentials behind firm barriers and walls, these are the many dangers to a robust world. Whether more traditionally conservative or more subtly paranoid in cancerous form, the result is generally the same, namely, a state of perpetual war and crisis, and the destruction of more potential than is unleashed in the process. Even the winners in such a game ultimately lose, for there is a devaluation of the potential of the systems in which they operate as a whole, even if their relative share of surplus always remains a tiny bit ahead in such an impoverished field. This manifests not only in overt forms, but even in more subtle ways in which meaning and value are determined so as to support those who often dominate precisely by their ability to manipulate these sorts of structural mechanics which create systems whereby people make themselves easy to divide and be conquered.

Divide and conquer is, unfortunately, the logic whereby domination has occurred throughout history. Likewise with its opposite. For it should not be thought that relational viewpoints and ways of acting are new, or arose with the Internet. Networks are simply an opening onto the potential for relational thinking and refractively emergent creativity which has always been there alongside more rigid and reifying modes of operation. Without this, in fact, there would be no robustness at all, and even reifying systems only ever attempt to harness the power that relationality unleashes on the world, and to keep the creative instability this generates as much as possible in the hands of whatever supports the status quo. In this sense, the Western notion of "the individual" is both cause and effect of one of the more massive attempts in history to go beyond traditional forms of territoriality, such as the family or nation, towards mega-corporations. Whether conservative or cancerous, however, the effects are equally constraining.

When examined in the larger context of worldviews produced across the globe and through history, however, it is in fact the philosophy of the isolated individual, of an objective observer working to know and control an outside world, which is an aberration. While dominant in the Euro-American context from Descartes and Kant forward, this notion needs to be seen as a fantasy which was in a feedback loop of cause and effect with contemporary logics of European industrialism, colonialism, capitalism, and modern science. For it is hardly a coincidence that the fantasy of objective observation in science, of calculations of pure profit in economics, and the study of the individual "against" the background of the rest of the world in philosophy came about at around the same time as Europe and then America began literally raping and pillaging the rest of the world.[56] Structures of reification such as exceptionalism and isolated individuality need therefore to be seen as part of a continuum of the mutation and development of forms of paranoid control whereby robustness has been contained and harnessed for ultimately centralizing ends.

There are, however, resources for rethinking these paradigms beyond the destabilizing aspects of contemporary relational technologies such as "networking." This project will therefore look for inspiration and strategies from logics of relationalism and emergence in pre-modern Western and non-Western sources, as well as from counter-traditions within the West. These can all help point beyond the philosophies of the reified individual, and all the more practical logics of consumption, decontextualized profit, xenophobias, ecological destruction, and other behaviors which the notion of the reified individual often serves to subtly suture together. None of which is to say that societies beyond the West are without their violences, but rather, that their philosophies and worldviews can provide roadmaps to help with the particular crises which have arisen from the dominance of Western models in the world today, in both Eastern and Western contexts. For ultimately, Eastern notions often also need to be transformed, because while they tend not to reify the individual, they are often tied into social logics which are their inverse. In all this it also needs to be taken into account that any reified notions of "East" and "West" are themselves products of the history of colonialism and violence, the legacies of which need to be problematized as much as possible at each step.

And so, while this project will draw upon Eastern notions, it will also work to transform and be transformed by them in the process, all with the goal of robust development in mind. While many non-Western sources will provide crucial inspiration for relational modes of thinking at work in this project, the emphasis upon changing the inner world will be coupled with an activist desire to unleash robust change, not only in the inner landscape, but in the outer world which feeds back into and develops this as both cause and effect as well. The hope is that in the process it may be possible to build something which networks in new ways, perversely drawing upon East and West, pre-, modern, and post-modern, from science and mathematics and beyond, so as to imagine new potential futures beyond contemporary turfs, zones of accumulation, and conservatively or cancerously enforced divides.

One difficulty which many in the West have with using non-Western sources, however, is the often theological or devotional nature of many of these insights. This Western bias is a legacy of the process of secularization which allowed the West to develop its forms of science. While clearly powerful, Western science and secularity are based on exclusions of wide swaths of the rest of human possibility. The same could be said for the notion of "profit" in "the market," or any other abstract standards of value and meaning, all of which only ever can be contextualized in regard to the evolutions which gave rise to them and of which they are a part. In this sense, notions such as "progress," "ratio-nality," or "God" are all aspects of the ways in which the world produces us as we produce our culture, with all of these feeding back into each other at multiple levels of scale at once. Rather than ask whether or not there is a "God" or anything like that, it might make more sense to begin to wonder precisely what this notion did for the West for so long, why it remains important for large portions of our globe in and through the development of capitalism and modern technology, and what this can tell us about ourselves that could help potentiate the development of greater robustness.

From such a view it may then be possible to see "God" as simply a way to try to think the world like any other, a refraction of the world in which we find ourselves. For if our brains are in many senses pattern completion machines,[57] then our notions of God can be seen as an attempt to complete the pattern of our world, with our conception of God as that of the largest pattern of which we can conceive. In this sense, if the whole world is a network of networks, then perhaps theological models from the past can help us theorize the world and all that is in it in an age in which all increasingly seems to be becoming one-in-many, and many-in-one, and networks of networks intertwining these. Perhaps even scientists and philosophers would find such notions of the divine less objectionable than the more transcendent models of the past, which had a tendency towards violence and blind faith, a tendency which more immanent, relational, and emergent modalities work to continually frustrate.

For while many non-relational notions of God present a reified, limited sense thereof, one which is both projection and screen for paranoid hopes and fears, a more relational and emergentist notion of the divine could potentially help us imagine ways to liberate ourselves from this. This would be something like a radically immanent notion of transcendence, a this-worldly pantheology. Such a notion of God would then simply be a name for the continually self-differing creativity of refraction whereby robustness potentiates itself in its process of thinking itself into a world. Rather than a theology of purity or exclusion, of the sorts which seem to thrive in relation to organized religious institutions or fundamentalist doctrines, this would be one which sees something like "God" everywhere and in everything, if ever more so in whatever attempt to link up the robustly differing emergence of each and any with that of all, each robustly refracting each.

It is for this reason that the networkological project can even be seen as endorsing a sort of theophanic pantheism,[58] in which all appearances of God which promote robustness are beneficial, a notion of the divine which could in fact come into sync with scientific and liberatory social perspectives. From such a perspective, the very stuff of this world, all of which is an aspect of some sort of original singularity or "Big Bang" which explores and develops itself in and through space and time as we know it, can be seen as holy, and increasingly so as it helps give rise to the emergence of greater sustainable complexity, in all senses of these terms, in regard to itself and what is around it. The infinite potential to transcend what is permeates the very fabric of our world and ourselves, we just have to learn how to see this and unleash this, even as the very structure of this world can help provide a roadmap which can teach us how to develop these potentials towards the better which we and our world could become.

It is essential to keep in mind in all of this, however, that networks should not simplistically be seen as the solution to all the world's problems, for as was made clear at the start of this work, it is evident that networks, both today and in the past, can be violent as well as constructive, often indiscriminately destroying as they create. This is particularly true with networks that are reflective in structure, and maintaining the refractive, distributed structure of networking which preserves and even promotes differences rather than destroying them often requires the sort of massive multi-layer feedback which exists in few places beyond the human brain. Refraction is something which must be grown, and with great difficulty, for paranoid reflection, whether conservative or cancerous, will always work to try to co-opt it to its own ends.

In this sense, once the human is removed from the center of all value, it is essential to find new values which can do the work this notion has done in protecting some of what is valuable in our world, while hopefully avoiding its more insidious effects. This becomes particularly important as the highly networked phenomenon of contemporary capitalism reworks prior forms of individuality underneath our feet, by means of advertising, social networking, digital prosthesis, and so much more. For if there is one thing capitalism is good at, it is its uncanny ability to outnetwork islands of more fair ways of life, or even eliminate the ways in which the traditionalisms of yesterday did protect some differences which were not always already designed for the extraction of profit.

This is why it is essential not to respond to contemporary capitalism with reactive conservatism, or half-hearted attempts at appeasement. Rather, the only way forward which has a chance at success is to outnetwork capital, to show the ways in which contemporary capital is simply not networked enough, and to beat it at a game which is ultimately not its own anyway. For contemporary cancerous and neo-conservative networks only deploy networked models for ultimately uniperspectival and reifying ends. Terrorist networks, the increasingly networked armies that fight them, and contemporary capitalism, all fundamentalisms of various sorts, are manifestations of the tendencies of reification which may use networked means, but are not networked and relational in themselves, for they end up producing paranoia, atomization, rigidification, and homogenization in their wake, running counter to the ways in which networks unleash potential for the networked emergence of robustness as such.

Fundamentalism of any sort, whether as particularist paranoia which seeks to defend particular aspects of the world against all change, or the production of cancerous growth machines which seek to reduce the world to one reflection of a hypertrophied same, is ultimately counter to the manner in which networks tend towards the distributed when given the opportunity. In a changing and diverse world, such approaches can only lead to violence, crisis, and collapse, whether cultural, financial, biological, or geological. While this can be seen most clearly in regard to fundamentalisms which make use of networks for traditional or neo-traditional aims, for example in first-world digital armies and their terrorist mirror-inverses, this applies as well to the ways in which a completely financialized world, a neo-fundamentalism which strangles the very resource bases and creative pockets that made it possible in the first place, ultimately halts evolution with its unique blend of unlimited flow and rigidified modes of value formation.

Few dangers are more profound today than that of market fundamentalism, an approach which uses networks for highly cancerous aims while speaking the language of evolution and democracy. While the fetishization of the market uses Darwinian language, it is ultimately a mockery of the radical diversity engine of physical and biological evolution which gave rise to it. For market fundamentalism values one thing alone, namely, financial capital, the reproduction of more power for more power here and now, abstract surplus, regardless of the cost to the quality of life or the future.[59] In the biological world, only locusts and other creatures that destroy their own foodbase live like this, and they do not tend to live long or develop much further in the long run. Radical market fundamentalism is in this sense anything but robust. It is anti-evolutionary, for it is what happens when feedback begins to get caught in its own circuit, unable to escape its own gravity, bringing the system crashing down on itself by feeding on the very contexts which allow it to thrive. Rather than produce greater emergence, such a system gives rise to ever more violent cascades and bubbles within virtual realities of currency and products, all with very real effects. The more unfettered such logics become, the more violent the mood swings, and the more crashes of entire ecosystems or organisms and cultures become a persistent reality. And after each crash, those left standing can often clean-up the spoils for a song, such that the engineering of crashes is now nearly an intentional art. Unfettered capitalism leads only to monopolization, such that only limited capitalism truly protects competition and growth which is not merely for more growth, but for better quantity and quality of emergence for any and all.[60]

Despite the dangers posed by such forms of capital, it should not be thought that it might be possible to fight cancerous modalities on their own turf with either appeasement or reactive nostalgia. Fundamentalism against fundamentalism always loses to fundamentalism in the end, even if in different form. The form of resistance must be refractive or not at all, and if there is any way to halt the massive subsumption of our world by the capitalist maw, it is by pushing it beyond its own game. For any of these cancerous modalities, by using networks, hold within them the secret to their own deconstruction, namely, the radical potential which networking presents, which itself tends towards refractive rather than reflective modalities, towards creation rather than reproduction of the paranoid same. The manner in which revolutions and information leaks have begun to use technologies designed by the powerful against their makers is just the start of this sort of co-evolutionary development. We have just begun to see the potentials that lie in this direction, though we need to work to continually deconstruct the ways in which the powers that be will always try to reify our modes of acting and thinking so as to divide us from the pulsing creative potentials which are the very fabric of which more rigid forma-tions are ultimately made.

We can always network differently, the problem is that we often do not see the potentials right in front of us; we prefer the meager recompense the megacorporations allow us. Truly emerging requires developing new forms of trust which we have been trained not to desire. Until we begin to experiment with new, more refractive forms of networked world-production, however, we will continue to be manipulated by systems of domination which arise from anywhere and nowhere, distributed agents more powerful than the figurehead technocrats who operate them for a nice chunk of the spoils. But they are hardly the masters of the show, which are quasi-living, transvidual tendencies bigger than any individual human or set of human agencies. Capitalism is ultimately a hyperorganism, and we need to evolve it to be more robust, lest it implode itself with us as well. Only refractive networks of resistance which learn to sync up, by means of their very differences, have any chance of shifting the terrain whereby this currently global organism directs energies of the reified, divided masses into the hands of the few.

There are lessons here which can be applied to the ecosystems of life in ponds as much as to economies. Learning to evolve ourselves individually and collectively towards robustness can help us not only to come into sync with the processes which brought us about from the physical and biological worlds, but also to tap into the processes in our world which seem to produce the best of all we love, in and beyond the parameters of the world we currently see. Studying the evolution of robustness in the world can help us better imagine ways to evolve increased robustness, not only in ourselves, but also in the world around us. It can also help us understand how to shift the parameters whereby evolution selects for some traits over others, such that it may be possible one day to out evolve capitalism along with our tendencies towards other paranoid structures in turn.

The networkological project aims to provide new lenses for looking at the world which can help imagine ways of acting which could make some of this possible. In all this, however, it should not be thought that the networkological project views itself as describing the only way of looking at the world. Rather, if philosophy is an attempt to understand the whole of the world of experience, even only as this appears to us here and now, then perhaps each age needs its own view of the whole to help it figure out simply what to do next. Philosophy should not merely describe the way the world is, but also the way the world can be. Such a view of philosophy does not aim for eternal truth as much as for the truth as it is and could be, from the perspective of the world as it appears right here and now. If we look at philosophies in the past this way, as the products of their ages and cultures, then it only makes sense to understand the attempt to produce new philosophies in this way as well.

Rather than place faith in ideal notions like certainty or proof, all of which remain outside justification themselves, the networkological project believes such approaches ultimately rely on non-relational foundations. Notions such as "logic" or "reason" have only ever been value terms to describe whatever the majority thinks is the best way to think. None of which is to say that the networkological project rejects any notion of reason or logic to its argumentation. It seeks to come into sync with the patterns, symmetries, and invariances which structure the world as it is and could be, rather than to develop a rigid, ideal, and impossible set of standards in regard to which the world will always be lacking or excessive. The world should be the standard for argumentation in philosophy, not the reverse. And if the world has created all that is of value, then valuing creation allows us to produce new meanings which can help us imagine new ways of acting which in turn, it is hoped, can resonantly sync with this creation, this emergent robustness, at ever deeper levels. Philosophy is only ever world-modeling which produces the potential for such sync, and as such, the networkological project sees itself as a description of the world as it is as much as a dream of what it could be.

Breaking down the barrier between reality and fantasy, the networkological project firmly believes that intervening in virtual reality impacts our actual futures, with wide ramifications for the practice of philosophy as the radical creation of new lenses with which to rework our ways of seeing how we act in relation to our worlds. This project will therefore see philosophy as composed of descriptions, rather than deductions or proofs. Taking inspiration from post-foundationalist approaches in mathematics and physics, as well as post-structuralist philosophy, the networkological project sees all theories as moves within a continually shifting series of networked games. Philosophy, mathematics, and other abstract disciplines have only ever been meta-gaming, just as could equally be said about capitalism and attempts at resistance against it. And all games have rules, even if these are often fuzzy or continually redefined, and these rules are the descriptions of the terms of its dynamics. In this sense, the only description which the networkological project cherishes more than others is that which says that only the rigid, paranoid, reifying descriptions and the modes of organization which they foster are truly dangerous. Refracting this exception in reverse to all it sees allows this project to intervene in a way which it hopes can potentiate ever more robust forms of networking.

In all this, networks are particularly well suited to redescribe the world in terms of robust emergence because they have difference at their relational core. Networks link together different aspects of the world in regard to those which are different from them. In this sense, networks are a means whereby this project weaves a new way of thinking about immanence, relation, refraction, emergence, and robustness, and in terms of the type of networks that have come to dominate the character of our age. Networks are a means to an end, a bridge which, once used to cross a ravine, can be thrown away, like a tool used to construct a building which then becomes part of the building itself and fades into the very structure which it was used to create.[61] And so, in regard to itself, this project does not aim to reproduce itself with some sort of fidelity, but rather to proliferate differences, its own deconstruction and reconstruction, in a manner which can hopefully help others to sustainably do the same. Take this project and use it, tear it to shreds, shatter and refract it to give rise to emergences more robustly. Robustness must be for any and all or it is hardly deserving of the name.

From Networks to Netlogics:
Diagramming the World

While the networkological project's goals are concrete in relation to the contemporary situation in the world, there is a highly abstract side to this project as well. By abstracting concepts to their limits, it is possible to see their ramifications in more extreme situations than those currently available in our everyday lives, a process which helps explore potential pitfalls before they arise in practice. Before bringing this introduction to a close, it is worth examining this more directly theoretical side of this project as well, an approach which describes what this project looks like from the lens of more traditional notions of philosophy, even if concrete examples will be used whenever possible in the process.

From an abstract, philosophical perspective, when networks intertwine with each other, they *grasp, or relate* with each other. This can happen in a series of ways, each corresponding to one of the primary aspects of networks, or elements, described in the preceding sections as nodes, links, grounds, and levels. These four elements are not only aspects of networks in the world, but, as concepts, they are elements of the concept of network itself. As was stated earlier, this concept, a concept of a type of diagram, is what will be referred to as the network diagram, which is composed of the four conceptual elements of node, link, ground, and level, the last of which is itself an element, or aspect, of emergence. Each of the elements of the network diagram describe one of the primary ways in which networks grasp each other, and as such, give rise to each other in the world. These modes of grasping are what produce nodes by noding, links by linking, grounds by grounding, and levels by leveling, all of which are produced by the emergence of networks from within each other in the world. These primary ways of emerging, these processes of grasping and modes of relating, are what the networkological process will refer to as *logics*. There are four primary logics described by the networkological project, those of node, link, ground, and emergence, of which level is an aspect.

Of these logics, the *logic of the node* is simplest. To grasp something according to the logic of the node is to isolate it, reify it, separate and abstract it from what is around it to the greatest extent possible. Eating a mouthful of food, picking up a stone, examining a society from the perspective of only one category, each of these approaches to the world is, in its way, a radical reduction of the complexity of the world, to whatever extent possible, to one particular aspect. This aspect can then be linked to others, and a network produced thereby. This action of carving up a section of the world, separating it off, and isolating it is what noding is, it is what gives rise to nodes. And so, the networkological project will refer to those processes which do this as operating according to the logic of the node. Nothing in the world is ever fully isolated, and as such, nodes are always composed of aspects to which they are linked, even as they link to others beyond them in turn. The *logic of the link* describes the ways in which aspects of networks, including but also going beyond nodes, connect and are connected to each other.

There is, however, a particular type of connection which exceeds the logic of the link even as it extends it from within, and this is the logic of grounds. Grounds are fundamentally peculiar, they are neither fully inside of networks nor fully outside of them. Grounds are a principle of indeterminacy, for they are always in the background, such that when foregrounded, they cease to be grounds, and show themselves to be composed of networks and their elements, rather than the hazy indeterminacy they often appear to be. Grounds are that which gives rise to networks, from which they separate themselves off, as well as that which maintains networks as their context and support. When networks change, they always do so in relation to their grounds, absorbing aspects back into these, or absorbing aspects from them. The manner in which that which is beyond the nodes and links in a network gives rise to, maintains, changes, or dissolves a network is the manner in which that context grounds that network. The attempt to understand why a network is formed the way it is an attempt to understand its relation to its contexts or how that context grounds it. When networks relate to each other in the mode of grounding, as contexts which are neither fully within the network nor without it, as neither nodes nor links but that which contextualizes these, this is described by the *logic of the ground.*

Grounds are the contexts of the foregrounds of networks, the nodes and often links, and yet, each ground is multiple, composed of grounds within grounds, networks within networks, whole and parts, and at multiple levels of scale, and even levels of scale can be seen as nodes within networks, which are linked together by others in turn. Nodes contain nodes, links link to more links, contexts always open onto other contexts, and levels contain more levels within each other, all at potentially infinite levels of scale. Where did this all come from? What are the processes that gave rise to all these? When contexts open on to the processes from which they emerged, the differentiations that gave rise to them, their larger contextualizations within the dynamic shifts within the world which produced them, what emerges is an attempt to grasp all the elements of networks, including nodes, links, grounds, and levels in regard to their relations to processes of emergence in the world as such. These processes are what grasp each other, and the patterns of stability which arise within this are what gives rise to nodes, links, grounds, and levels in and through this. Emergence is that which grasps itself, and networks and their elements are the result. To grasp a network or network element in this manner, which is to emerge in relation to it, is to grasp it according to the *logic of emergence.*

The opening of grasping, from relative isolation to connection to context to processes, is movement which the networkological project will trace in a wide variety of forms. This is the redescriptive movement, or diagramming, which refracts and is a refraction of the network diagram. In the process of this diagramming, this project will work to show how all aspects of the world which might seem isolated can be seen as aspects of the emergence of the self-differing stuff of the world from itself. This self-differing stuff, which, as mentioned earlier, will be called the oneand, is the matrix and flesh of experience, that of which any one is composed, and which yet also exceeds this. This excess, the *–andic* side of the oneand, is the emergence within relation which always pushes it beyond itself. The network diagram, which describes three elements, and one quasi-element, that which opens onto emergence which always exceeds itself in and beyond each of the original elements, is in this sense not a structure of three or even four aspects, but is beyond this. For this reason, the network diagram will also be known as *the fourand*, and its structure as *fourandic*. Since networks describe the manner in which the oneand manifests in the world, the networkological project can be seen as an attempt to describe the manner in which the oneand manifests in the fourand.

By showing how what appears to be composed of fixed nodes and links always has the oneand within and beyond it, the networkological project will work to show how attempts to limit, fix, determine, control, capture, or petrify aspects of the oneand into structures of ones, twos, or threes, miss the potential for radical creativity which it fundamentally is, and can be ever more intensely. Working to sync with the emergence of the oneand by means of liberating the fourand within any ones, twos, or threes in the world is what the networkological project is all about.

While this might sound incredibly abstract, there are ways in which the four netlogics can be described more concretely. For example, if you are typing on a computer, and you only take into account the computer as object in front of you, the way it feels and acts in isolation from the world around it, you are dealing with it according to the logic of the node. But if you begin to think about the computer as a meaningful entity, you see it as different from the table upon which it rests, the fingers you use to type on it, the dog sitting in the room next to you, the thoughts in your brain, and so much more. These systems of relational differences are so many modes of connection which have patterns at work in them which make them intelligible. Trying to interpret how the computer is different from or the same as what is around it is to grasp it according to the logic of the link.

And yet, there are so many ways to read a computer. A computer can be interpreted as a tool for use, the manifestation of scientific formulations and technological innovations, or as the product of industrial exploitation of populations across the globe. The intertwined lumps of silicon and plastic we call a "computer" is, of course, all of these. But determining which interpretations we use at any given moment to read this computer raises the question of why use one set of interpretations over others, and what makes us choose certain interpretations, or modes of action, as well as what similar processes gave rise to the computer in the first place. How do we justify our relation to this computer, and what reasons do we give to ourselves for this? How do we stop the slippages of potential meanings, and anchor our relation to the computer in one meaningful modality of thought and action over others? These are questions of value, and I am a valuing economy: I make choices based on my values, and the ways in which my culture, biology, and physical context evolved me to value according to its values. The abyss of grounding always ties into the processes of emergence. To see the computer as an aspect of various economies, including financial economies, discursive economies, labor economies, and living economies such as myself is to see it according to the logic of the ground.

But all of these economies came from somewhere, according to processes of evolution which link them in so many inter-twinings and unfoldings of potential, so many complexifications which emerge in the world. Linking up any particular set of experiences, meanings, and values to the larger processes which gave rise to them is to situate them in regard to questions of emergence, and ultimately, how emergence occurs as such. If we pursue such a chain of reasoning, we need to ask precisely what emergence is, how it comes about, why it comes about, and how we and the computer relate to these questions. Only such a questioning can help us fully situate in regard to how we ground our attempts at grounding, which will always lead, in one form or another, to the paradox of emergence as such, to the attempt to think the emergence of values, meaning, and experience, and the possibility of trying to come into sync with the emergence which gave rise to these, and which has the potential to go beyond these to potentiate further robust emergence. The emergence of the philosophy of networks is an attempt to deal with these issues, to produce the emergence of a philosophy which will foster emergence in the world.

Radical Relational Emergentism:
Philosophy as Refractive Crystallography

As a network of concepts, production of the networkological project will resemble that of the complex systems at work in the world it describes, its new creations emerging and mutating in relation to the growth of the complex whole. Each will be shifted by the refractions of what comes after, unworking and reworking the old and new from within, even as what remains will slowly link together, each partially destabilizing the others and the whole with each new addition. What emerges in this process is a conceptual architecture, a quasi-living complex which responds to each mutation even as it develops a gravity and weight of its own, much like a vortex responds to the stresses in a continually shifting pool. As such, this project will not reflect some core assumed at the start and proved at the end and imposed from center to parts throughout. Rather, it will produce itself as a shattered whole, giving rise to a wide variety of mutating local potentials, each sending ripples through part and whole with each addition, sometimes subtle and at other times profound, democratizing the process of creation between concepts and domains in the process, producing a philosophy which is as distributed as possible in regard to the world in which it finds itself.

While this book is the start, then, it is also the culmination of the inception of a larger project of networking which is only ever still beginning to become truly networked in relation to its contexts. In this sense, the philosophical apparatus of the networkological project aims to evolve itself from the world around it, to emerge as a meta-stable complex network, one which resonates with the form of what it seeks to describe, dynamically mutating as it goes beyond its own past forms of futuring. More like an organism than anything else, this philosophy will produce itself as an inorganic, conceptual organism, a strange machinic life which will grow like a crystal.[62]

The seed of this crystal, that which can be abstracted from the refractive process as a whole, which echoes and resonates with the refractions of the subject matters that provide its media of crystallization, is the notion of the network diagram itself. This concept, rewoven from various discourses of networking at work in the world today, is itself simply a diagrammatic refraction of the sub-concepts and descriptions of which it is both an abstraction and a guide. Including notions like node, link, ground, and level, along with the networkological principles, and many other concepts and descriptions in works to come, ultimately, its wholes and parts exceed each other, for this concept is nothing more than that of the complex networking of this project itself in its potential to sync with the world which gives rise to it.

As a conceptual machine for intertwining and radical differentiation, a structure which mutates both itself and its contexts with an aim towards fostering robustness, the network diagram is a prism for the refractive crystallization of conceptual models of worlds. Continually reworking how it manifests in regard to its contexts, the network diagram describes a mode of redescription which is flexible and distributed, a dispersed processing which seeks to foster robust emergence in the world by means of its engagement with ever more of its aspects. As an abstract description of a process, the network diagram is a way of moving and acting in the world, a diagramming world modeling which is never pure, but always in situation, always transforming and being transformed, always ever an abstraction from the very crystallizations which it produces in all it touches. Such a process creates the new by networking, fighting closure as well as dissolution except for where they can promote ever more robust forms of networking.

This project, these networkologies, are therefore not a single networkology, but a network of networkologies. In its commitment to robustness, the networkological project will produce a series of networked lenses for reviewing the world and its aspects. It will start by examining traditional lenses, and work to tease out the networks below the surface and waiting to emerge, even if beneath each of these are simply more networks, the potential for ever more fractally refractive networks. By means of its modes of redescription, this project will work to describe a mode of relating to the world which provides a glimpse of the refractory structure of the networked fabric of our world, that which gives rise to this all, yet differently in each case, this seedwork which is prismatic shimmering all the way down, layerings of kaleidoscopic mirrorings which shatter and crack each other continually to give rise to ever new patterns.

In the process, this project will also be, to some extent, its own demise, as it works to give rise to more robust emergences in and beyond itself. One goal of this project, then, is its own metabolizing by those networks beyond it, leading to new relational figures, beyond networks and not yet imagined, which radical creativity will produce from itself in ways to come. Networks are only a means to an end, a structure which, it is hoped, can diagram some of the potentials whereby a relational, immanent, refractive emergence of robustness can help describe the world in potentially liberatory ways, in relation to our networked age here and now.

This introduction began by mentioning notions of oneness, seen in many ancient traditions, such as "Everything is Connected," "All is One," and "The one in the many, the Many in the One." These notions are often reduced in complexity to indicate a unitary, overly-simplistic sense of oneness which radically reduces the meaning, or potential meanings, involved. This project nevertheless takes these claims seriously, working to describe a notion of oneness as robust emergence which is both the world we experience in all its complexity, and also the potential for more robust emergences within and composing the very fabric of all we are, do, and see. The goal of this endeavor, in and beyond any of its aspects, drawing upon science and mathematics, past and present, "East" and "West" and beyond, is to help think our potential relations to the world around us. The hope is to produce a philosophy of networks for our hyper-connected age, to help give rise in the process to an emergently robust set of networks, so many seeds for the future, these refractively and polymorphously proliferative networkologies.

Part Two

Networkologies: A Manifesto

Networks are everywhere, and increasingly so. With the rise of the Internet, mobile computing, globalization, digital finance, and social media, ours is an increasingly networked age. Networks are not only our present, but our past and future as well, for it seems more each day that the world was always already networked, as if simply waiting for the rise of new network formations, and the Internet in particular, for us to have the eyes to see this. Nevertheless, so many of the models we use to help understand our world, from economics to politics to ethics and beyond, are prenetworked not only in terms of content, but also form, products of a time before networks changed everything.

We need new models in sync with the needs, crises, and potentials of our age. Various branches of contemporary science, mathematics, and social science increasingly employ networked models, but there has yet to be an attempt to develop an entire worldview, a philosophy, based on networks.[1] Such a philosophy would have to take into account the massive advances of the technology, science, mathematics, and social sciences of networks. But it would also have to bring these quantitative approaches into sync with qualitative concerns related to meaning, interpretation, value, and power, so as to develop an ethics, aesthetics, and politics which could help us better navigate the challenges of our networked age.

This book, the first installment of "the networkological project," will begin to develop a general worldview based on networks, a philosophy not merely about networks, but *of* networks, in all senses of these terms. The basic notion of what makes up a network is simple: a network is anything composed of parts, connected to others, against a background, with each of these composed of more networks in turn at multiple levels of scale. In the terminology of networks, the parts are called nodes, they are connected by links, contextualized by grounds, and layered in levels, with nodes, links, grounds, and levels as the primary aspects, or elements, of networks.

From a networkological perspective, anything and everything can be seen as networks composed of networks. Atoms are networks, as are ordinary objects, societies, organisms, brains, concepts, thoughts, languages, and economies. The differences between these, however, is in the form of their networking. Networks can be homo- or heterogeneous, static or dynamic, centralizing, directional, or multi-centered. They can link to one another in a variety of ways, containing and differentiating, absorbing or producing one another, emerging spontaneously under some conditions, or produced for specific purposes in others. When aspects of a network come into sync with aspects of another, they diagram each other. Networks can give rise to intensities and complexifications, and grasp each other in various modes of experience, meaning, valuation, and thought. Deviously centralizing potentials or distributing them amongst one another, the various forms of networking have ramifications for technology, economics, ethics, politics, and beyond. Networks not only represent the world, they are the world; they not only unfold potential, they are potential; they not only describe thought, they are thought; they not only emerge from the world, they are this emergence. Understanding the different types of networks, their modes of structuration, interaction, intertwining, and formation, how they reflect and refract one another, as well as the meanings, values, actualities, and potentials which emerge from them is what the networkological project is all about.

This project is a thought experiment to see what the world could look like when viewed as composed of networks of branching networks. If anything and everything can be seen as networked, then networks are ultimately a way of looking at the world, a set of lenses which can show not only how everything can be seen as networked, but as having the potential within them for more intense forms of networking. Showing how and why this could be, as well as why we might want this, is the primary task this project sets for itself. To paraphrase a famous philosopher: *"To those who look at the world networkedly, the world will look networkedly back."*[2] This is the fundamental wager of this text. The networkological worldview takes the notion of the network and transforms it into a concept, diagram, ethic, and project. Welcome to the world of networkologies.

This manifesto will sketch, in hypercondensed, programmatic form, this project as a whole, describing in each section below not only how networks "are" in the present, but also how they could be if they network more intensely to liberate the potentials within them in the manner described by this project. In this sense, while not all networks "are" robust, they could be, and they tend towards this when not turned against ultimately networked ends by means of various forms of what will be described below as overreification. In addition, it should be kept in mind that, due to the form of this manifesto, the task of explaining and grounding the claims made in such a short text will necessarily need to be continued by future networkological texts.

> *nodes: access, science, mathematics, image of thought, process, complexity, emergence, relation, fractality, holography, spacetime, immanence, principles, experience, realities, (un)limits, semiotics, mediology, machinology, value, symbolic economies, robustness, practics, metaleptics, sync, understanding, evolution, meta-evolution, hyper-evolution, thinking, critique, deconstruction, reconstruction, post-foundation, refraction, diagram, difference, distributedness, historiography, psychology, panpsychism, liberation, commons, oppression, economics, political economics, politics, transviduality, post-anarchism, pantheism, theophanic post-theology, erotics, praxis, aesthetics, nothing, philosophy, meta-philosophy, history of philosophy, beginning, dream*

Networks are about access. The networkological project will address impasses in many fields, and draw upon recent advances at the cutting edge of science, mathematics, and technology, various branches of the social sciences, as well as philosophies present and past. Nevertheless, it will not engage in endless debates with specialists tied to narrow academic disciplinary modalities, rigid ideologies, or deadlocked partisan divides. Rather, it will emphasize the creation of the new, and the potential impact this can have upon our lives. And since change comes about when many can access new ideas, this project is designed with access in mind. For as this project will work to show, when not put to ultimately non-networked ends, networks tend towards the radical democratization of information, power, and potential. And so, unless specifically stated otherwise, networkological texts will be written so that no prior knowledge of science, mathematics, philosophy, or any specialized discipline will be required of readers, everything will be explained along the way. Due to the "manifesto" form of this text, however, what follows will necessarily be to some extent an exception to this, one which finds its full context, however, in relation of the rest of the networkological project itself.

Networks are a science. The networkological project finds inspiration in complex systems science, and the science of networks to which it gave rise during the second half of the twentieth century. Developing the implications of this new way of looking at physical, biological, and cultural phenomena, along with insights drawn from resonant approaches in a variety of other disciplines, this project will work to synthesize these to build an overall relational way of looking at the world, one which can help recast dualist, binary, reductionist, and otherwise non-relational models and practices which have led to impasses in a wide variety of fields, in and beyond the traditional domains of the sciences.

Drawing inspiration from emergent and embodied cognitions theories, as well as those related to "soft-computing" technologies, including fuzzy control systems, genetic and evolutionary algorithms, and artificial neural networks, this project will develop non-binary and networked models for dealing with a wide variety of phenomena.[3] This project will also build upon insights drawn from developments in epigenetic, autopoeitic, and multi-level selection theories in biology, non-substantialist models in philosophy of chemistry, and relational approaches to the radical findings of contemporary quantum physics, as described by notions such as spacetime smearing, Feynman networks, Gell-manian consistent histories, and David Bohm's notions of implicate folding.[4]

While this project will pull widely from various branches of contemporary science and mathematics, it will hardly accept the findings of these fields unquestioningly. Building upon work in science and mathematics studies by theorists such as Thomas Kuhn, Bruno Latour, Isabelle Stengers, Brian Rotman, Albert Lautman, Gilles Châtelet, and Fernando Zalamea, the networkological project views science and mathematics as social practices.[5] Rather than view interpretations and values within scientific and mathematical practices as biases to be one day removed, all model-making and experimentation will be seen as fundamentally perspectival and participatory, with biases serving as enabling conditions of these activities as such.

Intertwining relational approaches to mathematics and science with those in fields which pertain to meaning and value, this project will work to expand the potential implications of quantitative and qualitative approaches to the world, in order to show these as complementary aspects of not only our attempts to understand the world, but of the world itself. While some of what follows may therefore seem strange to those working in mathematical and scientific research, it should nevertheless be noted that nothing which follows will contradict the findings of contemporary science and mathematics, even as many of the assumptions at work in these practices will be reframed.

Networks are a mathematics. Working to sync with post-foundationalist movements in contemporary mathematics, as described
by group and category theories, this project will also draw from
many other aspects of contemporary mathematics, in fields such
as graph theory, set theory, analysis, post-Euclidean geometries
and topologies, topos theories, sheaf theories, and multi-valued
logics. In the process, it will work to show how networks can be
used to describe a wide variety of mathematical objects, from
sets to functions, categories to surfaces, and even numbers
themselves, and to indicate the ways in which non-linear models
provide a general interface between mathematical language and
the types of feedback indicative of complex systems in their
many forms.[6] In the process, this project will view mathematics
as a particularly abstract form of semiotically networked meta-
gaming, one more fold within the foldings whereby worlds
continue to emerge from themselves in forms abstract, concrete,
and everything in between by means of complex networking.

Networks are a new "image of thought."[7] Artificial neural
networks have shown that the primary elements of thought can
now be simulated on computers using networked models, and in
ways which are increasingly feeding back into neuroscientific
research on living brains.[8] Artificial neural networks learn,
guess, and forget in the manner of animal brains, and show, if in
radically simplified form, how the basic elements of animal and
human thought, such as the induction of patterns, memorization,
association, categorization, and temporal modulation can be
seen as types of networked wiring diagrams within complex
dynamic systems.

It is therefore possible to see thought and thinking as simply
what happens when matters intertwine in particularly complex
ways in dynamic systems, with the most complex forms of
matter, such as those found in the human brain, having the most
complex types of thought. The very form of artificial neural

networks and other modes of soft-computing, so different from that of the architecture of traditional serial computing, debunks many of the traditional myths about thought which have dominated philosophy and science, such as the notion that thought is somehow like human language, that it is linear, or that it is composed of binary switches. Researchers are increasingly coming to see complex forms of thought as taking a form which is non-linear, non-binary, and the result of emergent forms of sync which can occur between heterogeneous networks in relation to a relatively small set of wiring diagrams.

While the serial forms of computation at work in most computer hardware today provide us with incredibly fast tools which complement the limitations of human brains, serial computers are still massively simpler and less flexible than organic forms of computation present in even simple mammalian brains. Even the complex semiotic meta-networks of language and mathematics, which have made the engineering of computers possible, are much simpler than the brains that gave rise to them, which remain the most complex systems we know. While it may one day be possible to produce parallel computers which can exceed human computational abilities, this will likely require some sort of shift away from serial silicon chips to nano-, bio-, or quantum technologies which can change and grow in the manner of organisms. Soft-computation in its many forms, including fuzzy, networked, and evolutionary modalities, shows how this might be possible, beyond the limitations of binary, serial computation, which are simply the beginning of what synthetic minds will likely be able to do one day.

The implications of these changes is that it no longer makes sense to imagine, as many have this century,[9] that the most complex forms of thought we know take the form of a rapid linear series of binary computations. Rather, in the manner of the human brain, complex forms of thought can now be seen as the ability of a dynamic network to have some of its subnetworks come into sync with aspects of what is to be thought, so as to be able to change and develop in relation to it. This is something which animal brains do with massive rapidity and elegance all the time. Dominant conceptions of what it means to reason and to think, including assumptions based on these, which often guide our notions of logic, symbolic or otherwise, all need to be rethought in light of these new developments and the perspectives they provide.

Networks are a philosophy of process. Everything we experience in the world is only ever the same for a short while, with human scales of time mere flickers in the long durations of time at cosmic scales. Whatever manifests to us in our experience presents us with only a tiny fragment of the spacetime relevant to it, such that if one were to place something in a different set of conditions elsewhere in the universe it would be hard to say in advance precisely what it might do, or of what it might be capable. A sample of liquid water, for example, is always potential ice and steam, as well as part of a plant or a person, a star or a symphony. Everything we experience always was and will one day again be radically different than it is here and now in front of us, such that ultimately, anything is only ever a temporary stasis within patterns of processes. Nothing is then ever fully what it appears; all empiricism is to some extent always already an implicit idealism, and all physics always already partially metaphysics, for both empiricism and physics bracket what is beyond the here and how, even if these are always virtually present.[10] In this sense, to say that something "is" this or that, or is in this or that state, is only ever a convenient or useful fiction, for it describes, if often indirectly, the perspectival relation between an aspect of the world and those which grasp it in a particular context.

For these reasons, the networkological project is a philosophy of process. Drawing upon group and category theory in mathematics,[11] as well as the work of process philosophers[12] and theorists of scientific practice such as A.N. Whitehead, Gilbert Simondon, and Gilles Deleuze, the networkological project sees each experience of the world as a limited reification, literally "thing-ification," of the processes of differentiation, intertwining, and emergence which brought it about. While reification is necessary if there is to be interaction and experience in the world, practices or models which take these snapshots of more encompassing processes of change as somehow ultimate tend to radically simplify the way they relate to the world.

Rather than freezing the world into a collection of static images, this project views any aspect of the world as having been different in the past and likely the future, such that all entities, states, or reifications of other sorts conceal within them potentials, forces, and tendencies which are themselves result of others and will lead to others in turn. All networks and their elements are only ever patterns of symmetries, balances between forces which provide momentary localized stases within the dynamic changes at work in the world around them. Reifications always therefore need to be seen as related to contexts and processes of change beyond them, for failing to take the processural aspects of the world into account results in a lack of sync with the world, in practices as diverse as science and ethics. Overreification, which the networkological project will generally simply refer to as reification for the sake of simplicity, is in its many formations that which this project argues holds networks back from reaching many of their more robust potentials.

Networks are a philosophy of complexity. According to complex systems science, "complexity" is the manner in which "a whole exceeds the sum of its parts."[13] While a car can therefore be described as merely complicated, something like an organism, whose actions and reactions cannot be fully predicted from the form of its components, is complex. A tornado or convection cell, each of these has a form and potentials distinct from that of the components which give rise to it.

Complex systems are difficult to engineer; rather, they need to be grown, and complex systems science has shown that complexity tends to come about spontaneously in particular conditions. These generally include the presence of diverse materials, "meta-stable" conditions "on the edge of chaos" between stable equilibrium and unstable dissolution, relatively distributed or "small world" modes of organization between parts, and relations of feedback between the aspects that modulate the way they interact with each other and their contexts, whether internal or external, and often in a manner which is "scale-free" or fractal across levels of scale, thereby leading to the potential for sync in and through difference and change.[14]

In such conditions, new forms of organization which could not be predicted by the form of their parts, and as such have "non-linear" relations between earlier and later states, tend to emerge on their own, something which can be observed in various physical, biological, or cultural contexts.[15] A whirlpool in a draining pool of water, the swirling groupings in schools of fish, or the branching patterns in lightning are all self-organizing complex phenomena. Self-organization, often called "autopoeisis" or "emergence,"[16] not only comes about on its own in these conditions, but this process also tends to feed on itself and self-potentiate as well, giving rise to the very materials and conditions which support the development of even more complexity, up to and including the advent of life and the evolution of organisms. Complex systems also tend to adapt flexibly to the world around them. Put a stone near a whirlpool or a predator near a school of fish, and both whirlpool and fish will rework their patterns ways which are relatively decentralized, and whose form cannot be predicted from that of its individual elements.

Complex systems science explains "how newness enters the world,"[17] as well as how this newness can self-potentiate and adapt in the right conditions. Because each complex system can be seen as composed of networks of distributed agents which nevertheless often find ways to work together, the science of networks and complexity have developed in an intimately inter-twined manner.[18] Complex systems science will therefore be essential to the networkological project's efforts to describe how networking can give rise to a wide variety of experiences in our world.

Networks are a philosophy of emergence. Expanding upon the scientific usage of the notion of emergence, if in a way which does not conflict with the usage of this term in complex systems science, this project will develop a philosophy of emergence. And so, this project will view everything in the world as the result of self-organizing, self-potentiating, complex networking, or emergence, if to differing degrees and in different ways. From such a perspective, emergence is the very stuff of the world, its self-differing substance, that which emerges from itself by means of its differentiation and complex networking, and of which any particular network, including those which are merely compli-cated, are simply aspects. Emergence can then be seen as a principle of radical creativity, in and beyond any particular creation to which it gives rise, present within all we experience, yet only able to be unleashed by particular forms of differenti-ation and networking. Building upon philosophies of radical creativity, as described in the work of theorists such as Gilles Deleuze, Gilbert Simondon, or Henri Bergson,[19] this project will work to bring these into sync with complex systems science and the needs of our networked age, with a goal of giving rise to an emergence which is more than the sum of its parts.

Viewing the aspects of the world as various forms of networked emergence in this manner allows for them to be seen anew. From such a perspective, relatively static matter can then be seen as dormant emergence, while the actual or potential motion of matter, or energy, can be seen as active emergence. While energy is indistinguishable from matter at high energy levels, at lower energy levels it folds with itself to give rise to matter, which it can then move in ways which allow it to fold with other matters in ways which can give rise to qualitatively new and more complex forms of matter and energy in turn. As the networking of dynamic and stable matters and energies, all complexity, which is all potential for emergence in the future, is the result of emergence in the process of differentiating from and then networking back with itself. The result is the self-potentiation of complexity by itself, with matter, energy, actuality, and further potential for further emergence as so many aspects of this process.

While such notions may sound strange when phrased in abstract language, they nevertheless allow the world to be described in new ways, even in regard to everyday circumstances. For example, energy gives rise to new potentials by means of intertwining with matters of various sorts, such as the manner in which the sun gives rise to fuel, which can be used to produce electricity, which can build and run the computer used to write this book. All of these are examples of the emergences which come about when potentials of various sorts are renetworked back with themselves in particular ways. Beyond everyday circumstances, however, the approach to emergence described above can also make sense of the often counterintuitive findings of quantum physics, as well as the complex experiences which arise in networks such as the human brain, or a wide variety of social phenomena, and much of this project will be an attempt to describe how and why this might be.

From a networkological perspective, everything in the world of experience can be seen as aspects of emergence networking with itself. And in this sense, this project will itself emerge from the concept of emergence, even as it works to foster emergence in the world by means of this in the process. Showing how and why this expanded notion of emergence comes into sync with complex systems science, philosophies of radical creativity, and the needs of contemporary philosophy and society will be one of the primary tasks of this project as a whole.

Networks are a philosophy of relation. As a philosophy of emergence, the networkological project is also a philosophy of relation, for it views complexity as that which emerges as it differentiates and then intertwines, or networks, with itself. All reifications, disjunctions, or separations can then be seen as aspects of the manner in which the self-differing stuff of the world differentiates and intertwines with itself. From such a perspective, everything is then ultimately related to everything else, even if by its disjunction, a position which has strong support in quantum theories of cosmology.[20] According to this view of the origins of our world, all we have ever experienced comes from that which gave rise to the "Big Bang," a quantum singularity with the potential for our entire universe layered on top of itself in a superposed and entangled manner, smearing and condensing space, time, matter, and potential upon themselves. Our whole universe can therefore be seen as the manner in which this singularity explores itself in the process of its complex emerging by differentiating and renetworking with itself, moving from potential to actual, across and through the extended spacetime of our everyday experience.

Viewed as aspects of this singularity, as refractions of the same relational continuum which is both within and beyond spacetime as we know it, anything can be seen as related to all others, fractally and holographically, no matter how distantly they are separated in our everyday worlds of experience. As such, the potential for anything we have ever experienced or dreamed, and likely much more, should not be seen as coming from someplace radically distinct from us, but from the whole of relational emergence of which any aspect of the world is a part, for ultimately, even if our world is the result of another, we would have to be related to this other world in turn.[21] Each aspect of the world can then be seen as an aspect of a whole that gives rise continually to all we experience, and potentially much more. For if any of these only complexify by means of emergent networking, each then has the potential, in the right circumstances, to do the same and potentially more in both quality and quantity.

The networkological project therefore sees the potential for radical emergence as infinitely present, here and now, right in front of us. Potentially and certainly practically infinite potential is within the very fabric of the world, as the self-differing substance of emergence itself, even if this can only ever be unleashed by differentiation and networking, in a manner which nevertheless self-potentiates the more it complexifies. We can never know what an aspect of the world can do, for it is potentially and practically infinite in relation to how it networks, with the singularity as the most complex potentiality of which we know, the human brain as the most complex actuality of which we know, and everything else on a continuum of complexity between these. While these and other related insights in this section are described in relation to abstract physics and philosophy, the ramifications for political and social theory are manifold.

Networks are fractal. The networkological project views the manner in which emergence networks with its differentiations as fractal and holographic in form. Building on research in quantum physics on topics such as quantum foam and the divisibility of quarks, mathematical issues such as the divisibility of continua, as well as a wide variety of philosophical concerns, the networkological project views networks as always nested, or layered, into other networks, at potentially and practically infinite levels of scale.[22] Such a structure is what Benôit Mandelbrot famously described by means of the term "fractal."[23] Having no smallest or largest scale, such a "scale-free" view of the fabric of the world is "self-similar" in the manner whereby it differs from itself and its contexts, and it is intertwining of sameness and difference, differentiation and sync , which gives rise to the proliferation of qualities, entities, forms, and processes which comprise our world.

Drawing upon the notion of multiple intensities of infinity in transfinite set theory,[24] this project also views some aspects of the world as networking the infinite potential of its aspects into greater intensities than others, not only in terms of quantity, but qualitatively in relation to their differentiation and intertwining within networked emergence. When the networked fabric of the world contains itself more intensely in this manner, the result is potential which can emerge in practically and potentially infinite ways, in regard to the self-differing refraction of these potentials with themselves as matters and energies and all to which they give rise.

Networks are holographic. The networkological project views the relational self-similarity of self-differing as not only self-similarly fractal across levels of scale, but across space and time as well. This form of complex self-similarity, often called holography, describes the manner in which wholes and parts are complexly interdependent in a manner not unlike that of a living organism, and which, like fractals, exist between more traditional notions of dimensionality. Such a form is illustrated in the manner in which holographic images, which are able to represent an entity from multiple sides, are constructed by recording an interference pattern between parts and wholes.[25] And so, if a section of a holograph is examined, it will reproduce an image of the original whole, if with less clarity than the original whole holograph, for the parts of a holograph record not merely parts of what they represent, but the relation between these parts and the whole, as a whole, within and in relation to each part.

When holography and fractality intertwine in a manner which is emergently self-differing, they describe how complexity can manifest in the structural fabric of an entity, a notion which this project will describe as refraction. A refractive structure isn't one in which all its parts are like a hall of mirrors reflecting nothing but itself, but rather, is like a continually shifting, self-shatteringly differing crystal of emergence. The emergence of such a crystal within itself in one location ripples into others, with parts and wholes resonant with each other even if never fully the same.

The fractal and holographic refraction of self-differing describes the manner in which emergence manifests relationally, for fractals and holographs are fundamentally infinite in relation to more traditional notions of limitation, with fractals proliferating to potentially infinite levels of scale, and holographs made up of parts which only make sense as aspects of a whole which exceeds any part or even the sum of these, and which can be fractally subdivided as well.[26] Reifications can only ever grasp small aspects of such refractive structures, even as they can contribute to, yet also hinder, their processes of emerging. The world itself can be seen as such a refractive structure, in which the quantum singularity before the Big Bang explores itself in all its polychrome potentialities, with space, time, matter, energy and all these give rise to as its many aspects by means of this process.

Networks are a spacetime. The networkological project views spacetime as fundamentally networked. While the spacetime of most human physical worlds is commonly described in terms of three dimensions of space and one of time, our inner worlds do not follow these rules, nor do the phenomena of quantum physics, or the non-Euclidean and topological approaches to spacetime in contemporary mathematics. We need models of spacetime which can include the inner and outer experiences of our worlds, as well as the less everyday formations of mathematics and physics, while making room for the potential for alternate spacetime formations previously unknown.

Working backwards from lived physical experience on Earth today, we can surmise that space and time indicate forms of incompossibility and displacement which are exclusive to varying degrees, and which when intertwined with others give rise to extension, of which the spacetime of lived physical experience is merely one type. Intensive spacetime, which takes place within an entity, can be distinguished from extensive spacetime, which occurs outside of an entity, such that both intensive and extensive spacetime can be grasped from either within or without an entity capable of doing so. And so, an example of intensive spacetime, grasped from within, can be seen in the manner in which humans experience the flow of thoughts in an inner mental landscape, one which expands, condenses, jumps, loops, speeds up, slows down, and can produce many forms of containment and layering, and in regard to forms of motions which defy the parameters of the external physical world, giving rise to the various combinations of thoughts and feelings which determine the topologies of inner spacetime. All of this seems to be the result of the manner in which the patterns of activation in the brain come into sync with each other so as to feel the inner topology of the brain, at least from a perspective which, like that of the networkological project, does not firmly segregate mind and matter from each other. While inner spacetime would then simply be how it feels, from the inside, to activate particular aspects of the networks of the brain, this hardly changes the fact that the brain has a particular spacetime structure which, while contained in our standard four dimensions, is, in the manner of a subway system or computer network, hardly four dimensional when explored from within.[27]

When a human grasps the spacetime of the world beyond it, however, this tends to manifest as a relatively static domain in which loops, dilations, layerings, and many of the other relatively normal phenomena of internal spacetime are generally precluded, so long as the human remains in a relatively standard, non-accelerating inertial frame. However, in between intensive and extensive spacetime, quantum phenomena and spacetime seem to "smear" within each other, at least in regard to localized areas within more traditional, macroscopic, decoherent, "non-smeared" spacetime observed by humans. Time thereby becomes spatlialized, for quantum phenomena in such states are able to be in more than one space and time at once, at least in regard to those grasping them within the parameters of more traditional spacetime. In such cases, the law of the excluded middle falls out of the logics of the spacetime of these phenomena, and their appearance becomes fuzzy, a matter of degree of intensity rather than simple either/or, presence or absence. As a result, spacetime becomes branches of incompossibility and possibility of varying intensity in relation to those around them, breaking down many of the binaries which structure more limited types of manifestation in experience.[28] If extensive spacetime manifests in the networks formed by quantum events as they flicker in our worlds, quantum spacetime can be thought of as networking space and time within quantum phenomena, as intensities, even if this can be grasped externally for example, by an observing human, in the mode of clouds of probability.

The simpler forms of spacetime which dominate the world of lived physical experience on Earth today seem ultimately to derive from these branching networks of graspings, pathways, fields, and processes. As many theorists have argued, the "arrow" of our time,[29] whereby time flows only forwards and space can only be traversed in one direction at a time, likely derives from the flow of energy from the Big Bang, which pushes time in one direction and space into a relatively flat expanse. Without the continual flows of energy resulting from this originating event, which extended spacetime as we know it, there would be no need for time to only continue in one direction in the physical world. To complicate this picture, as relativity theory has shown, acceleration curves the parameters of spacetime, turning points into paths, paths into fields, and fields into processes which have fuzzy aspects of all of these as they increase in intensity. Energy and matter then seem to affect spacetime inversely, with the movement of energy compacting spacetime by means of acceleration, and material forces of repulsion (i.e.: electromagnetic, weak force) pushing against this to extend spacetime, thereby giving rise to spacing and timing within this. This has led some to even argue that matter is little more than spacetime knotted with itself by energy, such that the manifold forms of the world of experience as we know it, from the singularity to humans, are ultimately aspects of the differentiation and networked intertwining of one fundamental stuff.[30]

While it is ultimately impossible to describe the spacetime of a singularity such as the Big Bang, at least by means of bodies and languages adapted to the extended spacetime of relatively fixed points, linear paths, homologous fields, and metricizable patterned changes, it seems clear from what has been described that the networks of spacetime we see around us, based largely on four axes of relatively linear displacement, and idealized by means of the Cartesian grid, are only one particular case within the many potential spacetime mappings available. From the singularity to the brain, the networks of spacetime are much more complex.

Networks are immanent. If everything is related to everything else, and the fundamental stuff of the world is self-differing, there is no need to imagine that the source of the world and its potential to produce the new is elsewhere, somehow radically transcendent or separated off from the world of experience. Transcendence and immanence can therefore be seen as aspects of a continuum whereby aspects of the world continue to transcend themselves as aspects of the manner in which the radically immanent self-differing fabric of the world emerges from itself, with the potential for transcendence immanent within any and all.[31]

The networkological project therefore views any approach to the world which splits it into two or more types of fundamental substance, or which radically divides the world between mind and matter, mind and body, heaven and earth, divine and profane, human and animal, animate and inanimate, sensate and inert, us and them, or me and world as attempts to reify aspects of the world in ways which run the risk of losing sync with its refractively relational emergence. Rigid binary hierarchical reifications of this sort limit the emergence of potential by foreclosing possibilities, and have often been used to justify and promote worldviews and actions which reduce the world to tidy certainties, easily divided into good and evil, or that worth valuing and that which can be ignored or treated with contempt or neglect, with potentially disastrous consequences.

The world is and can be infinitely more complex than this. For these reasons, this project will work to recast binary models of the world as continua of intensities, moving from models based on "black and white" distinctions to "shades of grey." It will then show how the networked intertwining of these intensities, themselves the product of forces and tendencies within and yet also beyond otherwise reified matters, can be used to account for what binary models do, but in ways which can also tie these back into the contexts and processes of their production, thereby avoiding many of their otherwise often profound limitations.

Networks are a set of principles. The notions of immanence, relation, refraction, and emergence, briefly articulated in the preceding sections, describe the four principle ways in which the networkological project views the world of experience. These principles, abstracted from the redescriptions of the world which networks provide, can then be applied back to the world to produce more networked descriptions in turn, such that ultimately, they describe what this project means by networking.

To summarize, according to the principle of emergence, the basic stuff of the world is fundamentally emergent, self-differing, self-organizing, and self-potentiating in regard to conditions of diversity, distributed refraction, meta-stability, and feedback which can lead to sync. According to the principle of relation, all aspects of the world find their meaning and value relationally, in the contexts of their production, such that nothing in the world can be understood except relationally, with reification as an aspect of this process, but not its end. The principle of refraction describes how distributed forms of organization, between centralization and decentralization, which when manifested fractally and holographically, tend to potentiate emergence of complexity. And according to the principle of immanence, the stuff of the world, its fabric, is of one type, a notion which is only sensible in regard to the diversity of our world if this stuff is fundamentally emergent.

The principles of immanence, relation, refraction, and emergence, which correspond to the notions of node, link, ground, and level of emergence, are the primary descriptive principles of this project as a whole. The very concept of a network employed in this project is in this sense ultimately a shorthand for the manner in which the world can be described according to these principles, which are simply four aspects of what it means to network. From these principles, it is possible to describe the ways in which networks describe the world as it manifests to us as experience, meaning, value, and thought, and in a manner which, as will become clear, is itself a refraction of the valuation of robustness which grounds this project as a whole. The rest of this manifesto will articulate some of the ramifications of these principles, in regard to particular ways in which networks redescribe aspects of the world in fields as diverse as ethics, politics, aesthetics, and beyond.

Networks experience. In relation to the principles described above, the networkological project articulates a theory of experience. According to this perspective, each experiencer can be seen as having a networked world of experience which is carved into interconnected segments, known as worldslices. Each worldslice is a network of other worldslices, foregrounded against a background, which is composed of more networks of worldslices, and this is layered into levels at practically and potentially infinite levels of scale. Worldslices are abstractions from a given world of experience, even as each world of experience is also an abstraction in turn from the world of experience as such, that which exceeds yet manifests in all worlds, with each experiencer as a topologically non-orientable worldtwist between these.[32]

Each worldslice manifests as it does by means of the inter-twining of the networks of a given experiencer, those of other experiencers, and those of the world. This intertwining produces networks of reference which form the grammar of worldslices, which appear to an experiencer in a world at a given location in their spacetime, and upon which more networks of reference can be applied to produce multiple interpretations of networks of worldslices, depending on the complexity of the experiencer in question. Complex brains, for example, are able to layer networks of reference in this way. Nevertheless, since all networks are composed of other networks, all networks of experience and their networks of reference are ultimately layered at potentially infinite levels of scale.

As an immanent philosophy, this project sees all worldslices, from humans to atoms, as worldtwists, which is to say, experiencers, even if simple worldslices only experience the world in simple ways. Matters like atoms feel the world around them, even if they are not able to experience this experiencing reflexively, a more complex form of experience known as consciousness. Humans, however, are complex in this manner, and so can feel their brains, thereby producing thoughts, which are layered into the feedback between how they feel their brain and body, thereby producing feelings and emotions,[33] which are layered into the feedback of both of these with how they feel their bodies, thereby producing sensations. Those experiencers without a central control system like a brain nevertheless seem to only feel the way their bodies feel the world, in a relatively decentralized manner, and in a manner which cannot experience its own experiencing in the manner of conscious or self-conscious organisms.

It is important to note, however, that no experiencer can ever directly experience the experience of another, for they could only do so by being inside them, and so, the experiences of others can only ever be surmised by the ways in which these entities act, the structure of their bodies, and the patterns between these. From such a perspective, however, there is no need to imagine that simple matters, like stones or atoms, do not experience, but rather, that they experience simply, while more complex matters, such as organisms, experience more complexly. While such a perspective on the world cannot be proven, it is justified in the same manner in which humans surmise that each experiences the world in ways which are at least similar, and simply follows this reasoning to its conclusion, thereby avoiding the need for a dualist approach to the relation between mind and matter.

Networks are a theory of realities. When experiencers are able to coordinate their actions this is because of symmetries between how they experience their worlds. The areas of overlap and resonance between any group or set of worlds is known as a reality, while those areas which do not overlap between a set of worlds, which are reality excesses, manifest within these realities as sites of incoherence, inconsistency, or incompletion. This sort of networked layering of worlds and realities is fractal and holographic, for there are as many realities as there are groups of experiencers, just as there are as many worlds as there are individual experiencers.

From the excesses of a given reality or world, experiencers can learn about various ways in which other realities or worlds are in excess of their own, for excesses relevant to various realities can indicate, if indirectly, aspects which exceed them by means of incoherence, incompletion, or inconsistency. It is important to keep in mind, however, that worlds are always in excess to any realities of which they may be a part, just as the world is in excess to all the worlds of the various experiencers which experience it, for it only manifests within these indirectly. In this sense it is also possible to see those aspects of worlds which appear in more realities as having a greater degree of reality than others, just as those which appear in more worlds have a greater degree of appearance in the world of experience, even if we can never know if there is more to the world than the world of experience other than by indirect means. There are many implications of these issues, not only in regard to physical experience, but also for ethics and politics.

Networks have (un)limits. The excess of the world to worlds, and worlds to realities, are only aspects of the ways in which emergence can only ever be partially grasped; no network is ultimately ever able to fully grasp any aspect of the world, there are always excesses. These limitations do not prohibit access to the world, but rather, make it possible. Each limitation marks the site of excesses, which manifest as paradoxically uncloseable openings, or "(un)limits" within experience, which can be conceptualized as aspects of "the network paradox," which is abstracted from the way these (un)limits manifest in worlds and realities from the perspective described by networks.

The network paradox manifests most directly in the form of the paradox of the ground, the way in which grounds are always neither fully within nor outside a network. Whenever an effort is made by a network to grasp a ground, it becomes a network of networks, with other networks forming new grounds behind it, even if these are often indistinct.

Likewise, the boundaries of a network are only ever determined by other networks. And so, whenever a network attempts to grasp the manner in which its own networks impact what it experiences beyond it as grasped or ground, it can only do this by means of its own or other networks, which are themselves contextualized by grounds. Any attempt to grasp all of these, however, will run into difficulties, for there will always be more grounds. And so, while it is possible to determine the manner in which networks impact the experiencing of others in particular contexts, it is never possible to do this completely for any experience or context, for there are always more grounds which manifest whenever a network grasps another, and any attempt to grasp these will be altered by this very action to reveal more grounds in turn.

The paradox of levels indicates how there are always more levels within networks and their elements, and the paradox of the link indicates the manner in which links always connect to other additional links, such that nodes can be seen as simply what happens when links intertwine and bend. The paradox of the node describes the manner in which no aspect of the world can ever be fully grasped as a node or network, for more networks are always required to fully grasp something, in that a complete God's eye view of any aspect of the world, or of the world as a whole, is ultimately impossible. Bringing the paradox of the node, link, ground, and level together is that of emergence, which describes the self-potentiating incompletion of emergence as such. This paradox brings these all together, and the network paradox is simply the concept which articulates the manner in which the paradoxes of node, link, ground, and level describe the paradoxical manner in which emergence manifests in experience as networks of emergence as such.

Networks are a general semiotics. In addition to theorizing experience, networks are also a theory of meaning. All aspects of experience are always themselves and more, for they are always aspects of contexts that exceed them. The manner in which any particular aspect of our worlds of experience manifests in relation to others is known as meaning. Since all aspects of experience are always already meaningful, viewing the world through the lens of experience alone is only ever an abstraction from the networks of meaning of which they are a part, with networks of experience as aspects of the networks of meaning in the world.

Unlike many contemporary philosophies of meaning, the networkological project does not see the world as fundamentally divided between language and the world, meaning and matter, or signifier and signified, but rather, works to overcome these binaries. Building on the semiotic theories of Félix Guattari, C.S. Peirce, Louis Hjelmslev, Thomas Seebock, Yuri Lotman, and Vilém Flusser,[34] as well as contemporary trends in information theory,[35] this project works to show that all the world is a semiotics, full of meaning, with human language as one particularly complex formation, anchored in the complex memory machines which are human bodies, brains, and culture, within the simpler and often more aleatory meanings, grammars, and languages at work in the world.

In this sense, meaning can be seen in the world all around us, beyond language and human life. On a physical level, matters interpret the world around them when they react to each other, storing the results in the memory incarnated in their physical form, modulating the potentials they unfold in relation to what is around them in regard to this, reading and writing upon their physical form and that of others in turn. The physical world is in this sense full of rippling waves of metonymic impacts and metaphoric imprints, as well as continual processes of erasure, scripting, and rewriting. In more complex systems, these can then be intertwined to produce stable contexts which allow for the emergence of codes which can link readings and writings in complex memory systems over time. In living systems, material symbols become organic signs in complex relational networks of relays which regulate DNA protein feedback networks,[36] which can develop by means of evolution to produce neural networks which regulate loops of inputs and outputs in webs of feedback in complex organisms. By means of these, organisms are able to modify their physical form in relation to their surroundings, producing continually new writings on themselves, their brains, and the world in the process.

Humans have taken these processes of complexifying meaning in memory systems the furthest, not only by means of language, but also by the modification of the physical environment and production of meaningful objects, processes which then feedback into evolution. Human forms of meaning making, however, are ultimately only complexifications of the processes of reading, writing, translation, and interpretation, which are ultimately aspects of a wider prose of the world, with human language as abstractions thereof. From this, it is possible to then see the world as having a grammar of which human grammars are merely a part. Intensities of qualities produced by tendencies are like the world's adjectives, entities produced by the patterned knotting of these together are like the world's nouns, grammars of relations which sediment from relations between these are like the world's linking words (i.e.: conjunctions, prepositions, copula, etc.), while the processes of which these are only ever so many reifications are like the world's verbs, with human meanings as abstractions of the meanings within the world of experience in which we find ourselves.[37]

Human sign systems are in this sense extensions of the various ways in which molecules read each other, cells read enzymes, organisms read sensations, and all write upon each other. Language is neither prison-house nor glass house, [38] for our world is full of layers of mediation which each reveal and conceal the worlds and realities they present at potentially infinite levels of scale, with human meaning-making as simply abstractions of abstractions which grasp each other in layers which are practically and potentially without end. Within this, human images are two-dimensional signs for aspects of our four-dimensional experiences, a slice of worldslices, and languages systems of abstract conventions represented by matters in the world such as bits of sound or squiggles on paper or screens. Like any other worldslices, those which form images and words in their many forms produce networks of meanings which can impact the patterns of networks of neurons whereby we store memories in our brains, and in ways which can help us sync with our worlds and each other as we learn how to read languages, images, and our experiences in relation to our memories as children. Our worlds of objects and gestures, architecture and sounds, all these are meaningful because they are patterned, and by means of comparing patterned relations between aspects and contexts in the present and the past we learn to come into sync with aspects of our worlds to differing degrees.

From such a perspective, even mathematics can be seen as simply an extremely abstract form of the process whereby humans link abstractions and meta-abstractions into systems of memory in relation to cultural systems of meaningful matters which feedback into these. Mathematics is simply the most abstract form of this, in which signs are stripped of all but the most abstract qualities present in our relations with the world. Building on notions developed by theorists such as Albert

Lautman, George Lakoff, Gilles Châtelet, Brian Rotman, and Fernando Zalamea,[39] the networkological project will therefore see figure in geometry as abstraction from lived space, quantity and number as abstraction from counting, and algebras and problem-solving techniques of various sorts based on these as abstractions from the problem-solving activities of our embodied lives.

Mathematical formalizations are in this sense merely specialized languages for dealing with particularly abstract situations and meta-situations derived from the world, and ultimately only meaningful in relation to these. As such, even symbolic logics and the law of the excluded middle need to be seen as contingent as the notion of orientability in geometry, which is to say, as abstractions of the world as it generally manifests itself to us, even if quantum physics demonstrates that these are ultimately restrictions of the various ways the world can be.[40] In all this, the radical effectiveness of language and mathematics should not then be seen as indicating their transcendent existence, nor that they cut us off from the meaningfulness of the world, but rather, the manner in which they echo aspects of the world of which they are ultimately aspects. For they are simply various forms of tools which evolve in relation to our own evolution in relation to our worlds.[41]

Networks are a mediology. Networks grasp aspects of each other, such that no aspect of a network should be seen as the result of only one network, but rather, as an intersection or symmetry whereby many aspects grasp aspects of each other. In this sense, any aspect shared by networks can be seen as a form of mediation, or betweenness, and hence, as an interface or media device.

Media interfaces abound in our world, from the distributed mediation provided by screens, to that of our biological sense organs, or the chemical reactions that make the physical world a continual process of reading, writing, and translation, which are all forms of mediation. Media transform what they connect, always connecting and separating in disjunctive syntheses, and can be as simple as a physical connection between things, such as the manner in which a wall mediates the relation between roof, floor, and other walls in a house, to the complex chain of mediations whereby my eye mediates the relation between light and my optic nerve, then my optic nerve to my visual cortexes, and my visual cortexes to various other aspects of my brain, each an interface for the others. And just as physical and biological phenomena are complex media ecologies, so are language, economies, and various other cultural formations. The study of media logics, which Régis Debray has called "mediology," provides a lens on the world by means of which it can be transformed into networks of so many mediologies which take a variety of physical, biological, and cultural forms.[42]

Networks are a general machinology. The networkological project views all aspects of the world of experience not only as meaningful signs connected in signifying media systems, but also as machines whose forms represent not only meanings, but also values. Signs and their meaningful contexts are aspects of combinatories, media machines which transform flows of potentials into actions, giving rise to themselves in the process of transforming inputs into outputs in this manner, making choices and partially determining the potentials for future choices in the process.

Whether complex machines, known as complexes, or complicated machines, known as complicates, machines transform potentials, which is how emergence manifests in particular contexts, into aspects of processes, or actions, thereby giving rise to meanings and values. Each machine has its own grammar of codes which transform matters into meaningful functions, using memory stored at one level to potentiate meaning at the next, and all according to what that system and those which gave rise to it value. Grammars of codes within these can be represented by meta-signifiers of meaning, allowing for the transformation of meanings into functions within machines, while the potential for the comparison and evaluation of codes themselves can be represented by means of meta-meta-signifiers, or hyper-signifiers.[43] These hyper-signifiers of value, or currencies, incarnate and represent what that system values, and the investment of currencies, as well as their stores in the forms of "capitals," forms of accumulation of surplus currencies, are what allow systems to evaluate particular aspects of its world by means of its actions, including those of interpretation, and hence, the production of meaning.

In this way, systems can use meta-signifiers to evaluate the ways in which meanings are produced, and hyper-signifiers to evaluate how values are produced. Examples of how meta-signifiers operate at more than one level of meaning can be seen in the manner in which biological meaning is regulated by stop-codons in DNA, how linguistic meaning is regulated by particular grammatical functions which also play a role in this language (i.e.: the word "I"), or how cultural meaning is regulated by the ways in which grounding terms (i.e.: "God," "truth," "reality," "proof") function to regulate how cultural discourses relate meanings with values to guide actions. In terms of value, biological systems regulate their various economies by means of ATP, similar to the ways in which cultural economies use money. Building on the work of Félix Guattari and Régis Debray, this project works to show how semiotics, machinology, mediology, and ultimately economics are varying aspects of the same.[44]

Networks value. All systems are economies which value many things, qualities, modes of relating, and processes, in regard to the systems which evolved them to value in these ways according to their values in turn. From this, it is possible to develop a networkological theory of value. Building on the productivist theories of value in the Marxist tradition, the symbolic economics of Jean-Joseph Goux, David Graeber's social action theory of value, attention theories of value in the work of Jonathan Beller, and the econophysics of Octavian Ksenzhek and Doyne Farmer,[45] the networkological project views valuation as the manner in which potential unfolds into action, with that which is valued being that in relation to which potential is unfolded. In this sense, value is retroactively determined by the action of a system in relation to its contexts.

As aspects of processes, actions unfold potentials in regard to the values of a system in relation to those of its contexts, according to its interpretation of the meanings at work in and around it. All complex systems value the production of themselves and their own potential for growth as primary valuation, with all other forms of value derived from this, while complicated machines indirectly express the values of others as their quasi-values, which manifest according to the ways in which they were designed. All forms of value, however, are representations of the open-ended potential of a system, which is potentially and practically infinite in regard to the way it networks with its contexts, with the ultimate grounding value as the potential for emergence as such: that which gives rise to various subforms of value. While simple systems, such as molecules and simple matters, tend to value whatever their contexts of emergence value, the more complex a system, the more potential it has for emergence from its contexts, and hence, to evaluate aspects of its world relatively independently from values of the actions which brought it about. If all value is ultimately a manifestation of emergence, what emergence ultimately values in and through its many forms is the potential for emergence from emergence, with so many subforms of value as aspects thereof.

Within particular contexts, value and its representations can take as many forms as there are potentials. In physical systems there are many forms of energy, such as heat, electricity, magnetism, and nuclear forces which can be seen as so many currencies which move matters, or can be stored as capital in the forms of matter, which can itself then be moved and thereby express forces at higher levels of scale. Living systems also have particular currencies, such as the nutrients and molecules needed to keep that organism alive, and all living systems are complex networks of economies that work to regulate each other. In regard to human social systems, these value many aspects of the world beyond money, and demonstrate this by means of allocating prizes, positions, jobs, degrees, relations, prestige, commodities, properties, etc.

The more centralized a system, the more one particular form of value comes to represent the value of particular currencies in relation to one another, with varying intensities of this currency shifting in relation to the evaluation of these currencies by the system. Such a centralized value system can help the system modulate its relation to various value systems, and coordinate various sub-systems and currencies within itself. ATP in living organisms or money in human society are examples of currencies which modulate the relations between other forms of value in regard to the systems in question. A similar situation can be seen in the ways in which particular terms organize meanings in human discourses, with notions like truth, freedom, God, or love functioning as various qualitative currencies which modulate the way other terms are valued in various semiotic economies, even if they do not generally do this quantitatively in the mode of money or ATP. While the ability of ATP to perform its function relates to its form, fully financial economies which have gone off the gold-standard, such as those of most economies today, do so in relation to pure regulatory function, allowing for the creation of new forms of feedback, but also making them particularly susceptible to feedback crises.

Networks are symbolic economies. In all its forms, value is always fundamentally intertwined with meanings, for meaning and value are obverse sides of each other. Valuation is the ground of meaning, for meaning describes the ways in which patterns emerge in the ways in which a system intertwines its actions with those of the world, even if these patterns then feedback into processes of valuation in the ways in which they produce interpretations. If the meaning of any particular entity is its position within a particular context (i.e.: "what" that thing is in regard to its contexts), value describes that which indicates which context is used to determine how action relates to these meanings in regard to the unfolding of potential (i.e.: "how" to act in regard to that thing in the context of a more fundamental "why"). While meaning is in this sense the position which one entity has in a context in relation to a meta-context, value is the meaning of this meaning in regard to another meta-context, which relates this meaning to a system which values according to processes which unfold potential into action. Just as experience is an abstraction from meaning, so meaning is an abstraction from the values of the systems which gave rise to it.

Attempts to completely centralize and control systems of meanings and values tend to lead to crises, and since meaning and value are so intimately intertwined, crises in meaning tend to become crises of values when taken to the extreme, and vice-versa, for both are ultimately always about the potentials for emergence in regard to experience. Paranoid conservatism, cancerous reproduction, idolatrous absorption, and chaotic dissolution are so many ways in which potential can unravel in this way, while evolution is the process which attempts to learn from past mistakes and learn to avoid such crises in the future. Ultimately, such crises can be seen as manifestations of the ways in which the attempts to bypass the network paradox arises as so many limit-effects in regard to particular systems, even if this notion is itself simply an abstraction from these.

Networks value robustness. As a meaningful system like any
other, the networkological project is itself a manifestation of
values. Rather than pretend it has no values, this project will
work to show how the relation between its values and meanings
are an integral part of the way it attempts to relate to the world
around it. In contrast to those systems which base their values on
some sort of transcendent source beyond the world of experience,
this project will ground its values, as well as the ethics and
politics which it derives from these, in an immanent manner, by
means of abstraction from the best of the world in front of us. For
if ethics is the study of what we should value, an immanent
approach to ethics needs to base itself on that within the world
which has the potential to give rise to an even better world than
we currently experience. Since the best of everything in the
world, and even the potential to pose questions of value itself,
seems to be potentiated by the self-potentiation of emergence
itself, this project will value that which can give rise to this, and
not only in the present, but emergently, in the future as well.

As such, this project will not value those aspects of the world
which are merely complexly emergent, but those which emerge
the most sustainably in relation to their contexts, which continue
to emerge as emergence, a notion which complex systems science
calls "robustness."[46] Robustness is never growth of mere
quantity, for any aspect of emergence only ever potentiates itself
by qualitatively differing with itself, either by differentiating
from and renetworking with itself, by transforming itself so as to
intertwine with differing aspects of its contexts, or both, since
ultimately, these are aspects of each other. Robustness is also
never simply short-term growth which sabotages itself in the
long-term, and so robustness must also work to foster its
contexts. Robustness is emergence in its most relational form,
and ultimately, is the emergence of emergence from its own
limitations so as to emerge more intensely, not only in the past
and present, but future as well, not only in one location, but also

in many locations in space and time at once.

Considered as enrichment and development in the widest possible senses, robustness is an increase in complexity, in terms of quality, quantity, quantity of qualities, and quality of quantities, and in a relational manner, which is to say, ecological and sustainable in regard to its contexts for the long haul. In terms of organisms, robustness is life lived more abundantly, for any and all, for its own sake and for what it can become, beyond any attempts to reify it in regard to particular organisms, contexts, goals, or communities. Robustness can never be for the few, for this is always self-defeating in the long run, and leads to pain, suffering, and destruction of complexity and potential, which are ultimately aspects of the same. As the source of all that makes life worth experiencing, robustness is the primary value of this project, and fostering maximum robustness is one of the key tasks of network ethics. Building on the implicit valuation of robustness at work in complex systems science, the networkological project will describe robustness as the grounding value of the networkological project and its values as such.

Networks are a practics. Based on what is described above, the grounding maxim of network ethics can be formulated as follows: "Let all your networks operate at maximum robustness." Robustness, the sustainable emergence of complexity, can only occur in a relation of mutual sustainable emergence with your networks, which are ultimately all networks, if to differing degrees, starting with those most relevant to your own potentials for robust emergence. While we cannot know the consequences of our actions in any ultimate sense, if we all promoted robustness in regard to whatever is near and relevant to us, our world would be a much better and more robust place, for ourselves and all relevant to us, for little acts can exceed the mere sum of their parts if they reach a critical mass.

Beyond the grounding maxim, there are many refractions of

this which indicate sub-valuations of this project. For example, since organisms experience pain whenever they experience a destruction of their complexity, and complexity in its many diverse forms potentiates the emergence of robustness, the reduction of pain and suffering is one of the values of this project as well, at least to the extent that it does not supervene the valuation of robustness. While some forms of pain may be necessary to produce overall gains in complexity and robustness, reduction of pain in the overall remains one of the goals of this project, since pain is an indication of the destruction of complexity. And since fear of pain gives rise to tension in organisms, the reduction of this sort of lessened suffering is also a goal, just as the reduction of the destruction of complexity in regard to the physical world, which likely produces some sort of proto-pain, are sub-goals as well, once again, to the extent to which they do not contradict the valuation of robustness.

The attempt to develop tools for dealing with the sorts of issues which arise when the grounding maxim articulates with particular situation is the task of practical ethics, or practics. In order to help imagine robust ways of dealing with the challenges the world presents to us, the networkological project advocates studying robust systems in the world, to see how they react to situations in ways which potentiate their robustness, so as to abstract potential strategies which can relate to our own challenges. These guides can give rise to principles, that which can help guide our intuitions and model-making in regard to aspects of the world which go beyond our knowledge. And these can help us to determine which aspects of the world can serve as models to help us imagine new strategies to evolve more robust ways of acting in our world. Since the human brain is the most complex entity on the planet, and potentially the most robust as well, the radical democratic socialism at work in the brain can therefore serve as an ethical, political, and aesthetic model, one which can not only describe the complexities which could come to be in the world beyond the brain, but provide potential roadmaps for strategies to help evolve these in the world beyond the brain as well, a complex issue which will be described at length in future texts.

There are many lessons to be learned from the ways in which complexity has emerged from the quantum singularity, the most complex potential we know, to matter up to life, and from life to the brain, the most complex actuality we know. Particular values, decisions, actions, and the way these inform particular meaningful practices in the world, can be framed in relation to the ways of approaching the world this general orientation describes. Practics is the task of applying the general principles ethics abstracts from the world, which are never ultimately unrelated to how that world is interpreted, and the values and processes underlying this. In this sense, ethics and practics should be seen, as with all meaningful, descriptive, or philosophical practices, as aspects of the processes of which they are all a part, which is to say, the manner in which the world emerges from itself, and in ways which, it is hoped, can give rise to greater robustness in the future.

Networks are metaleptic. The valuation of robustness which grounds this project should not be seen as grounded merely in the here and now. Rather, any attempt to determine not only what we value, but also what criterion we should use to intervene in the process of determining which values we should value in the future, which is to say, the question of ethics, needs to get a more comprehensive sense of precisely what is at issue with such a question, and what could bring it about in relation to value and the emergence of valuation as such. This requires an attempt to ground the question of value and valuation in regard to the contexts and processes which gave rise to their possibility, as well as the possibility of their being questioned and influenced by this, and the values at stake in relation to these.

Human valuation is produced by human evolution, and human evolution is itself the result of the various evolutionary processes that gave rise to it in turn. Since anything we could value was produced by the various processes which gave rise to the world around us, understanding the contexts which lead to the evolution of the world around us, as well as the relation this has to our own evolution, can help us understand what might be at issue with this sort of questioning. For by understanding this, we get a better sense of what it means for us to value, both in the past and the present, as well as the stakes of what it means to value in the future. It can also help us get a sense of the potential limitations which our evolution, including that of our ability to value, may have produced in us in the process, as well as potential pathways beyond these. For ultimately, evolution has sculpted us to think, value, interpret, and experience in particular ways, and only when we understand what this means can we begin to get a sense of what it could mean to understand our experiences, interpretations, values, and thoughts in ways which potentially go beyond this.

Moving from valuation to the processes which gave rise to these, the networkological project will work to show that not only are all experiences meanings, and all meanings values, but all values are aspects of processes which can be seen as forms of thinking. In the process, this project will work to think of what it might mean to engage in a thinking which emerges from itself in robustness. Describing what it desires to see in the future as potential within its own past, a process which rhetorical theory has at times referred to as metalepsis,[47] this project will work to self-potentiate itself, in the manner of all emergence, jumping over its own shadow to frame the emergence of robustness as both the source and end of all valuation, like a snake eating its own tail and emerging fractally out of the other side. It will do so with its eyes set upon action which can proleptically then bring about that which it metaleptically desires to see as its own potential future pasts, past futures, and robustly emergent present. As paradoxical as this may seem, this is simply resonant with the structure of the emergence of complexity in the world itself. Such a post-teleological form of metaleptic self-narrativization not only serves to ground the ethics of this project, but also in fact, the way the ethics of this project grounds the manner in which this project thinks its relation to its world in the process. It will do this by means of describing the process of the evolution of valuation and thinking which attempts to understand what it could mean to emerge robustly in relation to these.

Networks sync. As detailed earlier in this manifesto, networks describe a new image of thought. From the perspective of neural networks, artificial and biological, thinking can be seen as what happens when aspects of networks come into sync with each other in ways which potentiate robustness. For example, when a human senses an obstacle in its path, this occurs because aspects of its networks of sensory neurons come into sync with that of incoming data from the obstacle. The patterns of activation in sensory neurons then work to come into sync with those in memory which can recognize the object, and these work to come into sync with those linked to potential solutions, such as moving to avoid the object. These then work to come into sync with other aspects of the brain which control motion, in relation to the continuing stream of incoming data which keeps tabs on how this process of reaction is going. The result is actions which, if all goes well, sync with the challenges presented by that environment.

Sync describes the manner in which diverse and distributed aspects of the world are able to work together in ways which potentiate robustness. The most complexly robust forms of sync are those which manifest sameness within difference, and are radically distributed in nature, which is to say, they are complex. In the example described above, none of the neural populations involved are the same, nor are they the same as the obstacle, or the muscles and bones involved. While the brain does centralize processing, it is radically distributed in its modes of organization, and in regard to the body and environment which could make sense of its electrochemical pulses. Because of the widely divergent scenarios with which humans can come into sync, and the highly complex problems we are able to solve, humans and their incredible brains present the most complex forms of potential for sync of which we know.

From the evolution of simple forms of sync, such as present between sub-atomic particles, to that whereby complex brains can come into sync with aspects of themselves and their world so as to emerge more robustly, this project will work to produce an account of the evolution of thinking which metaleptically bring its potential futures and remembered pasts into sync in ways which potentiate robust emergence in the process of this thinking.

Networks are a theory of understanding. Building on the work of theorists of embodied and emergent cognition, as well as theorists of the evolution of cognition such as Eric Baum and Gilbert Simondon, the networkological project will view the simplest manner in which thinking occurs as the manner in which processes give rise to simple forms of memory which then feedback into these very processes.[48] From such a perspective, all physical form, even at the most basic level, is a repetition of a pattern of symmetry between materio-energetic forces, and this is the simplest manner in which memory manifests in the physical world. Physical form is, in this sense, a recording of a pattern of balance within a much more complex dynamic network of influences, even though this is ultimately an interpretation of the contexts and processes which give rise to it. From this, material form emerges as a knot or residue which then serves to modulate these contexts in regard to this particular aspect in the future, and in a way which can potentiate new and potentially robust emergences. While some memories may fade when conditions change, those which remain the same are able to form the basis for more complex forms of memory which can then give rise to more complex forms of sync.

Memory in this sense is a form of knowledge, for it is an abstract and condensed recording of aspects of an environment which can serve as a foundation for potential sync between that aspect and others in the future. That is, this recording of aspects of its contexts can then help that aspect to coordinate, work with, or sync, with aspects of its world that are resonantly similar to those which give rise to this form, such that conditions which potentiate emergence in the future are not wasted, but can build upon these complexifications of the past, stored in memory, to produce new complex emergences, and potentially more robust emergences, in the future. In this sense, it is possible to say that the knowledge stored in the memory of the body of a physical matter potentiates its ability to know how to work with aspects of its future contexts in ways which tend towards the evolution of greater complexity. This know-how is reified as knowledge in memory, but is the result of processes past which can potentiate the emergence of more complex processes in the future in a process this project will refer to as understanding. In this sense it is possible to say that a hammer understands nails better than dirt, and its ability to produce a house in relation to nails and other materials is the result of this. Likewise, the body of a fish understands water better than that of humans, and this is because of the knowledge stored in the forms of the matters of their bodies, which allows them to know how to deal with their contexts, which is to say, understand them in ways which can potentiate their future emergences. Understanding in this sense is that which gives rise to knowledge which can then potentiate the complexification and emergence of greater understanding, even if only when that knowledge reintertwines with the world to produce new forms of understanding.

While simple matters cannot read what their environments have written on them, complex systems can compare the patterns at work within these. Simple matters only have the memories written on the form of their bodies, but these are erased each time a matter changes its form, such that only complex systems of matters are able to store multiple memories within them, and hence, to be able to sync with dynamically changing situations. Genetic material is an example of how this can happen, for DNA is a form of meta-writing which uses the position of particular formed matters within dynamic patterned sets of moving matters to produce positional, functional meta-meaning on top of more limited, static formal meanings. By means of this, matters assume functions in addition to their physical forms within the complex system of an organism.

The result is that organisms can modify the form of their body so as to sync with a wider degree of situations in their environment than before, evidencing an increase in their knowledge of the world, and hence, their ability to understand more of its aspects in the process. As organisms complexify, they tend to differentiate, specialize, and renetwork, ultimately giving rise to distinct organs for reading, interpreting, and writing in relation to the world, which leads to the development of sense organs, neural networks, and motor organs, respectively. Building from basic chemical messengers, the differentiated evolution of specialized organs leads to the production of specialized organs for sync production, with neural networks as the result, for it is the role of neural networks to help create sync within the organism and to sync this with the world without by means of the body in a way which can maintain, if not increase, the complexity of the organism in question.[49]

Networks evolve. All sync in the world as we know it comes about, in one form or another, from a process of evolution.

Building on modern evolutionary theory and models of evolutionary computation, as articulated by thinkers such as Daniel Dennett, Gerald Edelman, Edward O. Wilson, and Martin Nowak,[50] the networkological project views evolution as a problem-solving algorithm, operating in a multi-dimensional fitness "landscape" of potentials. Such a notion is hardly linear or teleological in the sense of older evolutionary models. Rather, it views evolution as a multi-agent search operation, with many potential pathways towards an ever mutating set of peaks of fitness, nested within a variety of layered landscapes which operate in regard to many potential levels of selection, in potentially infinite levels of scale of evolutionary processes operating within each other.

From such a perspective, it is possible to see evolution as the attempt by the world to think itself, which is to say, to differentiate with itself so as to unfold its potentials in a manner which is able to sync with its own robust emergence from itself. And if this is the case, then the problem which evolution works to solve by means of this thinking is robustness, with experience, meaning, valuation, sync, and more complex forms of thinking as aspects thereof.

This occurs in several stages. All simple physical matters act to maintain their complexity, as seen in the principle of least action in physics,[51] and yet, given the opportunity, tend to complexify spontaneously. In this sense, it is possible to say that physical matters value their complexity, yet the process of physical evolution which can come about in relation to these in the right conditions values emergence. And this process of physical evolution is what leads, ultimately, to the production of living organisms, which value not only the maintenance of their complexity, in the manner of all matter, but its growth as well, which is to say, their emergence from the complexity they already possess in the form of continuing to live and even grow. And while individual organisms value their life and growth in this manner, the evolution of life which brings them about values not only that organisms live and grow, but that they do not go extinct in the process, which is to say, evolutionary populations and biological evolution itself values robustness. Biological evolution exists within the gap between the valuation of emergence and that of robustness, just as physical evolution exists within the gap between the valuation of complexity and that of emergence.

In the process of evolving organisms which value what it values, biological evolution has given rise to a wide variety of mechanisms to bring this about. Instincts keep organisms programmed to follow specific instructions, but because evolution cannot anticipate all the changes possible in a dynamic environment, evolution has built pattern-completing brains. These brains record relevant aspects of the environment, store these in neural patterns, and try to bring these into sync with new, incoming patterns to trigger actions that have led to good outcomes in the past. This is the process of learning. To keep animals from straying too far from the goals of evolution, however, evolution has produced value systems,[52] such as hormones, and in complex organisms the limbic system, which creates sensations of tension and satisfaction, by means of various chemicals, when the organism goes against or follows the goals of evolution, respectively. None of this, however, world work if there were not some sort of sensitivity to pain and pleasure already within living organisms, as part of their flesh, since satisfaction is generally triggered in complex organisms whenever there is pleasure or the expectation thereof, and the same in regard to tension and pain. It does not seem unlikely then that simple, non-living matters might even feel something like proto- pain or pleasure, even if explicitly not aware of this in the manner of higher organisms, for they certainly act in ways which demonstrate a valuation of at least the maintenance of their complexity. Such a view further collapses the need to differentiate mind and matter, a notion supported by the development of artificial neural networks.

If value systems keep an organism on the path set by evolution, complex memory-prediction systems such as the brain, while intertwined with this, allow the organism to intervene in its world, and this ultimately feeds back into the evolutionary process, potentiating it while changing it in the process. Complex planning, for example, is intertwined with the evolution of the ability to conceptualize potential future states of the organism, its ability to imagine itself as if grasped in the mode of an object, a basic aspect of self-consciousness. By means of such a process of recursion, not only is complex planning possible, but also the self-questioning which gives rise to learning, which can eventually lead organisms to question a wide variety of things, and to challenge yet also potentiate their evolutionary programming.

The development of recursion in complex organisms is intimately tied in human evolution to what is potentially the most powerful product of biological evolution after the evolution of the brain, for in addition to storing memory in our bodies, DNA, and brains, we have also developed external memory storage, our "wideware."[53] These distributed networks of memory, stored in gestures, tools, images, and words, have radically potentiated our evolution, and have produced feedback effects which have led to massive increases in the complexity of our physical brains, and ultimately, more advanced forms of wideware, such as language.[54] The evolution of wideware is part of what this project will refer to as cultural evolution, for wideware is inherently distributed and social, it happens over a "wide" distribution of locations in space and time, and in a manner which is profoundly social. In this sense, wideware builds upon the evolution of sociality which is present in only a handful of species, such as social insects, where the individual not only values itself, but the population as well, in a process known as "inclusive fitness."[55] Radical advances in complexity are potentiated by the cooperation which wideware makes possible, and massive increases in the brain can be seen as aspects of the ways in which cultural evolution has emerged from biological evolution and ultimately radically potentiated it. In many senses, wideware and culture are aspects of each other, the former the materialization of the latter. As with physical and biological evolution, cultural evolution has infinite potential pathways and levels of scale, and all of these are valuable, for diversity potentiates robustness.

Networks meta-evolve. Evolution has produced the most complex, emergent, and robust creature we know, which is to say, humans, and this has been potentiated by our abilities to plan and question, to self-consciously imagine ourselves changing in the future, and to develop gestures, tools, images, and language which can help us modify the world in our own refracted images. While evolution values the production of robust populations, and in this sense, values robustness, we do not, for like all life, we value our complexity and its increase as emergence, which is to say, our life and growth. While we are self-conscious, in that we are able to represent ourselves to ourselves, and in this sense, come into sync with aspects of our past and future selves, evolution can only do this through us, for it is ultimately only a form of quasi-life, distributed networks of populations which have living beings as its wideware. And yet, evolution acts in a way which indicates that it values robustness, and it has given rise to our self-consciousness in an attempt to potentiate this. Our ability to think about ourselves self-consciously, and to question our own behaviors by means of this, even to the point of questioning our values and to imagine potential changes in relation to these, needs to be seen in this light, and in regard to the potentials for robustness to which this could lead.

The radical potentials which emerge in light of this only

become apparent in regard to the ways in which evolution itself has shifted over the course of human evolution, for the human evolution of wideware has not only complexified our bodies and brains, but has also given us the power to affect the very environments which provide the contexts of our own evolution. Such a process of meta-evolution began simply, with the production of tools and images, but as we developed architecture and agriculture, language and weapons, we quickly began to modify our environment in radical ways. We are now coming to the point where we will be able to not only modify the conditions of our cultural and physical environments, but also the very genetic writing whereby biological evolution evolves us.

The ability to take over our own evolution as meta-evolution is already occurring. And yet, we still only ever think, value, interpret, and experience in the manner in which evolution evolved us to. While our cultural evolution has potentiated our physical evolution, this is now out of sync with our biological evolution, and the result is that we are slaves to the paranoid and aggressive programming of our limbic systems which protected us early in our evolution by giving rise to the "flight or fight" programming which helped us to avoid predators. But once we outwitted our predators and solved the problem of our own food production by means of organized agriculture, we have replaced our predators with ourselves, even as the situation on earth only requires this because we perpetuate it.

And so we are caught in a feedback loop of our own making, in which paranoia and aggression are both cause and effect. While evolution has given us a massive neocortex which can plan and even understand evolution itself, we remain restricted by the limbic system the cortico-adrenal circuits, which hold back the oxytocin systems which could lead us to greater desire, curiosity, trust, and cooperation. While we may realize intellectually that we should be less destructive towards each other, we do not desire this, and until we do, little is likely to change.[56] We need to cultivate new desires, then, as well as new technologies, and this can only happen if we desire to give rise to the evolutionary conditions which could make this possible. This has been the case since early human evolution. But now that we can destroy everything on the planet, and will soon have power over our own genetic code, the need to deal with this problem is beyond urgent.

Networks hyper-evolve. To truly understand our situation, we need to understand the contexts and processes which gave rise to it, so as to influence not only this situation, but the way it produces us as well. This would be to come into sync with it in a manner which allows us to robustly emerge in relation to it, which is to say, to think robustly in relation to it. For to think evolution would be to evolve in relation to it, and by means of it. It would be, in fact, to take over evolution, to liberate us from the way it manipulates us to value, interpret, experience, and think in certain ways. Such a coincidence of thinking and thinker, of evolution and evolved, is similar to the manner in which a population of neurons in the brain is able to participate in the process of thinking at multiple levels of scale, and to feedback into itself, to meta- and proleptically influence its own becoming by means of affecting the situation which determines it, in a way which attempts to understand itself, its contexts, and the contexts of its contexts: a thinking that works to potentiate the robust emergence of itself in relation to these.

In regard to human evolution, such a process would only be possible if we truly understood evolution, and that towards which it tends, the limitations and potentials within it and us, and the manner in which we could bring physical, biological, and cultural evolution into sync so as to robustly emerge from and in relation to these. Such a thinking of evolution would put its resources at our disposal, and would sync our thought with that of evolution itself even as it became part of our thinking.

164

Thinking with evolution in this manner would be the first time in biological evolution in which the products of evolution and the process of evolution came into sync by valuing the same thing, a process which is not only a meta-evolution, but the potential for the robust emergence of evolution from itself, in the manner in which physical evolution gave rise to the evolution of life. In this sense, such a self-conscious meta-evolution, in sync with the values of its own evolution, a thinking that seeks to robustly emerge from its own evolution, could then be seen as a form of hyper-evolution.

This would then be an attempt to evolve ourselves, by means of evolution, towards the self-conscious valuation of the evolution of our emergent robustness. Put in simpler terms, it would be the attempt to question how we could work to evolve ourselves to be not only more robust, but more valuing of robustness, which is to say, more open, curious, desirous, and altruistic, and less paranoid, defensive, acquisitive, territorial, defensive, and aggressive. Of course, simply deciding we want this will not do much. Nor will the attempt to impose this on others have any chance of success. Change comes about not because of the decision or desire of any individual or even group, but rather, a shift in the processes which evolve us.

We need to build new social structures which evolve us towards greater trust, which promote those things which lead to robustness and its self-conscious valuation, such as diversity, meta-stability, feedback and questioning across levels of scale, and the long-term relational outlook which helps produce sustainability. That is, we need to build the sort of world which will make us the sort of people we know we should be and wish we could be. This could only happen if we self-consciously agreed, as a society and a species, that we wanted this, and if we actually and truly did. Learning to stop sabotaging oneself, as an individual and community, is part of what therapy and education, as practices of liberation, are about. We need to learn, as a species, to liberate ourselves from the chains of the paranoia and defensiveness which were adaptive to our evolution but which now restrain us. We need, as a species, to heal from the traumas and scars of our own evolution, so as to liberate ourselves from ourselves, our own worst enemy.

The only way to do this, however, is by means of a self-potentiating "tiger's leap" into the future, a proleptic metaleptics, one which sees the potentials in our moment and learns how to develop these so as to help liberate ourselves from ourselves.[57] Change of this sort can never be applied top down; we have hopefully learned the lesson of the failure of violent attempts to make a better world which always end in more violence. It is impossible to solve violence with more violence, rather, there is a need to build trust to give rise to more trust. As any therapist will tell you, people do not change and become less self-sabotaging unless they feel safe enough to be vulnerable, to let their defenses down, to learn from others how they may have wronged them, and to develop ways to work with others better in the future. This is only done when the therapist creates a relational context which functions as a safe-space in an often terrifying world, where the person can begin this process of self-questioning, healing, and growth. Any attempts at a shortcut to this process will, as history has shown us, on an individual or collective level, necessarily backfire.

Distributed, refractive, democratic, socialist modes of change, starting small and growing slowly, provide the sort of structures which make people feel less the need to prey on each other, or to create social structures, such as multinational capital, which do this to us with an agency which often appears beyond us, and which make people more likely to experiment with trusting each other. This process is self-potentiating, and it does not need to start at a governmental level. It can start in the way we treat those around us, how we raise our children, how we create small-scale social groups. Altruism is self-potentiating as much as paranoia.

At some point, we have to hope that, when the evolutionary fitness landscape allows, we may reach a tipping point in our own evolution, and hopefully we can then tip the scale in a more robust direction, and away from destruction. Only if we prepare the ground now will this ever be possible. Helping to encourage this way of looking at the world, so as to give rise to more robust emergences, refractively different from this yet robustly resonant with it in its own way, is what this project is about.

All of which is to say that the time has come to liberate ourselves from the baggage of our evolutionary history, to bring the biological evolution of our limbic system up to speed with our cultural wideware and the brain, and particularly the hyper-democractically socialist neocortex which gave rise to it. And the only adversary to this process is ourselves. G.W.F. Hegel famously argued that evil is the particular when sundered from the universal,[58] but time has shown that the universal has its evils as well, at least when these are particular universals. But beyond any particular universal is the emergence of robustness as such, that which gives rise to singulars, particulars, and universals, which is only ever reified and reifying in part, which can come into sync with itself only by sustaining its ability to differ from itself to give rise to yet greater robust emergences of complexity. Or, put differently, we need to realize, as Guattari has argued, that "everyone wants to be a fascist,"[59] which is to say, everybody wants to be a despot of their own paranoid kingdom, as well as one of the wealthier cogs in the capitalist infosphere. The lures of paranoia, and the continual need for more, these fears and the defensive postures which relate to these, are part of our biological hardware. Evil is never primarily in the other, unless we project it there. We are always what we fear, and should fear, most, for no one can ever hurt us more than ourselves.

It is time we took over our own education, our own therapy, our own liberation. Evolution is a brutal process, feeding the spawn of one species to that of another, herbivores to predators, remorselessly producing a ratchet to ever greater complexity. But altruism and cooperation, in the forms of multicellular organisms, colonies of insects, herds of animals, and ultimately, the radical cooperation of the human brain, are the apogee of its development. New stages in our evolution can only arise if we overcome, as a species, the scars of our evolutionary past. And this can only come about if we want it to, and begin to develop the world which can evolve us to be able to better work together rather than destroy each other.

The desire for destruction, for the pain of others, sadism and evil, these are all inside each one of us. Only by recognizing this can we learn that it is not ever the other's evils which are those we need to worry about, but only our own. For only when we develop a radical practice of listening to others, to try to understand what we have done against them, in the past and potentially in the present and future, can we begin to change. It is only by such a practice of radical listening,[60] not to any universal other, but to the particular others around us, and even to the ways in which we hurt ourselves, can we begin to get beyond the destructive ways which we needed to evolve, both as individuals and as groups, but which now make it impossible for us to grow in ways which are not destructive of others, and ultimately, ourselves. The affects of terror, disgust, rage, what do these ever give us but a spiral of pain? And yet, we cannot wean ourselves from them. Only by creating a world which requires less of them, by recreating ourselves to require these less in relation to each other, might this be possible.

And we need not wallow in self-hatred or guilt, but learn from our own tendencies, and realize that the desire to lord over others, or to grow at all costs, will always be part of us. Understanding this is the key to our futures. But we cannot merely tell ourselves, intellectually , that we should want this, we need to actually desire this, in our core. How to cultivate new desires in ourselves? The first step is always one of faith, the gesture of the outstretched hand, the principle of openness, of fostering robustness within yourself and all around you, with no expectation of an immediate return, other than the joy which that which leads to robustness always brings.

As paradoxical as this may sound, only by means of this can we, at this juncture in our evolution, increase our power, and our pleasure. The most selfish strategy would be, in this sense, the most altruistic. And in this process, we would become more like the neocortexes of our brains, radically democratic and socialist robustness machines, which have the potential to bring this liberation to any and all, so long as we can learn to shed the shells of our evolutionary pasts. Beyond selfishness and altruism, and building on a Spinozist approach to questions of power and pleasure,[61] as well as the forms of sync with our worlds needed to increase these, this project argues that the more we come into sync with the evolutionary tendencies of the world around us, the more it will open before us, providing greater power and pleasure in regard to ourselves and our worlds. To sync with evolution in this manner is to outthink it, to evolve ourselves so as to supersede it from within, to radically differ from ourselves and it in a way which potentiates even more of this robust growth in the process. To never be satisfied with our understanding of the pain we have caused, are causing, or will cause ourselves or others, we become better at learning how to learn from ourselves, and we emerge, more powerful, more pleasureful, in a world more in sync with its own radical self-differing in and through our own, each transcending the other in the process of immanent thinking.

Networks think. If thinking is an attempt to emerge robustly by coming into sync with aspects of something, then part of what it means to think would be to try to understand how evolution evolved us to think in certain ways. We need to come into sync with evolution, to think by means of it, and in this, to emerge from and in relation to it. Only this would be a thinking of evolution, of robust emergence, and ultimately, ourselves and our processes of thinking.

Such a thinking would radically potentiate not only our own power but our pleasure as well. For rather than pitting ourselves against the world and each other, we would realize we no longer need to do so, and that the only reason why a paranoid disposition makes sense today is because of the fact that there are other humans with similar dispositions in the world along with us. By coming into greater sync with each other in the self-conscious valuation of robustness, in an ever more complex relation to internal and external differences, we think in and with evolution, not only in relation to each other, but to ourselves and the wider world as well, which would put us back into sync with it in the process.

Such a form of sync would necessarily go beyond the binaries which could be used to describe it, for it is fundamentally multiplicitous and non-dual,[62] beyond rigid distinctions such as necessity and freedom, internal and external, differing and sync, activity and passivity, and ultimately, the reifications of language and embodiment which are only ever aspects of the processes of robust emergence of which our thinking can be the most robust part. It is an evolution of thinking and evolution itself, and ultimately, a manifestation of emergence as robustness itself. It would be to emerge in and as thinking in a way that could change the world which thinks us by means of this, and vice-versa.

Such a controversial notion has much in common with many easily misunderstood notions in the history of philosophy, such as the Stoic love of fate, Baruch Spinoza's *amor intellectus dei*, Hegel's notion of grasping one's concept both as substance and subject, Marx's notion of becoming the subject-object of history, as well as Taoist notions of *wu-wei* (non-action), Sufi notions of *fana'*, Hindu notions of realizing that *Atman* is *Brahman*, and

Mahayana and particularly Vajrayana Buddhist notions of entering a non-dual state with the Buddha-embryo/matrix (*tathagathagarbha*) which is both the potential for liberation and the fabric of experience itself. [63] In contrast with the Eastern aspects of this, however, this project will nevertheless argue for the need for an active transformation of the world which brings self and others, past and future into sync in a way which does not simply focus on the personal transcendence of this world nor absorption in some larger power by means of a hypostatization of the present. Unlike Western aspects of this, however, it will not view transformation of the world beyond the self by means of the filters of reified individuality. The firm separation of self and world needs to be superseded by a process of more radically robust thinking before our species destroys itself and its world. To think in this way is to go beyond thinking in reified form, abstractly, in the form of an experience which can be memorized and known, which is to say, in the mode of objectification. It is to come into sync with the liberation of thinking from its own less complex forms of prior development.[64]

This project works to do just that. Experience, or the simplest form of thinking, describes the manner in which the world reflects upon its own workings to feel itself: and the networkological project views all matter as feeling itself in relation to its world, no matter how simply. When we abstract meaning, value, and processes from this, we feel the world simply in a more developed, human form of immediacy which finds its antecedent in this mode of thought, one which this project will view as analogous to thinking in terms of nodes, of the reification of thinking which can produce mere knowledge at best.

Meaning comes about, however, when aspects of the world are read in relation to a wider context. All experience is always already meaningful, but simple matters can only feel themselves and other aspects of the world through this, and hence, cannot read the meanings that they themselves feel and are. Only complex dynamic systems can compare and contrast in order to grasp the samenesses and differences which can relate an aspect to a wider set of contexts, and to read it in relation to these, and then, by means of the evolution of this, to write an interpretation on its body, then on its bodyplan, then on its bodily actions, then on its neural network, then on its wideware. When humans grasp any aspect of the world in relation to others, they do so in a manner of seeing all aspects of the world as the result of linkages between aspects, as manifestations of forces, analogous to seeing the world composed of nets of links. This can help humans to better understand the world around them in regard to a particular set of circumstances or needs. By comparing multiple contexts, modes of interpretations, ways of linking and even forming nodes and links with grounds beyond them, however, the limitations of this way of thinking can soon become apparent.

Meaning is always already intertwined with valuation, for all meaningful systems are formed in order to help systems unfold potentials in ways which can help produce sync in relation to an often dramatically changing set of circumstances. If organisms find meaning in their world, they always do so in regard to the instincts which program them to value particular interpretations and actions over others. Only organisms with self-consciousness, however, seem to be able to grasp their interpretations and actions, as well as the meanings and values behind these, and ask about what grounds these. This continual questioning of grounding contexts, of comparing and nesting these in each other, is to see the world as a set of contexts in relation to each other, and is analogous to seeing all aspects of the world as networks of grounds. The questioning of values and self-reflexivity in this sense, however, reaches a limitation unless it begins to think in terms of the processes which brought these contexts about, including the ability to question the values of meanings and values.

Going beyond the attempt to grasp the world as valuation,

thinking requires understanding processes nested in processes, in which values emerge as expressions of nested networks of evolutions of which the very questioning of values, meanings, and experiences is a part. Doing so does not seek to merely grasp thinking as an abstract experienced thing, to understand its meaning to determine the appropriate response, or to evaluate it in regard to deeper or even self-questioning values, but to emerge in relation to it. For the question of the value of valuing, and the questioning of even the value of questioning, brings about the question of the potential of these processes in relation to the whole, which is to say, the potentials of emergence here and now in relation to emergence as such. Such a thinking can only emerge from itself and in relation to itself as the self-conscious valuation of the emergence of robustness. In regard to human evolution, this would require the attempt to move beyond the ways in which our own evolution continues to hinder our ability to do just this, so as to begin to evolve new ways to more robustly evolve ourselves by means of our world.

This section has worked to show that all aspects of the world can be seen as an experience in a world, a meaning in language, value in an economy, and a thought within an embodied dispersed thinker, or a brain. Each of these networked ways of diagramming the world is hardly a stable, reified, completed entity, for each upon closer examination opens on to the others, refracting and shattering in relation to each other, the world, and so many other potentials. Each resonates with aspects of the network diagram, of node, link, ground, level, and emergence, each refracting the other. This project works to think emergence by such a process of diagramming, by thinking thought as diagramming, so as to come into sync with emergence to emerge from it more robustly in and as thinking. The rest of this manifesto will attempt to describe ramifications of this way of thinking the world.

Networks critique. Viewing all meaning as expressions of sedimented values, all values as sedimentations of valuing processes, and all valuing processes as reifications of processes of emergence, this project will work to show how a redescription of the world from the perspective of robustness can not only describe the world potentially more adequately than other models, but in a way which can help it self-potentiate in the process as well. Such a mode of description not only works to resonate with the world as it is, but also the world as it could be, which is to say, more robustly. And so, this project will work to show how it is possible to redescribe our world in ways which minimize the need to rely upon reified and reifying concepts and models, displacing by more networked forms those conceptual models which use relatively isolated individual elements, static hierarchical binaries, monocausal explanations, rigid proofs, linear histories, axiomatic or transcendent foundations, or other forms of decontextualized, non-processural disconnection. The critique of reified and non-relational forms of modeling gives this project its critical edge.

Networks deconstruct. In an effort to move beyond the skeptical nihilism which has gripped philosophy in general for much of the late-twentieth century, particularly in regard to highly self-reflexive philosophies of "the linguistic turn,"[65] and the deconstructive modalities which work to dissolve these and traditional philosophies without putting something new in their place, the networkological project puts deconstruction in the service of reconstruction. Beyond the incoherence of deconstructive skeptical nihilism, the incompletion of paranoid traditionalism, or the inconsistency of the cynical *realpolitik* which emerges from an oscillation between these, the networkological project will recontextualize these as what happens whenever social paradigms have foundational crises which question the values of their meanings and the meanings of their values, and approach the sort of reflexivity which allows for the potential thought of and as emergence, which can manifest as opportunity, crisis, or both, whether on a personal or social level.

Such a crisis occurred in most forms of human meaning production during the twentieth century, reviving the ancient threat of skepticism, something which occurs whenever cultures try to deal with radical changes in their worlds by searching for new paradigms, often bringing on paranoid and cynical defensive structures in the process. Taken to their extreme, such crises can cease to be adaptive, and lead to self-perpetuating cascades of feedback which can destroy physical or living systems, such as when a microphone nears a speaker system, or a cancer develops in an organism, both cases in which feedback does not help a system to regulate its development in relation to its contexts, but rather overwhelms its attempts to adapt and transform itself, leading to either feedback in the service of isolation and rigidity, or growth and expansion without adaptation.

Rather than try to move beyond such crises, this project takes these as part of its own grounding, working to learn from and integrate them into its own structure rather than simply repeat them.[66] Synthesizing paranoid traditionalism, deconstructionist skepticism, cynical *realpolitik*, as well as the seduction of the belief that new paradigms will not be subject to the same sorts of crises in turn, the networkological project instead works to come to sync with the emergence of robustness in and beyond itself by constructing a philosophy of radical creativity which continually reconstructs itself. Assuming that any and all systems must risk dissolution whenever they try to change, this project will view all social paradigms, including philosophies, as able to be deconstructed in regard to any of their grounding conditions, such as language, the body, the economy, and beyond, any of which can lead to the paradoxes which occur whenever an attempt is made to grasp emergence as a whole. The question then it not whether a paradigm is grounded or not, but why it is grounded in one way over another, a question of values, and how its system of values relates to its contexts of emergence. The networkological project will therefore view the need for a new, networked paradigm as an opportunity to relate to paradigms and their groundings differently from the way reified and reifying world-views have done so in the past, so as to produce a post-foundational philosophy and praxis not merely about emergence at the level of context, but of emergence as well, in regard to both content and form.

Networks reconstruct. Viewing the ground of any aspect of discourse to be its potential to foster robustness in particular situations, the networkological project espouses a continually shifting "experimental pragmatics" in place of notions like proof or any other sort of ultimate justification.[67] This project will then view all its own concepts as potentially deconstructible, and will only retain any of them to the extent that they foster robustness; even its primary concepts, such as robustness and emergence, will continually deconstruct and reconstruct, shifting in meaning and ultimately value as this project modifies in the process of producing new descriptions of the world and itself. As a meta-stable post-foundation, the particular way in which emergence and robustness articulate other concepts in this project will therefore be perpetually tentative and fluid, even if always grounded in the attempt to maintain and foster the most robust notions of what these concepts can become as a form of refractive self-potentiation. Framing the lack of certainty in the world as an opening towards the production of meta-stable evolution of greater robustness, the networkological project therefore works to evolve itself from its contexts in the same way. Rather than look for any sort of secure, final, ultimate, or otherworldly foundation, nor simply repeat the fascinating tragedy of its impossibility, the networkological project recontextualizes deconstruction and reconstruction as aspects of the more encompassing process of the robust emergence of complexity in the world, up to and including the emergence of the networkological project itself.

Networks are post-foundational. In the process of its emergent refraction, the networkological project works to reintegrate aspects of the world which other worldviews tend to segregate off as either exceptions to all rules, or as transcendent guarantees or repositories of meaning which are always ever incomplete, incoherent, or inconsistent. Exceptionalisms, such as notions that the human soul or mind are radically distinct from the rest of the world from which they emerged, will therefore be reworked to produce relational models. This also applies to discourses which try to "prove" themselves by assuming "axiomatic foundations"[68] which somehow do not need to be justified in turn, or which depend on foundations in what has never been experienced, such as otherworldly promises of something like heaven, or a God who makes sure our proofs are secure. We can only ever justify our actions and descriptions in regard to the world from which these emerge, of which proof and otherworldly foundations are a part, even if the benefits of such notions are ultimately a question of the values these promote.

Rather than condemn this world, or the flesh of our bodies, or other ethnic groups, matter, animals, or systems which do not ignore the full complexity of the world as sinful, unworthy, inferior, or unproven, the networkological project sees this world as the source and locus of all values. As such, it evaluates descriptions of the world not against preconceived notions of value or truth, but rather, the degree to which they sync with the project of emerging more robustly in relation to the world in which we find ourselves, which is always ever the product of the cultural, biological, and physical conditions of its emergence. Such an always already situated process of contextualizing views the networkological project itself as a product of contexts, which provide the very means for its attempt to think its relation to the world as such.

Networks redescribe to refract. In the process of articulating itself the networkological project will produce a series of crystalline,[69] fractal redescriptions of whatever subject matters it touches, from economics to politics, evolution to language, philosophy to neuroscience, from the science of networks to various philosophies and beyond. By keeping its commitments tentative, and continually unraveling itself to reconstruct itself anew, the networkological project will describe how the emergence of the self-differing fabric of the world can immanently and refractively give rise to the complexity of the world of experience, up to and including that of the networkological project itself. This will be done by getting inside more traditional ways of describing the world, and exploding them from within, by showing the networks waiting to emerge under the surface of their reifications, and in the process producing new, networked redescriptions which go beyond the limitations of discourses of the past. But rather than hold on to these new networked redescriptions as firm foundations, this project will then do the same thing to its own redescriptions as it articulates them. It will shatter whatever new lenses it produces from within, showing how even these relationally and refractively structured networks of description contain yet more networks within them, which can then be renetworked with shards of more traditional description which have been similarly shattered from within, so as to give rise to yet more, new, networked forms of description in turn. The result will be a fractal proliferation of networked lenses, each of which describes the world from a particular perspective, some more complex than others, all networked to each other, and with all of these ultimately unraveling the notion of emergence, and vice-versa. Any and all of the networked lenses produced in this process are able to be subjected to the same process of shattering and redescription, of any and all their elements, changing the relation between these in the process, all in relation to the general value of robustness, new processes of redescription, and potentially changing circumstances in the world.

Networks diagram. In the process of refractively producing itself by means of its redescriptions, the networkological project abstracts its organizing concept, the concept of the network diagram. Composed of the sub-concepts of node, link, ground, and level of emergence, the network diagram is the continually mutating yet fundamentally refractively opening seed of emergence which manifests in yet is fully contained in none of the networks which it describes or to which it gives rise. The network diagram is a structure for the production of emergent networks, an abstraction from and guide for the networkological practice of redescription which has a commitment to the robust emergence of the potential for ever more radical creativity as its ethical, political, aesthetic, descriptive, and conceptual core.

Rather than function as a unitary master logic, the network diagram refracts within each other a general commitment to robustness with the singularity of a wide variety of contexts, producing its particular redescriptions in the process, potentiating and grounding itself in the process. The results are so many proliferative and proliferating networkologies which provide new ways of looking at various aspects of the world, each of which then reshatters to give rise to ever more refractive networkologies in, around, and in relation to those already in the process of emerging.

Radically productive and never quite where it seems to be, the network diagram is always ever emerging differently, even as it resonates with networks in the world which do the same, if to varying degrees. The network diagram is a concept for a diagramming which emerges from itself, and emergence, robustness, and all the other concepts of the networkological project are only ever aspects of this process. The networkological project emerges from the world and itself in a manner which values robustness and promotes this in the world, not only in terms of its content, but also its form. And so, the redescriptive diagramming of the network diagram, which gives rise to this project does not then produce anything like a single networkology, but rather, only an ever increasing refraction of networkologies.

Networks embrace difference. If the world is fundamentally self-differing, any attempt to fully grasp any of its aspects, or even the whole of it, will lead to frustration, for any such attempt will ultimately be incomplete, incoherent, or inconsistent with the way any and all aspects of the world differ from themselves in the present, past, or future. Building on the theories of Kurt Gödel, Douglas Hofstadter, Jacques Lacan, and David Bohm, the networkological project views any attempt to fully organize, describe, evaluate, or think any aspect of the world, or the world as a whole, as a paradoxical endeavor. Organization, description, valuation, and thinking are recursive modes of action which are always in between fixed states, and attempts to fix them, in part or whole, or bring them to some sort of complete or reified end, seem to always lead to frustration. That is, whatever the cause, the world appears to ultimately resist extreme reification, and this can be seen in the manner in which quantum events do not seem to allow themselves to be ever fully reified, axiomatic systems in mathematics are not able to be recursively grounded, complex systems exceed the sums of their parts, and rigid and exclusionary modes of psychological and social organization inevitably lead to symptom formations.[70]

For this reason, this project works to avoid what it calls reflective forms of organization, description, evaluation, and thought. Reflective structures try to bring parts and wholes into perfect resonance, producing coherence, consistency, and completion at the cost of expelling that which undermines these outside of itself. This results in the need for defensive operations which seek to maintain coherency, consistency, and completion, at the expense of potential which could be used to foster robust growth rather than maintain guard against the systemic possibility of potentially destructive crises. In contrast to reflective structures, refractive structures embrace differing, both within and beyond themselves, and work to promote difference, both within and without, to the extent to which it enriches robustness.

By making differing central to the fabric of its logics, such a mode of organization is only ever partially coherent, consistent, and complete, but what is gained is greater potential for robustness. This is not to say that refractive systems are disorganized, but rather, that their modes of organization are open, adaptive, similar yet not the same throughout, with "family resemblances"[71] between various local autonomies as that which helps them cohere, as opposed to the centralizing logics of reflective systems. And ultimately, the only fundamental exclusion upon which these systems are based then is that of the extremes which can undermine robustness, whether in the form of extreme disorganization which can lead to dissolution, or extreme organization in the form of reflective structuration, in either reproductive or conservative modalities. Of the organized, reflective modalities which do not destroy organization outright, the first requires complete sameness in organization, while the second allows for differing only so long as it ultimately serves to always promote growth of a particular type of structuration. This sort of cancerous reflective structuration, as opposed to conservative structuration, is still reflective, and while more flexible, it can be equally as destructive to a system in the long run. For rather than expel difference and then expend energy on defense against internal and external forms of differing, at ultimately great cost and leading to perpetual threat of crises, refractive structures work to incorporate differing within them by emerging in relation to difference in a manner which frustrates extreme reification. While refractive structures give up the false sense of security which rigid, centralizing, reifying, conservative reflective structures tend to bring, or the often startling cycle of growth and collapse which tends to accompany cancerously reflective structures, refractive structures make up for this in flexible and stable growth. From the mathematical to the psychological, refractive modes of organization indicate a roadmap to more democratic, adaptive, robust futures.

Networks are distributed. Networks tend towards robustness, but there are networks in the world which maintain and foster the tendency to reification by means of various forms of centralization and monopolization of control and potential. While many of these networks may thrive in the world, and may even use distributed, robust network formations for centralizing ends, these networks are ultimately not networked enough, and ultimately undermine their own robustness, as well as that of the contexts which support them. This is not to say that there might not be times in which centralization is necessary for survival, but since tendencies to centralization and distributedness self-potentiate, these states have a tendency to overstay their usefulness. In such situations, these network formations may make radical advances in the short run, while devastating aspects of their contexts that could ultimately support their own robustness in the future.

Between forms of centralization and decentralization, which would tend to destabilize a system, there is a zone of distributedness in which a system is likely to evolve to further complexity. There is wide leeway, however, within this zone between those approaches which are more and less robust. The world as it is currently constructed seems designed to maximize the degree of reification possible to evolve complexity for the smallest group possible without risking total collapse, even as the world would be the most robust if it maximized decentralization without risking total collapse, a state of maximum distributedness which, based on the science of networks, tends to lead to the greatest self-potentiation of robustness. The promotion of maximal distributedness, or the minimum necessary centralization, is part of the practics of the networkological project.

Networks are a historiography. In order to understand the stakes of the present moment, it is necessary to historicize the times in which we live by producing narratives, even if these are continually adjusted in a process of renarrativization. Rather than see this process in terms of traditional, reified notions of historiography, the networkological project works to develop a more relational approach to this process. History never moves in straight lines, nor does it simply connect reified influences, periodizations, or unitary causes to produce tidy narratives. Our readings of the past are always selective, inflected with our desires for the future, and both past and future only ever are refractions of our present. Attempts to reduce history to simple relations of cause or effect, or linear narratives which are not multidetermined by forces and entities with multiple potentials is to reify what history is and can be.

Rather than try to ignore these enabling conditions of writing history, this project views the production of narratives as the intertwining of multidetermined networks of influences in regard to aspects of past, present, and future which intertwine to produce new networks which we can use to help interpret the multiplicity of influences upon us in the worlds in which we find ourselves. This is a continual process of renarrativization, of meta-historicization, which is ultimately networked to the core. Advocating a "constellatory" rather than linearizing view of history,[72] one which views time as having many potential forms and any history as necessarily inflected by the perspectival meanings and values of its production, the networkological project views the notion of objectivity as being a dangerous fiction not only in historiography, but also in journalism, science, anthropology, and beyond. Rather than aim for objectivity, this project aims to help to understand and work with how our perspectives necessarily inflect our ways of narrativizing our present, pasts, and potential futures in relation to our values, and in ways which perpetually recreate them. Rather than attempt to remove the bias at work in the production of narratives, this project attempts to reflect upon how we network with these to help produce the narratives which can help us best foster robustness in regard to both the world of the past and the futures we hope will be.

Networks are a psychology. Not only do societies attempt to understand how they relate to their worlds, but individual organisms do as well, and so the networkological project is not only a theory of society, but a psychology as well. As an immanent and relational worldview, rather than one which views thought and emotion as radically distinct, the networkological project understands thought as how the brain feels itself, emotion as how the brain feels itself in relation to how it feels its body, and sensation as how it feels its body. All of these are intertwined aspects of each other, even if only some aspects of these are available to conscious awareness at any moment. Bringing together insights from networked artificial intelligence and cognitive neuroscience with relational approaches to psychotherapy, the networkological project views the inter-twining of affective states and meanings in individual, trans-vidual, and collective formations as varying sides of the same. Building on the work of theorists such as John Dewey, Maurice Merleau-Ponty, and R.W. Fairbairn,[73] this project works to develop networked models of processes of thought and emotion which can help us intervene in what we do so as to best help those of us who suffer or hurt others, which is all of us, if differently and in differing degrees, so as to develop more robustly in relation to our worlds and each other.

Networks are panpsychist. As a non-binary approach to the world, the networkological project does not separate mind and matter in traditional ways. Much of the cutting edge research in artificial intelligence and cognitive neuroscience is increasingly moving beyond dualist approaches to the world which divide mind from body, or even mind from matter. Working to show how human forms of thought could emerge from the intertwining of dynamic systems of networked matters, complex systems science show how matter and mind, or "psyche," can be seen as aspects of the same, like two sides of a sheet of paper.

Such a perspective is generally known as "panpsychism," an approach to the world which has nothing to do with psychics or the paranormal, but rather, philosophy and science.[74]

A panpsychist view of the world sees all matter as feeling and experiencing, if in a manner much less complex than that seen in living organisms and human beings. If mind is simply how matter feels itself, then more complex minds come about when matter complexifies. As a result, there is no need to consider life or humans as fundamentally different from what is around it, but rather, as results of emergent complexity. Moving beyond the hierarchical dualisms and human exceptionalisms which have been used to justify everything from the denigration of sex and the body to incredible violences against our environment, animals, and groups of people considered less special than others, such an approach views the world as composed of shades of grey rather than overly simplistic and conceptually violent hierarchies, so as to help us imagine more complex and less destructive futures.

Networks are a pedagogics and therapeutics of liberation. As a philosophy of emergence, the networkological project views self-liberation in relation to others as an ethical, political, and social responsibility and goal. And yet, practices of liberation, which in theory should include education, individual or group psychotherapy, and various artistic and reflective practices, are often reduced to institutionalized structures which work to make such practices harmless to the dominant social status-quo.

And so, the institution of education today has become a machine for the production of social hierarchy which reduces teachers to tools, students to recording machines, and learning to abstract hurdles which only the privileged have enough time and resources to master. All this is a parody of education. We are never educated, we only ever educate ourselves, and teachers are only ever life-long learners who work to create the sorts of environments which help others to more robustly emerge on their own. Education should therefore move from models of discipline, storage, and testing to that of rigorous play and pleasurable experimentation, with a goal of the emergence of robust complexity in and between individuals and groups. Rather than teach specific bodies of knowledge, education should provide supports to help students teach themselves about the world in relation to their desires and goals, a process which can lead to any sort of knowledge or skill production in the future, even as it works to introduce learners to new avenues for potential creativity.

All of this applies equally to therapy, for by providing the type of environment which supports emergence, people will not only teach themselves, but heal themselves as well. Therapy should exist to promote happiness and reduce suffering according to the desires of the client, rather than promote normalization according to the values of dominant society, and the same with education on a larger scale. Therapists and teachers need to learn from their clients and students about their desires and goals, and work to find ways to create environments for experimentation with new modes of living which can help develop the means to emerge in relation to these.

Drawing upon the pedagogical and political theorizings of John Dewey, Lev Vygotsky, Paulo Freire, Stuart Hall, Enrique Dussel, and bell hooks,[75] as well as psychodynamic psychotherapies from relational, intersubjective, and gestalt modalities,[76] the networkological project believes we have yet to learn how to liberate and grow ourselves as individuals and collectives. By studying the emergence of robust complexity in the past, including that of the natural and physical world, as well as modes of organizational, educational, and collective experimentation in the present, we learn how to better heal, develop, and evolve ourselves and those around us, and the networkological project is committed to the furtherance of this goal. And since people grow best when they feel safe, for it is only then that they are able to question their own destructive behaviors, and potentially take risks by experimenting with new ways of acting, this project views the creation of safe spaces to learn and grow, in education, therapy, and society at large, as one of its primary concerns.

It should be kept in mind that there are many forms of therapy beyond the sort developed in the West. Of these, the various Buddhist paths of meditation practice indicate a form of therapeutics as developed as any Western psychotherapies. Many of these ultimately reify the development of the self from that of society and world nearly as much as Western therapies do, and in this sense, there is a need to image what more collective forms of these therapeutics might look like. While Vajranaya Buddhism seems an attempt to do this with Tibetan society, if one with many problems, the question of what a revolutionary activist, world-changing therapeutics and/or meditation practice would look like remains to be seen. Building on the work of Engaged Buddhists, particularly the work of Thich Naht Hanh, this project works to foster these sorts of projects in relation to the wider world.

Networks are a theory of commons. Bridging social theory and theories of value is the theory of enclosure, capture, and commons. There are limited resources of potential in our world, and the manner in which potential is distributed determines in part the potential for development in the future. The binding of potential into particular forms affects the way it can play out in the future, with more distributed forms allowing for greater potentials for robust emergences.

Networks are produced by processes of differentiation and emergence which give rise to fields whose interfaces produce overlappings and boundaries between them, which can then give rise to bounded solids and nodes, including singularities which act as points of symmetry between multiple systems. All these change in regard to the condensations, expansions, dissolutions, and emergences of potential as it actualizes, becomes dormant, reemerges, and complexifies in relation to other aspects of its contexts. In the process, nodes can separate off, link up to similar nodes, which are often produced or modified by similar circumstances, each share traits in common with others by means of similarity of physical form. When this happens in a meta-stable environment, these nodes can then circulate and become part of dynamic networks of flows, digital rather than analog forms of connectivity, and these circulations of formed matters can then give rise to ever more complex forms of networking. Economies and languages, or the complex webs of chemicals seen in living organisms, are examples of such digital networks.

Digital networks form domains and fields of flows, and these can give rise to various types of dominance, resonance, and play, the dynamic interplay of which can influence the unfolding and refolding of potential as these processes influence others in turn. The result is that potential is often enclosed in particular forms, described by singularities, boundaries, territories, and dynamic landscapes, which incarnate patterns whose production and reproduction determine, in part, those of the future. Mapping these structures, as well as the ways in which they determine potentials in various contexts, can help us understand the power dynamics of these situations. From state and phase diagrams in the physical sciences, to the evolutionary fitness landscape diagrams used by biologists and increasingly economists to understand evolutionary processes both living and cultural, understanding how potential is unfolded and refolded, distributed or hoarded, channeled and shaped, can help us not only understand the way power produces and reproduces itself, often in hardly robust ways, but how to best try to intervene to make these structures more distributedly robust in the future.

Capture of potential, the shaping of its products and flows, the biasing of territories towards certain forms of production and reproduction, all these are crucial to the ways in which dominant powers remain in dominance today. The study of the formation and maintenance of fields of play which foster robustness, which many theorists today have called "commons,"[77] as well as how various types of commons are drained, undermined, and reworked to benefit particular paranoid or cancerous power structures, in ways which limit the sort of distributed organization which tends to foster the sustainable development of complexity for all, is essential to the networkological task of promoting all which can help robustness grow in our world. Describing the ways in which various types of commons, whether physical, biological, or cultural, can be produced and reproduced, as well as how they are often unraveled and captured by various paranoid or cancerous mechanisms, works to help develop forms of potential intervention within these situations, as well as imagine new means for production of new types of commons which can offset non-robust forms of capture and enclosure. Working to increase the distributedness of flows of potential and the structures to which they give rise is one of the primary goals of this project, and working to help foster the production, reproduction, expansion, and robust transformation of various forms of commons is a crucial part of this.

Networks work to be a discourse of the oppressed.[78]
Discrimination, racism, homophobia, misogyny, religious perse-
cution, transphobia, ethnocentrism, xenophobia, so many hatreds
in our world rely upon hierarchical, binary division, reified
categories, fundamentalist reductionisms, paranoid fantasies,
and dogmatisms of all sorts. The networkological project
therefore works to learn to be continually reworked and
expanded by post-colonial, anti-racist, feminist, anti-poverty, and
queer discourses, as well as discourses of those oppressed in
ways to come. In fact, this project advocates a continual listening
for new forms of oppression which emerge from our ever new
ways of acting, or which were previously submerged by various
power structures which have only now loosened, for it is only by
such an attentive listening that we grow as individuals and
societies. From this attentive listening, this project will work to
develop its concepts with the hope that their structure makes it
possible for them to be put to work by the various discourses and
movements of the oppressed, for in many senses, this is an
indication that these discourses are in fact truly what our world
needs.

In relation to these concerns, the networkological project will
work to help articulate a mode of discourse which can help
continually refractively intertwine with those of the oppressed to
produce a continually mutating set of discourses of the
oppressed. In its valuation of robustness, the networkological
project views maximum diversity, so long as this does not push a
system into dissolution, as a condition which fosters robustness.
Ever proliferating forms of diversification are necessary if our
world is to grow, and diversity in all its forms needs to be
protected, fostered, nurtured; for learning to intertwine with
diversity on its own terms is the manner in which the robust
emergence of complexity occurs. The same can be said of

refractive, distributed concentrations of surplus, power, and potential in their varying forms. Too much concentration of resources is as bad for growth as too little. These conditions can only come about, however, when there is meta-stability which keeps the formations in society changing, as well the conditions of feedback between parts, to help learn about both the beneficial and detrimental effects these changes may cause in the various aspects of society in the process, so as to help us modulate these processes.

In all of this, the oppressed can always teach the world how it can be more robust by liberating the potentials it has repressed in the process of its prior complexifications.[79] While this may result in lowered relative complexity for the few who do the oppressing, it actually increases even their overall robustness, for it potentiates them in the long-term. In this sense, learning from those aspects of the world and ourselves which are different, and allowing ourselves to be transformed by these, to the extent to which any of these promote robustness, is the school and therapy of the world, the practice of liberation for us all, and is in fact emergence of robustness itself in its socio-psychological form. The liberation of the oppressed liberates the world, and teaches the world, and us with it, how to better liberate ourselves from our self-constructed cages.

No particular oppressed group, however, should be seen as ultimately holding the key to liberating the world from itself, and history is full of oppressed who failed to learn the lesson of their own oppression, who oppressed others through or following their own oppression.[80] Working for your own liber-ation can only ever achieve so much, what is needed is a "cross-activism" in which one works for the liberation of others on their own terms, not merely for the end of one's own oppression, but towards the lessening of oppression as such in its many forms. Even those aspects of yourself and your world which hate you and which you hate contain the lesson to your own liberation, for continual listening and attentiveness to the pain of the world is the pathway towards learning to grow. The continual production of discourses and practices of learning about oppression and the potential for liberation can therefore help us all emerge more robustly. And this applies to those with privilege in our world, as well as those with less, for it is only when the oppressed refract in each other can they transform the world, for power ultimately tends to work by making the oppressed hate each other more than they hate those who oppress them. And this applies to the parts of oneself as well. In all this, it is always to the oppressed and to those in pain that we must listen, learn from, and be taught, in and through our own oppressions, within and beyond ourselves, for only in this way can we liberate ourselves and our world from ourselves.

Networks are an economics. Cultural evolution produces various forms of social technology, various wideware networks, or "plexes," such as our educational, banking, or economic systems, including markets. As products of evolution, markets are simply evolutionary systems which generate social structures in regard to the cultural fitness landscapes of regulations, currencies, modes of production, and various other social and political formations within a society. While all systems code the world into in regard to the ways in which its aspects can contribute to the maintenance and increase of the complexity of the system in question, contemporary financial markets prioritize highly abstract notions of value, cut off from more qualitative modes of valuation. Rather than modulate the relations of value between these, they try to absorb all other currencies and the meaningful systems these describe into themselves, a tendency which can lead to feedback crises which can liquidate all aspects of society beyond pure quantitative reproduction at worst, or give rise to crashes, which lead to the massive destruction of potential and centralization of the system as a whole at best. All of this describes a condition analogous to the way in which cancer can overpower biological systems, or the manner in which too much feedback in physical systems can drown out the signal it would otherwise amplify. At the other extreme, favoring stability over growth or hoarding of currencies can lead systems to dangerous imbalances as well, not of growth, but lack thereof. Between the two extremes are more distributed and refractive modes of organization which lead to more robust forms of growth.

While physical and biological evolutionary processes tend to manage their modes of organization by means of evolution within fitness landscapes whose contours are largely beyond the control of the organisms in question, humans have enormous ability to sculpt the fitness landscapes in which our cultural products evolve. In regard to economics, modifying the structural parameters in which markets operate is to change what determines fitness in a particular market, and in this sense, not only what they value, but also the meaning of the value of particular currencies and markets in regard to their contexts. That is, if short-term earnings are valued by corporate governors above all else, then markets will evolve corporations which structurally produce this above all else, but change the conditions of selection, for example, by means of changes in the governmental regulatory structure, or the manner in which boards of directors are themselves hired or compensated, and the situation itself will change on its own.

Our corporations and markets, and the social institutions to which they give rise, are ultimately the products of our own values, even if we often pretend otherwise, or convince ourselves that they are simply too complex and must be left to their own devices. If this is so, it is because we have made them this way, and it is in our power to change this. Ideologies of the free market, however, imagine the market as ideally without bias, and when this is valued, the result is a system which promotes unlimited quantitative growth of the qualitative status quo, without other forms of feedback to prevent this from becoming cancerous to the system as a whole. Rather than see markets as beyond human control or logic, economics need to be seen as an attempt to produce the types of fitness landscapes in which the most robust social structures can emerge on their own in relation to conditions which are always at least partially of our own making.

Rather than assume that economic and social systems have to take particular forms, we need to study robust systems in the world, gain insights in what tends to help evolve robust physical and living systems, and try to imagine cultural analogs that can help evolve robust cultural systems as well. Such an approach is one which would necessarily prioritize a more distributed form of organization than that present in contemporary forms of transnational monopoly capitalism, with its distorting effects of unlimited accumulation, and the horrible injustices this produces. [81]

Networks are a political economics. Neoliberalism and austerity doctrines are based on the notion that the economy can run out of money. But money is simply a representation of the potential within people and the environment, and credit simply the faith people have in their ability to make this into action. Recession, financial crises, and value crashes in today's world, in which external factors play a minimized role, are generally artificially produced by the hoarding of surpluses or cancerous pursuit thereof. These are practices which value stability or growth at all costs over the evolution of structures which can produce robust growth for all, rather than the crash and burn growth cycles which serve to pump surplus to the few, or the practices which prevent the greater distribution or these. It is not possible for society or an economy to be broke, only bullied, for an economy is only ever the potential for action and change, and money only ever a particularly abstract representation of this when stripped of all the qualities which, in theory, money should help us to produce.

Economies are about trust and time, labor and action, and debt is only ever a form of slavery, a fiction but with very real results, one often used to keep people laboring within systems which ultimately oppress them, and anyone who tries to tell you otherwise is simply trying to manipulate you thereby. Humans and their labor, along with the physical potentials of the world, are where value comes from, and we have the right to evaluate our values, rework them, and determine what they should be. The economy is not determined by forces beyond our comprehension, or by equations which only the few can understand. We are the economy, and we can and should determine the fitness landscapes upon which markets are allowed to evolve, and in ways which are in accord with our values, which for this project, means robustness for any and all.

Building on the work of Naomi Klein, Mark Taylor, Philip Ball, David Graeber, and Eric Beinhocker, the networkological project takes a complex systems view on political economy.[82] Our world has more than enough ability to provide the basics of life and happiness to everyone, including food, health care, housing, education, and employment. Until all have these basics, luxury is theft from the robustness of all, and the only debt worth talking about is the social debt we have to the welfare of each other. Rather than develop fitness landscapes which value rapid yet unsustainable bursts of growth which then crash and destroy complexity in the process, we need to build structures to last for the many rather than the few. We need to invest in human beings, and the only way to do this is to design fitness landscapes, so that our cultural search algorithms, including markets, find fitness not in cancerous growth in quantity but in sustainable growth in quantity and quality in a robust manner. This requires value-based interventions in fitness landscapes, by means of rethinking institutions. Commons shares, carbon credits, and other alternative currencies are one way to change the ways in which markets function so that they value what society values, rather than have these values dictated by financial capital.[83]

Networks are a politics. Complex systems scientists often describe complexity as that which self-organizes "at the edge of chaos."[84] There are radical political implications to this, even if these tend to remain under-thought by many of those who restrict their investigations to the sciences. The networkological project views the study of networks in the world, whether physical, biological or cultural, as necessary to learn strategies that can help us promote robustness in our own networks. And if maximum sustainable diversity, distributedness, and multi-level feedback, when supported by meta-stable energetic conditions, tend to support robustness in the world, then radical democratic socialism is the form of organization which is most likely to promote this in human societies.

Building upon contemporary evolutionary theory, with its notions of fitness landscapes and search algorithms, this project works to imagine less oppressive and more robust ways of evolving our social networks so as to help produce a better world. Viewing society as having been most robust in the past when small local organizations spurred each other to creation, so long as there is both a strong safety net and anti-monopoly conditions in place which could prevent the centralization of potential, the networkological project views contemporary formations such as nation-states with rigid borders, joint-stock corporations, monopoly currencies and forms of capital, oppressive debt instruments, restrictive forms of representation, traditional forms of wage labor and private property, and all reifying social structures as potentially in need of refractive redescription and renetworking. With the human brain as political and ethical model and source of organizational inspiration, this project sees flexible roles, shifting configurations, mobility within networks, and relations across levels of scale as so many strategies to combat reification, hierarchization, and monopolization of surpluses. All elections and changes in governments happen because of shifts in the ways in which populations evolve in relation to the various networks to which they are connected in various fitness landscapes. Revolutions and elections are hardly an exception, and these only ultimately lead to robustness when the fitness landscapes in which they operate further these values.

Intimately intertwined with these issues are those of power and belief. The networkological approach to these issues, as with those of value, is to find a way to describe these which can be found in simpler forms in simpler systems, and in more complex forms in complex systems, and in ways which harmonize with the account of value already described. If value describes the manner in which economies unfold potentials into actions, then power is their ability to unfold potentials into actuals, with belief as the degree of unity and unanimity with which it can do this. In complex cultural systems, however, power is often modulated by the manner in which systems believe that others control what is of value, just as belief describes the degree to which a system agrees with itself in regard to its interpretations of the factors involved with its attempts to actualize potentials. An animal eats, for example, because it believes that this will alleviate hunger, and hence help it better achieve its goals. Just as action describes what a system values, the presuppositions which underlie the linkage between these actions and contexts indicate what a system believes.

In this sense, a system in which there is lack of unanimity of purpose is one of diversity of beliefs. While this can be a source of robustness, it can also be disorganizing, and robust evolution requires a modulation of these issues accordingly. Conflicting beliefs in a human society occur when there are conflicting values which cause aspects of that society to see holding these

beliefs as worthwhile in regard to their contexts. While state-
ments are actions which indicate valued beliefs, they always only
exist within the context of the other actions of the system. A
person who says they dismiss something as a rumor but still act
as if they do not "just in case" is someone who acts multiply, and
hence, believes multiply.

All of these issues have ramifications for how systems change.
Changing the ways others value, believe, or act is unlikely to
occur if the underlying value systems do not change, even if these
only ever unfold potentials in regard to beliefs which link interpretations of contexts to actions. Change tends to come about,
however, when beliefs need to be changed because they no longer
are able to effectively link potential to action in ways which help
the system achieve its goals according to its values. While in
physical systems this is often a simple, mechanical process of the
conservation of energy, this is much more complex with more
advanced organisms such as humans. Nevertheless, the basics
are the same. Create a more robust situation, and people will be
more likely to change their values and ideas to become a part of
it. If you want to change what you believe, then change what you
do, or the situations in which you put yourself, and belief will
generally follow. If it does not, this indicates you did not actually
want to change what you believe in the first place, and that you
would need to understand this first, and potentially alter your
relation to this resistance if any additional change in this
direction is likely to occur.[85] Change ultimately comes about not
because of what people say they desire, value, or believe, but
what they do, as well as the values and beliefs which arise
because of this, and the power which shifts in regard to the
perception of what this means. While political change describes
the way societies manage their more directly extreme forms of
violence, such as wars and imprisonment, political structures are
always ever one set of networks in regard to those of the economy
and culture at large, and change in one network is likely to lead

to change in another, even if in a "non-linear" manner which is difficult to predict due to all the factors involved.

While the networkological project advocates radical democratic socialism, it does not believe this could ever be imposed, but merely grown, from the bottom up, refractively. We need to enhance those aspects of society which could make such a distributed, diverse, meta-stable form of feedback and sync possible, and ultimately, this change is more likely to come first in the realm of culture than from those more obdurate forms of political structure, such as governments, themselves. Rather, we should expect these to change last.

Nevertheless, there are moments in which the fitness landscapes converge, and small changes can have oversized impacts for generations to come.[86] Various forms of political organization can help take advantage at such times to help bring about the potential for a better world. However, such change will only ultimately last if the cultural ground is properly prepared for it, and resorting to force to sustain such an organization is always only a self-defeating tactic. As small world networks show us, the real battle for a better world is always within oneself first, one's immediate contexts next, and more distant contexts last, and if we all made the world better in our immediate environments like this, radical democratic socialism would ultimately emerge on its own.

Networks are transvidual. Society is, and always has been, more than individuals and collectives, but this tendency is increasing. We are networks of living processes intertwined with wideware plexes of various sorts, making each of us repositories of images, words, affects, ideas, actions, algorithms, and so much more, and at many, many levels of scale. Each of these is individual, and each is collective. What is more, our world is increasingly one in which new collective intelligences are forming, a result of our newly networked digital computing technologies. We process affects on a collective level by means of social networking software, we think collectively by evolving new visual and verbal memes, and we act collectively by means of various distributed agencies. We live in times of decentralized ideological cells and new modes of organization which can swarm and disperse seemingly at will.

We need to think of new ways of interacting which take these into account. The human microphone from the "Occupy" protests is one new such formation, a mode of collective amplification which can emerge and collapse like that of complex systems in the world, between traditional notions of collective and individual.[87] In an age of faceless corporations and aleatory resistance modalities, of what Michael Hardt and Antonio Negri have called "empire" and "multitude," we need to think beyond the individual and collective, at the level of what Félix Guattari, Gilbert Simondon, and Gilles Deleuze have, in varying forms, referred to as the transvidual.[88] While these new formations are potentially liberatory, they have so far generally led to new atomizations, increased ethnocentric hatreds, more policing of borders, and overall paranoid responses to change. Understanding why this is and what we can do about this, despite and through ourselves, remains the challenge of our networked times. And if, barring collapse, the long arc of history truly is towards justice, for it evolves in the crucible of the evolution of complexity, the question then is, how much pain and suffering must occur along the way, and at what risk of collapse, with no guarantees for success?

Networks are radically democratic, socialist, consensivist, and post-anarchist political practice. Democracy is the manner in which distributedness manifests in systems in regard to power, and socialism in regard to potential, such that ultimately, these are varying sides of the same. Working to promote democracy and socialism in all their forms is then to work to promote conditions which potentiate robustness. For these reasons, the networkological project takes an experimental, pragmatic, and postevolutionary approach to political and social theorizing and organizing, with a goal of helping produce the conditions which could help foster the emergence of radical democratic socialism. Surveying the landscape of contemporary social theory and practice, the networkological project finds it has much in common with contemporary "post-anarchist" modes of theorizing and organizing, those which emphasize democracy and socialism not only as goals, but as guidelines for theorizing, organizing, and action as well.

The term "anarchist," often used provocatively, and widely misunderstood even by those who might find many of its ideas amenable, is simply a call for a radicalization of contemporary notions of social democracy, and hardly an espousal of chaos. Even classical "anarchist" theorists were generally not against order, but merely the attempt to monopolize the decision on which forms of order were best by a powerful few, whether in government, corporate offices, or even a tyranny of the majority. Contemporary post-anarchists question many of the assumptions of traditional anarchists, often combining their insights with those from contemporary post-structuralist and postmodern philosophy and theory. Many post-anarchist groups, from the Zapatistas to the anti-globalization and "Occupy" movements of the recent past, have drawn upon Quaker meeting practices to form new consensus-based modes of organizing to produce experiments in collective liberation. All of these take a commitment to the twin principles of radical democracy, namely, opposition to the tyranny of the majority, and advocacy of social and economic justice for all, as the foundation of their worldview.

Working to promote bottom-up, horizontal, experimental practices to find new modes of social organization, the networkological project therefore looks to inspiration in various forms of cooperatives, communes, spokescouncils, affinity groups, alternative currencies and markets, and many other experiments in social organizing which seek to operate alongside or outside contemporary forms of dominant social organization. Many of these forms of social organization are organized emergently, value robustness in all but terminology, are refractive in structure, and are networked to the core. This is in contrast to hierarchical, centralized, and reifying structures of contemporary governments and multinational institutions, or even revolutionary political parties which tend to sediment into reification and control so as to gain the benefits mostly for themselves, thereby limiting robust emergence of the whole.

Network socialism and radical "consensivist" democracy are varying aspects of the same, and the anarchist critique of modern forms of government, as well as post-anarchist anarcho-socialist democratic methods, provide potential roadmaps to more robust forms of social organization. Inspired by the classical "anarchist" theorists such as William Godwin and Emma Goldman, contemporary post-anarchist theorists such as David Graeber, Hakim Bey, and Saul Newman,[89] and working cooperatives, communes, and experimental social formations new and old, the networkological project works to learn from these and continuing experiments to bring about a more just, equitable, less violent, and more emergent future in all its proliferating forms.

Networks are pantheistic. While there is a history of radical political formations and religions being at odds with each other, this is because both of these, as well as contemporary philosophical and scientific discourses, tend to have a rather restricted and reifying notion of what it might mean to speak of the divine. Rather than dispense with transcendence completely, the networkological project views radical immanence as a pathway towards rethinking this notion in relation to the divine. In opposition to not only those who see any notion of God as dangerous and irrational superstition, but also fundamentalists or orthodox dogmatists who try to monopolize conceptions of God to promote rigid exclusionary ideologies, the networkological project refuses to cede the notion of the divine to those who show a lack of breadth and imagination in regard to what the divine could mean.

Beyond vague deism and rigid atheism is the radical potential which comes about when God is conceived in terms which are theophanic, which believe that God takes many forms and appearances, as well as pantheist, which believe that God is in all, is all, but is most intensely in the best within all.[90] Such an approach to God differs from anthropomorphic images of the divine, even as it views all faces of God which promote robustness, anthropomorphic or otherwise, as beneficial to our world, for there is no otherworldly ground upon which to judge the truth or certainty of the appearances of God. Rather, there are only appearances which promote robustness more than others, a conception of the world which views God as fundamentally heterodox, appearing differently to each aspect of the world as that which draws it on to emerge more robustly than it already is, a God with many faces and forms indeed.

From such a perspective, any and all who go forth and present new visions of the divine should be encouraged to do so to the extent that these help foster robustness in the world, for that which reveals pathways towards greater robustness is a more powerful face of a fundamentally multiplicitous divine, and we can all learn from and be inspired in turn by these. Drawing inspiration from perennialist theorists such as Aldous Huxley, Frithjof Schuon, and Henry Corbin, radically pluralized versions of Islamic Sufism, Vedantic Hinduism, and Mahayana and Vajrayana Buddhism, as well as the work of philosophers such as Aristotle, Ibn 'Arabi, Baruch Spinoza, Ju Mipham, A.N. Whitehead, Emmanuel Lévinas, and, Jean-Luc Marion, and with many affinities with the works of Pierre Hadot, Sri Aurobindo,

Pierre Teilhard de Chardin, Seyyed Hossein Nasr, Robert Wright, Jiddu Krishnamurti, and various process and liberation theologies, the networkological project is a radical materialism which is also a non-dual post-theological pantheism of the divine flesh of the world.[91] While this may sound radically different from the concerns of contemporary science described earlier, not only does it not conflict with the findings of science, it is in many ways simply an extrapolation of the logics inherent in contemporary sciences of complexity themselves when applied to different concerns. Overcoming the need to separate philosophy, theology, and science, the networkological project works to reimagine what the stakes of these terms could be.

Networks are a theophanic post-theology. As a theophanic pantheism, the networkological project believes that every aspect of the world, down to its fabric, is an aspect of God. As such, all is divine, sacred, and holy, even if those aspects of the world which are the most robustly emergent in relation to their contexts are more godlike, divine, sacred, and holy than others, and hence, manifest God's face more intensely. For God's face is the face of love, it is the manner in which the world loves us, and calls to us to liberate ourselves from our self-created chains.[92] The face of God in its many forms shines throughout the world, but most clearly in those aspects of the world which are the most robustly emergent, for the more an aspect of the world develops its potentials by developing those around them, the more it provides a model for others which can refract their own potentials back at them. These are those aspects of the world which are more loving and cooperative, transcending the distinction between self and other, freedom and necessity, and in this sense, the more Godlike aspects of the world. And while these differ radically from those which destroy, constrict, create unnecessary pain or violence, or otherwise reduce the robustness of the world, all these are ultimately also aspects of God, which need to be loved and learned from as well. Good and evil in our world, that which promotes and that which destroys robustness, both can show us ways to be more robustly emergent, even if they do so differently. It is ultimately only by loving each and all can we grow, even by helping the most damaged and evil aspects of our world to heal and work towards the robustness of all, for in doing so, we teach ourselves and our world how to be more robustly emergent in the process.

In these senses, all pathways lead back to God, but some are more painful and destructive than others. For if God is the emergence of robustness, and an aspect of God is more godlike as it emerges more robustly, then pain is evidence of the destruction of complexity, and only pain which ultimately serves the emergence of robustness can be something other than sin. Those who endure pain for the sake of robustness are then saints in this world. And redeeming sin by learning from pain to foster robustness is our task, and in this sense, all aspects of God have the potential to reveal a face of God, for all can teach us how to better foster robustness, and even those idols of pain can become icons of the holy, even as they try to lead us astray. Redemption, the transformation of idols to icons,[93] of sin to robustness, is an endless task which must be renewed at each moment, and it does not do away with the pain and violence of the present or the past. And yet, this must spur us to greater robustness still, for the complexity which has been given to us came at great cost. We must have righteous anger at the pain we have caused ourselves in our emergence, and channel this to the creation of a better world by the healing of any and all of the pain we have caused.

We owe the world an infinite debt, for all who suffered and died due to violence in the past, which made our emergence possible, and only an infinite effort to promote robustness and reduce the pain and suffering involved in this process in the future begins to show the gratitude we owe for the infinite gift of our emergence. We owe it to the pain and suffering of present, past, and future to work to redeem the present and future to whatever sense possible by learning from the past, and working to reduce pain and suffering in the present and future. The tortures and genocides can never be made right, the cries of pain will endure, the horrors will continue to exist as scars in our collective past, wrongs which can never be made right, pits of evil which cannot ever be erased. But if we learn from them, learn their terrible lessons, as individuals and groups, forever more, then this prevents anything like them from happening again, and in this manner, they will not have been in vain. We owe those saints who suffered pain to make their suffering our teacher, and we can only hope that each death and moment of pain will one day teach us this terrible lesson deeply enough so they will never occur again, a task of remembering and learning to which we must perpetually dedicate ourselves.

But we need not only learn by transforming idols into icons, we can learn by more divine icons of the holy, those aspects of God which inspire us not by the horror they present to us, but by hope. These are the guides which help us imagine how a better world might be possible. Of these, the most powerful are the quantum singularity at the start of our universe and the human brain, one a potential which produced matter, and the other the most robust evolution of the freedoms of this potential within actual matter. These are two of the most holy faces of God which we know, for they teach us how to emerge robustly by evolving towards life, cooperation, and liberation, towards greater power and freedom in regard to the limitations at work in the world of which we are a part.

We are all aspects of the singularity as it explores its ability to actualize all its potentials in matter, just as space, time, matter, mind, and the world are so many aspects of this.

The singularity is the radically non-dual, multiplicitous face of God which shines through all else, such that the world is simply God's love of itself, and the human brain its most powerful gift to the world we have yet known, even as all these are aspects of God as it liberates itself from itself, a process of which we are a part. While the human brain, the most robustly complex emergent yet known, has given rise to the most robust forms of love and cooperation, complexification and sync yet known, it has also given rise to forms of violence and cruelty unknown in the animal world, something which evolution needed to understand if it is to evolve beyond it. In the forms of potential for love evolution has given us, we have the potential to overcome these, to self-consciously work to learn to evolve the need for these out of our own self-evolution. Learning what this could mean is the task we have before us. For we are most in sync with ourselves and the world when we liberate our flesh, our intertwining with our worlds, to emerge with greater robustness, to love the flesh of the world as it loves us, and we owe the gift of the world to us to learn from it how to produce the maximum robustness with the minimum pain to the world, of which we are a part.

Networks are an erotics. If all aspects of the world are divine, and the most robust are the most holy, then the human body, of which the brain is merely a part, is one of the most holy aspects of the world there is. Its pains are its sins, and its pleasures its potentials for redemption, even if there are pains and pleasures which have more potential for robustness, and hence, are more holy, than others, for those pleasures which can foster more in the future are more robust than those which are intense yet fleeting. In this sense, the evolution of robustness can be seen as a form of radically intelligent hedonism which works to maximize the evolution of the pleasures of the flesh of the world.

We do not yet know what pleasures a body can feel,[94] but we know that for too long bodies have been denigrated by varying attempts to reify and control them. The flesh is holy, the body is holy, and pleasure, in all its forms, is how we have been evolved to know when something is likely to provide us with potential complexity, even if not potential robustness. And so, while some pleasures lead us to harm, the networkological project views any pleasure as beneficial unless it somehow hinders robustness. This project therefore views queer, kink, transgender, intersex, asexual, and other erotic and interpersonal modalities, so long as they do not also do harm, as new explorations of the flesh which can teach us more about ourselves, each other, and how we can better emerge with each other.

The networkological project is committed to an experimental erotics of which the valuation of robustness, and a consensivist socialist democratization of pleasures and feedback, is the only general limitation of this. None of which is to endorse a form of hedonism which is simple, however, for there are pleasures which are intellectual and emotional, which rival and potentially surpass those of the more physical side of our bodies, and ultimately, to neglect any of these would be to limit not only our pleasure, but our power and potential as well.

Networks are a praxis. Discourses are practices which produce descriptions to help us model the world around us and to orient our actions in the world in regard to projects which sync with our values and systems of valuation. Science is a discourse which aims to describe our physical world and produce experimental practices and new technologies, just as cultural discourses aim to do the same in regard to society and culture, with mathematics being the particular discourse which straddles these by limiting itself to pure quantity. Theorizing is the practice of reflecting upon practices to transform themselves into praxes, and philoso-phizing is the practice of the theorizing of theorizing itself in relation to our praxes. All of these practices intertwine with insti-tutions, objects, and agents and their attempts to make sense of their world and transform it in line with their values. The networkological project is itself a praxis, one which works to emerge from itself and the world, in and through praxes of scientific, cultural, and philosophical discourses, practices, and praxes, all of which can learn to grow more robustly in relation to the potential to imagine new worlds revealed by artistic praxes.

Networks are an aesthetics. Art is the practice which abstracts aspects of the world and reforms them, without immediately subsuming these to concerns of action, description, or reflection, but with the aim of exploration, the attempt to see the limits of what can be created and experienced. Art helps us imagine new potential aspects of any or all of the rest of the world, providing raw materials for the production of new potential worlds and world-aspects in the process. Only when art is liberated to explore is it generally able to do so, but only when art is in discourse with its surroundings, that which is not restricted to being art, does it do this well. Like science, mathematics, discourse, philosophy, practice, reflection, and praxis of many sorts, art is never pure, it always mixes abstract and concrete, actual and potential, meaning and value, ethics and politics. When art intertwines with these, it helps potentiate robustness, and it is here that it ultimately finds its value.

As products of robust emergence ourselves, we tend to find resonance with that which intertwines order and chaos in complexity in creations, which is generally known as beauty, even as we also resonate with the limitations of our relative reifications in regard to the sheer potential of emergence, which is sublimity. When we experience art which creates new aspects of its medium, we not only take pleasure in the new creations to which it gives rise, but to the manner in which art resonates with our own forms of ourselves and the world around us, and in ways which inspire us to be analogously productive in relation to our worlds as well. In this sense, art is that which intertwines beauty and sublimity in ways which can potentiate the emergence of robustness. It is those artworks which help us to emerge in new and robust ways in relation to them and the wider world which, like the most complex forms of thinking, are the most robust manifestations of art in our world, and are hence able to spur us to create ourselves and our worlds anew.

Networks are a theory of nothing. If networks describe every-thing as networks of relation, and any particular thing is simply a network of others, then there is clearly something paradoxical about networks themselves, something that slips away any time an attempt is made to grasp a network, refracting the attempt to reify any given network to the contexts and processes of which it is an aspect. This is precisely what a worldview which views emergence as the fundamental stuff of the world sees as the manner in which the emergence of emergence from itself gives rise to the distinction between something and nothing which complexifies in relation to itself by refracting fractally, holographically, and emergently to give rise to the world we see.

This position, while paradoxical in many ways, is not neces-sarily new. Scientists have come to realize that the quantum materials of which our world is composed seem fractal in nature, down to quantum foam and potentially beyond. Atoms are composed mostly of empty space, and some theorists have even argued that the multiplicity of particles we see in our world could all ultimately be refractions of the same, a notion which makes sense in light of the way quantum particles are able to, in a sense, fold and network spacetime within them, rather than vice-versa, when they are in an entangled, superposed state. In regard to all these issues, if our universe emerged from something, that something has more in common with nothing than anything we have ever experienced, even as all our somethings seem more like nothings the more closely we examine them.[95] In regard to mathematics, few disciplines are more fundamentally about nothing, from the infinitessimals of calculus, to Frege's number theory and Cantor's set theory, such that all number and form can be seen as simply a play between a void and the parentheses which refract this voiding in a variety of ways, from numbers to spacetime, sets, groups, categories, and beyond. Many approaches to semiotics have argued the same, from Jacques Derrida's notions of originary repetition, spacing, and deferral to Jacques Lacan's purloined cybernetic semiotics.[96]

These notions have a long history in varied forms of philosophy as well, from F.W.J. Schelling's notions of the unconditioned, G.W.F. Hegel's notions of the concept as the manner in which the world grasps itself in and through ever more complex forms of negation, A.N. Whitehead's notion of spacetime as extension within the creative advance of the universe, or Gilles Deleuze's notion of disjunctive synthesis of the repetition of pure difference as that which produces the differentiations of repetition and vice-versa. Economists have long argued that banks "create money" by sleight of hand, and we have long seen the ways in which fictitious capital powers economies. In more devotional contexts, Vedantic conceptions of *brahman* speaking itself into being as *atman*, Mahayana Buddhist notions of nothingness (*shunyata*) and the Buddha-embryo/matrix (*tathagatagarbha*), or voiding in Isaac Luria's version of Kaballah all present notions which are similar in many ways to what is advocated here. From such a perspective, perhaps it is not so strange to see networks as composed of more networks, which are themselves ultimately the self-differing and renetworking stuff of the world emerging in relation to itself, at potentially infinite levels of scale and complexity, nothing and something emerging from themselves and each other, and refracting in complexity in ways which give rise to the world we experience.[97]

Networks are a philosophy. The networkological project does not play many of the traditional philosophical games, and as such, it recasts ontology as so many logics of experience, fractalizes epistemology by extending Jakob von Uexküll's[98] notions of worlds of experiencing in relation to C.S. Peirce's notions of a universal semiotics of interpretation, and intertwines metaphysics and physics in a radically self-differing emergentism, all with the crystalline seed of the network diagram to organize it. This diagram, a conceptualization of the process of refractive diagramming at work in networkological texts, has several aspects which can be abstracted and conceptualized.

The network diagram is composed of three primary elements, or sub-concepts, of the node, link, and ground, along with the paradoxical element of the level, which opens on to process and emergence. Each of these elements describes a way of relating to the world and its aspects, which this project will call logics, each of which opens on to the next until the final logic opens on to the infinite of emergence itself. The logic of the node describes reification, while the logic of the link describes the relation of nodes within meaningful contexts. The logic of the ground describes how systems produce, evaluate, and transform meaningful contexts in regard to their potentials for emergence, all in ways which echo that described by Gilles Deleuze with the notion of "disjunctive synthesis" and semiotics as "double articulation," that which can give rise to the new within existing structures by producing meaning and value from potential.[99] And the logic of emergence describes the manner in which each of these manifests an aspect of the emergence of emergence from itself by means of these logics.

Between finite and infinite, reification and emergence, from noding to linking to grounding and leveling and emerging, from one to the radical "–and," between all these elements and logics, and bringing them together, is the tendency of the –and of emergence itself. This manifests differentially as the "four-andic" structure of "the fourand" of the network diagram, as well as emergently within and beyond each of its elements and logics as "the oneand" of emergence. In this sense, the fourand of the network diagram manifests the oneand, that which is always beyond any particular one yet also always within it, the flesh of the world and the matrix of all experience, by means of the one(and) of the node, the two(and) of the link, the three(and) of the ground, and the four(and) of networks within networks and the leveling which opens onto the fourand of the oneand of emergence.

In this sense, if "the one" is the dominant logic in traditional notions of experience, with its emphasis upon the reification of experience, the networkological project works to open this onto the one(and) of refractive experience. Likewise, "the two" is the dominant logic of traditional notions of meaning, of the one-to-one correspondence of signifier and signified, and this project works to open this to the two(and) of the multiplicities of inter-pretations. Value in its traditional form manifests in regard to the three of exchange, which this project works to open to the three(and) of process. Thought as traditionally conceived, in the mode of dialectics, takes the structure of a synthesis and a remainder which keeps it going as a process of development, and yet, emergence exceeds this by thinking the manner in which thought evolves beyond its own reifications, meanings, values, and processes to potentiate the radically new in and beyond itself in relation to emergence as robustness itself. In this sense, this project will work to liberate the oneand from the one(and), the twoand from the two(and), the threeand from the three(and), the fourand from the four(and), and the –andic from the onetofour, thereby manifesting the oneand by means of the fourand of the network diagram.

Building upon this, the networkological project is also a theory of graspings. Any reification of emergence is a symmetry, stability, and event which is also a working together, a sync, a commons which is also a capture, a stasis, and limitation, yet also a new potential, a starting point for new growth and new networking. The most extreme form of reification in this sense, that which is most stable, static, contractive, and recalcitrant to change, is a node, that of which the differences and samenesses, displacements and repetitions, describe any notion of space or time relevant to these.

Links and grounds are that which connect these, links as extended nodes and nodes as contracted links,[100] and grounds as what remains, subsists, and emerges between these, the fields from which either and all are drawn, from which they emerge and return. These processes, these emergences and intertwinings, absorptions and differentiations, are those from which graspings emerge and transform, dissipate and grow, and are all aspects, as are the graspings, of that which necessarily has many names. Emergence, the oneand, experience, the matrix of appearances, these are so many words for that which has emerged, emerges, and has the potential to emerge, and all of these, robustly, in these and infinitely other potential forms, if only relatively so in regard to any of its particular aspects.

These notions, abstracted from the refractive redescriptions this project produces from whatever it touches, and complexly intertwined as the network diagram, guide the formation of new refractions in this project as its principle core, one which reimagines the world as refractive diagramming which always works to emerge more robustly from itself. Logic is the work of abstracting these models from the world, ethics the attempt to come into sync with this, and practics the work of applying this back to the world, bringing together induction, deduction, abduction,[101] and action in a work of radically emergent creativity, a philosophically refractive networkological praxis. Our modeling of the world, whether via the equations of mathematics, the theories of science or philosophy, or the dreams of art, are always a sort of virtual reality wrestling with the world, all of which attempt to understand the world and learn how to interact with it better. Developing the potentials of the network diagram in relation to the world is what the networkological project is all about.

Networks are a meta-philosophy. The networkological project is a philosophy of description. This is opposed to philosophies of certainty, which view their descriptions of the world as somehow true, proven, certain, or beyond the impact of their conditions, such as the material, biological, and cultural contexts of their production. On the contrary, a philosophy of description views all philosophies as composed of descriptions produced by some aspects of the world to help them navigate the challenges their world presents to them in better line with their values. In this sense, all descriptions which a discourse, model, worldview, or philosophy produce are only ever also descriptions of the contexts of their production, with any attempts at proof, justification, or grounding as yet more descriptions in turn, meaningful modelings produced by the values of the systems which evolved them.

For this reason, the networkological project sees all models as composed of differing types of descriptions, some of which ground others. Primary descriptions are the most deeply held descriptions in a model of the world, and are often implicit, for these describe the contexts and processes which gave rise to the very descriptions which attempt to grasp them, which is often quite difficult and requires enormous complexity on the part of the system in question. Secondary descriptions are the general descriptions of the world and its aspects based upon the perspective described by primary descriptions, while tertiary descriptions are those descriptions which comes about when secondary descriptions are applied to singular aspects of the world to describe them in particular ways. For example, when this project describes an economy as a network, it uses network notions, which are secondary descriptions, to produce a tertiary description of a network, while it does this in relation to the primary descriptions which are the convictions about the world which ground the production of the theories of networks in the first place.[102]

Philosophies of certainty tend to describe their primary descriptions as more than simply descriptions, and instead, frame these as the most true or proven thing which can be known in regard to a given context, and the result tends to be paradox in the form of incoherence, incompletion, or inconsistency. Philosophies of description, on the contrary, tend to describe their primary descriptions as the notion that all descriptions are merely descriptions, and that even this description cannot be proven, but it is the description of the world in which there should be, for a variety of reasons, the most confidence, for it tends to avoid the crises which more extreme manifestations of incoherence, incompletion, and inconsistency tend to bring when philosophies of certainty are rigidly employed. While philosophies of certainty are reflectively organized, with central core beliefs from which others are produced, philosophies of description are refractively organized. Descriptive philosophies believe most certainly in the rejection of reflective organization around reflective modes of certain belief, with all other local descriptions produced by means of the refractions of this refusal of certainty, with the embrace of refraction this brings, in regard to particular situations. While philosophies of certainty have their uses, they tend to resonate with conservative or cancerous modes of organization, with philosophies of description having more in common with distributed modalities.

Building on the meta-philosophical works of theorists such as Hegel, Friedrich Nietzsche, the American Pragmatists, and Wittgenstein, the networkological project views philosophical production as not only discovering the logics of our modes of relation to ourselves and our worlds, but as creating these as well. Philosophy is then as much a product of what is as it is a product of what can or should be, and is as much intertwined with issues of invariance in our world as with desire, hope, and potential. History is full of stories and dreams that changed the world, and philosophy is as much a dream as science, which acts on the faith that our senses are to be trusted, and the social contract of a community of experimenters, just as much as religion and philosophy are the products of faiths and communities in their own ways. Even mathematics only makes sense in a world in which there are communities willing to agree on counting and measuring, assuming and proving.[103] World-modeling is always description of what is and can be, and it is at the cusp between these that we can imagine better ways of describing our worlds which can help contribute to making them not only technically more proficient, but more robust, in all potential senses of this word.

Networks are a new history of philosophy. Working to displace the tradition of philosophies of the individual produced by Descartes and Kant, the networkological project works to show how relational philosophies of the past, from Plotinus to Mulla Sadra, Maimonides and Spinoza in the Jewish tradition, and Aquinas and Ockham in the Christian tradition, as well as in non-Western traditions, are the rule rather than exception in the history of philosophy, even if only a minor tradition in the West from Descartes forward. These relational philosophies, often overlooked, nevertheless provide crucial resources for constructing relational philosophies in the present. Some of these relational philosophies are even networked in form, as seen in the work of Leibniz, even if they are rarely also philosophies of emergence in both form and content. There are, however, some notable exceptions, such as seen in the work of Spinoza, Ibn 'Arabi, Mipham,

Bergson, and Deleuze. All these thinkers attempted to develop an immanent, relational, refractive, and emergent philosophy in regard to the situations in which they found themselves, and hence can serve as crucial sources of potential inspiration.

Networks are only a beginning. As a philosophy of emergence, the networkological project hardly sees itself as final. Networks are only one way of articulating immanence, relation, refraction, emergence, and robustness. These practical, logical, ethical, and reflective principles exist throughout the history of thought, and will hardly stop here, giving rise to the potentials for new and different robust and refractive models which speak to our worlds in the future. This project is only the attempt to describe how the whole appears from the here and now of its articulation, and should only be seen as a refraction of the physical, biological, and cultural contexts of its production. That is, while this project shows how everything in the world can be seen as a network of experiences, a language of meanings, an economy of values, and a process of thinking, this is all ultimately little more than the manner in which the world refracts through the networks which gave rise to it. In this sense, this project is as much the autobiography of these as anything else,[104] and the only merits it has beyond these should be seen in the potential it has to resonate with the those of others in ways which can bring about more robust emergence.

And so, if this project inspires others to articulate new worldviews in ways which promote the emergence of robustness, giving rise to new and sustainable complex emergences, in and beyond new networkologies, then this project is in the process of what it hopes it can become, which is to say, fuel for ever more emergences which will decompose and recompose its aspects according to their needs.

Networks dream. Such a provocative networking of concerns from so many domains, from science and mathematics to philosophy, theology, pedagogy, ethics, erotics, politics and beyond, is bound to be controversial, and this is the intent. Networks think differently, they force and help us to find new connections, they intertwine what seemed distinct, mutate what seemed fixed, push us to reimagine the way the world has been, and to rethink how it could be. By means of describing networked lenses, which allow for redescriptions of notions of experience, meaning, value, emergence, and beyond, this project works to show how it might be possible to describe the world in a manner that works to emerge in and through thinking it, potentiating its further robust emergence.

The rest of this project will work to describe why and how all that was briefly sketched above hangs together, which is to say, why and how networks bring together these varied concerns in this particular way. However, as a non-binary approach to the world, this project sees the difference between reality and fantasy as one of degree, and views its own production as a worldview as not only a refraction of the way the world may be, but also what it could become. Many dreams have influenced this world more than its so-called realities, and most realities are not what they seem.

Networks are a reality which are also a dream, one which – if enough believe in them and create their own networkologies, which is to say, create their own differing refractive philosophies and practices of emergent robustness – could become ever more intensely and creatively our reality. At the cusp of dream and reality, networks are a potentiality in the world for a world that yet could be.

Reference Matter

Notes to *Introduction*

1. This position is described at length in Manuel Castells' *The Networked Society: The Information Age – Economy, Society, and Culture, Vol. 1*, (Wiley Blackwell, 2ⁿᵈ ed., 2000).

2. For more on how complex networks pervade biology, see *Signs of Life: How Complexity Pervades Biology*, by Ricard Solé and Brian Goodwin (Farrar, Strauss, and Giroux, 2006), or Stuart Kauffman's *The Origins of Order: Self Organization and Selection in Evolution* (Oxford, 1993). For applications to the physical world, see Flake (note 7).

3. I first encountered this notion in the works of David Graeber, although the exact citation has eluded me.

4. This notion echoes that of A.N. Whitehead in *Process and Reality* (Free Press, 1978), pp. 4-6.

5. More on the crisis of meaning suffered by philosophy and many other fields during the mid-twentieth century can be found in "Postmodernism and Philosophy," by Stuart Sim (note 49).

6. Karl Marx famously argued that the "the philosophers have only interpreted the world, the point is to change it" (*The Marx and Engels Reader*, ed. Robert C. Tucker, Norton, 2nd ed., 1978), p. 107. Pierre Hadot also presents a scathing critique of the way philosophy has become tamed by universities in *What is Ancient Philosophy?* (Belknap, 2005).

7. The classic history of complex systems science can be found in M. Mitchell Waldrop's *Complexity: The Emerging Science at the Edge of Chaos* (Simon and Schuster, 1993). A more recent overview of the field can be found in Melanie Mitchell's *Complexity: A Guided Tour* (Oxford, 2009), while the most accessible introduction is likely Neil Johnson's *Simply*

Complexity: A Clear Guide to Complexity Theory (Oneworld, 2007). Another excellent, wide-ranging, and enjoyable introduction to complexity is Philip Ball's *Critical Mass: How One Thing Leads to Another* (Farrar, Strauss, and Giroux, 2004). For those wanting a more technical introduction, a good place to start is *The Computational Beauty of Nature: Computer Explorations of Fractals, Chaos, Complex Systems Science, and Adaptation*, by Gary William Flake (Bradford, 1998), as well as Yaneer Bar-Yam's *Dynamics of Complex Systems* (Perseus, 2006) and Sunny Auyang's *Foundations of Complex System Theories: In Economics, Evolutionary Biology, and Statistical Physics* (Cambridge, 1999).

8. For an accessible overview of the critique of reductionism by complex systems scientists, see, for example, the preface in Mitchell (note 7).

9. A general introduction to artificial neural networks and their implications can be found in the chapter on "Connectionism" in *Mindware: An Introduction to the Philosophy of Cognitive Science*, by Andy Clark (Oxford, 2001). For a book which describes the theory behind artificial neural networks in imaginative, largely non-technical language, see Marvin Minsky's *The Society of Mind* (Simon and Schuster, 1988). For more on the specific types of artificial neural networks and how they relate to the study of the brain, see Manfred Spitzer's *The Mind Within the Net: Models of Thinking, Learning, and Acting* (MIT, 1999) and Rodney Cotterill's *Enchanted Looms: Conscious Networks in Brains and Computers* (Cambridge, 2000). A book which relates these to complex systems science in a wide sense is Klaus Mainzer's *Thinking in Complexity: The Computational Dynamics of Matter, Mind, and Mankind* (Springer, 5th ed., 2007), especially pp. 227-300. For the classic, and still great, text on the historical and technical issues related to the development of artificial neural networks, see Abrahamson

and Bechtel's *Connectionism and the Mind: Parallel Processing, Dynamics, and Evolution in Networks*, (Blackwell, 2nd ed., 2002). Those seeking a contemporary account of the massive successes of artificial neural networks, also at times called "deep learning," should see "Scientists See Promise in Deep-Learning Programs," by John Markoff, *The New York Times*, November 23, 2012. For more on how the basic wiring types of artificial neural networks simulate basic aspects of animal cognition, see pp. 26-7, 119-35 in Spitzer (*ibid.*) for induction in back-propagation networks with hidden layers, pp. 170-4 for pattern-completion memory in Hopfield networks, pp. 224-235 for association by means of feedback wiring between Hopfield networks, pp. 97-106 for recognition and categorization in Kohonen networks, and pp. 174-6 for temporal integration in Elman networks. A slightly more technical account of these types and functions can be found in section 2.1 of "Connectionist Architectures" in Bechtel and Abrahamson, *ibid.*, pp. 19-28.

10. Networked and related forms of non-binary "soft-computing" will be explained in my forthcoming text *The Networked Mind: Artificial Intelligence, Soft-Computing, and the Future of Philosophy*. For more on how these issues relate to fuzzy control systems, see Arturo Sangalli's *The Importance of Being Fuzzy* (Princeton, 1998). More on these technologies in general can be found in Andrea Tattamanzi and Marco Tomassini's *Soft Computing: Integrating Evolutionary, Neural, and Fuzzy Systems* (Springer, 2001).

11. For more on these notions in relation to history and philosophy of science, see Bruno Latour's *Science in Action: How to Follow Scientists And Engineers Through Society* (Harvard, 1988), Isabelle Stenger's "The Invention of Mechanics" in *Cosmopolitics I* (Univ. of Minnesota, 2010), and in regard to history and philosophy of mathematics, Brian Rotman's *Ad Infinitum... The Ghost in Turing's Machine:*

*Taking God Out of Mathematics and Putting the Body Back In –
An Essay on Corporeal Semiotics* (Stanford, 1993), Gilles
Chatelet's *Figuring Space: Philosophy, Mathematics, and
Physics* (Springer, 1999), Albert Lautman's *Mathematics,
Ideas, and the Physical Real* (Continuum, 2011), and Fernando
Zalamea's *Synthetic Philosophy of Contemporary Mathematics*
(Urbanomic/Sequence, 2012).

12. The mathematical study of networks, known as graph
theory, and how this relates to complex systems science, can
be found in Martin van Steen's excellent, accessible, and
self-published text *Graph Theory and Complex Networks* (van
Steen, 2010).

13. For more on the semiotic issues mentioned here, see
Semiotics: The Basics, by Daniel Chandler (Routledge, 2nd
ed., 2002). The work of Yuri Lotman, less known outside the
former Soviet sphere of influence than he should be, can be
found in *Universe of Mind: A Semiotic Theory of Culture*
(Indiana Univ. Press, 2001), while the work of Thomas
Seebok, working in a tradition at least partly distinct from
that of Saussure and Peirce, can be found in *Signs: An
Introduction to Semiotics* (Univ. of Toronto, 1994). The work
of Louis Hjelmslev can be found in *Prolegomena to a Theory
of Language* (Univ. of Wisconsin, revised, 1961). The relation
between Hjelmslev's theories and those of Deleuze and
Guattari's theories of language is nicely explained by Brian
Massumi in *A User's Guide to Capitalism and Schizophrenia*
(MIT, Swerve ed., 1992), pp. 47-92.

14. For those looking for a general introduction to the scientific
study of networks, there are many excellent and user-
friendly introductions, each emphasizing different aspects
of this field in relation to complex systems science,
including Albert-Lázsló Barbási's *Linked: How Everything is
Connected to Everything Else and What It Means* (Plume, 2003),
Duncan Watt's *Six Degrees: The Science of a Connected Age*

(Norton, 2nd ed., 2004). For those looking for a more technical introduction, see Mark Newman's *Networks: An Introduction* (Oxford, 2010). For texts which link complex systems science, networks, and issues in contemporary post-structuralist philosophies and cultural theory, see *Mark Taylor's The Moment of Complexity: Emerging Network Culture* (Univ. of Chicago Press, 2003) and Brian Rotman's *Becoming Beside Ourselves: The Alphabet, Ghosts, and Distributed Human Being* (Duke, 2008).

15. See "The Phenomenon of Reification," by Gyorgy Lukàcs, in *History and Class Consciousness: Studies in Marxist Dialectics* (MIT, 1999), pp. 83-109, as well as *Reification: A New Look at An Old Idea*, (ed. Axel Honneth, Oxford, 2008).

16. For example, Melanie Mitchell (note 7), p. x.

17. For a book-length treatment of the notion of emergence, see *Emergence: The Connected Lives of Ants, Brains, Cities, and Software*, by Steven Johnson (Touchstone, 2001), or *Emergence: From Chaos to Order* by John Holland (Basic Books, 1999). A text on emergence which links this with many of the other philosophical and scientific concerns of this project is Manuel De Landa's *Philosophy and Simulation: The Emergence of Synthetic Reason* (Continuum, 2011).

18. For more on dissipative systems, and how this notion relates complex systems theories to notions of temporality and entropy, see Auyang (note 7), pp. 228-68.

19. See preceding note.

20. More on robustness can be found, for example, in Scott Page's *Diversity and Complexity* (Princeton, 2010), pp. 3-21. For a book-length treatment of this notion, see Andreas Wagner's *Robustness and Evolvability in Living Systems* (Princeton, 2007).

21. See note 9.

22. See note 9.

23. For more on the distributed nature of mind and

consciousness, see the sections on "Consciousness and Complexity" and "The Dynamic Core," pp. 125-56, in Edelman and Tononi (note 31).

24. More on embodied cognition theories, in experimental robotics and beyond, can be found in Gallagher, Pffeifer and Bongard in note 45.

25. David Bohm develops his notion of implicate folding in regard to quantum mechanics in a manner similar to that being argued here in *Wholeness and the Implicate Order* (Routledge, 1980), pp. 218-272.

26. While many working in contemporary cognitive neuroscience and artificial neural networks advocate something like panpsychism, it is generally philosophers who have made use of this term. For an example of contemporary philosophical discourse on panpsychism, see William Seager's "Consciousness, Information, and Panpsychism" in *Explaining Consciousness: The Hard Problem*, (ed. by Jonathan Shear, Oxford, 1997), pp. 269-286. For more on the notion of panpsychism in the history of philosophy, see David Skrbina, *Panpsychism in the West* (Bradford, 2007). Antonio Damasio is an example of a prominent neuroscientist and theorist who argues against mind/body dualism in what could be called a panpsychist manner, for example, in books such as *Descartes' Error: Emotion, Reason, and the Human Brain* (Penguin, 2005) or *Looking for Spinoza: Joy, Sorrow, and the Feeling Brain* (Harcourt, 2003). In addition, artificial neural networks themselves can be seen as part of a larger argument for panpsychism. David Bohm's endorsement of an essentially panpsychist position can be found in the book he wrote with Basil Hiley, *The Undivided Universe: An Ontological Interpretation of Quantum Theory* (Routledge, 1993), p. 386.

27. More on how distributed and refractive organization produce the effects they do can be found in the following note.

28. For more on network topologies, see "Why Do We Like Networks?" in Peter Csermely's *Weak Links: The Universal Key to the Stability of Networks and Complex Systems* (Springer, 2006), pp. 5-46. For more on how topologies impact transitions in dynamic networks, see pp. 74-9. It should be noted that the notions of weak-links, small worlds, and distributed organization are in many ways aspects of the same, in that weak-links give rise to distributed "small world" networks. These notions are also closely tied to the notion of "scale-free organization" seen in much of the literature on networks. Scale-free organization is another way of saying self-similar or fractal organization across a given number of levels of scale, and it is only when distributedness is truly scale-free that it is able to manifest its most beneficial effects, for this allows for feedback effects within the system across levels of scale. It should also be noted that refractive modes of organization are often referred to in network literature as "degeneracy," for they arise when there are many similar yet not identical systems in loose sync, often called "loose coupling," with each other. All of these issues are discussed in the excerpt from Csermely indicated above. For more on refraction as degeneracy, see Cseremly pp. 108-9.

29. "Small world" network topologies are addressed in the preceding note.

30. For more on meta-stability often described as a state "at the edge of chaos", see, for example, Ball (note 7), pp. 163-172, 292-3, 321-8.

31. See Donella Meadow's "System Structure and Behavior" for more on how feedback impacts complex systems, in *Thinking in Systems: A Primer* (Chelsea Green, 2008), pp. 11-74. In regard to how this relates to temporality in dissipative systems, see Auyang (note 7), pp. 228-68. For more on how feedback is essential to recursion in neural networks in the form of reentry, see Gerald Edelman and Giulio Tononi's *A*

Universe of Consciousness: How Matter Becomes Imagination (Basic, 2001), pp. 48-9, 118-9, 166-7.

32. The notion of cancerous reproduction in the sense described here, with implications for social issues, can be found in many forms in the work of Gilles Deleuze and Félix Guattari, for example, *A Thousand Plateaus: Capitalism and Schizophrenia* (Univ. of Minnesota, 1987), pp. 68, 165, 215.

33. Sigmund Freud's notions of a "life" and "death" instinct can be found in "Beyond the Pleasure Principle," in Peter Gay's *The Freud Reader* (Norton, Reprint, 1995), pp. 594-625, as well as the commentary on this presented by Jean Laplanche in his influential text *Life and Death in Psychoanalysis* (Johns Hopkins, 1985). For an introduction to Gilles Deleuze's notions of difference and repetition, see Joe Hughes' *Difference and Repetition: A Reader's Guide* (Continuum, 2009), or alternately, Deleuze's *Difference and Repetition* (Columbia Univ., 1995).

34. An introduction to Bergson's notions of radical creativity can be found in his lecture series *The Creative Mind: An Introduction to Metaphysics* (Dover, 1946). Deleuze's take on this, in relation to Bergson and beyond, can be found in *Bergsonism* (Zone, reissue, 1990). Gilbert Simondon, a crucial influence on Deleuze, develops related notions in his theories of individuation, and meta-stability is in fact a crucial notion for Simondon. While most of his works are currently being translated into English as of the printing of this book, the first full-length study of Simondon's work in English is Muriel Combes' *Gilbert Simondon and the Philosophy of the Transindividual* (MIT, 2012). For a text which brings Deleuze's Bergsonian philosophy together with complex systems science, see Manuel De Landa's *Intensive Science and Virtual Philosophy* (Continuum, 2002).

35. At all levels of scale yet known, even down to the quantum level, all forces seem to be conveyed by moving matters. For

more, see Leon Lederman and Christopher Hill, *Symmetry and the Beautiful Universe* (Prometheus, 2008), p. 261.

36. More on econophysics can be found in Octavian Ksenshek's *Money: Virtual Energy – Energy Through the Prism of Thermodynamics* (Universal Publishers, 2007), or in the work of Doyne Farmer at the Santa Fe Institute at http:// tuvalu.santafe.edu/~jdf/SFI%20Template/About%20Me. html.

37. For more on autopoëtics, see Livingston (note 54).

38. For more on the notion that all forces are the result of moving particles, see Leon Lederman, *Symmetry and the Beautiful Universe* (Prometheus, 2004), p. 361.

39. The principle of least action in physics is the subject of Chapter 6, "Least Action," in John Taylor's *Hidden Unity in Nature's Laws* (Cambridge, 2001), pp. 175-190.

40. For more on money as a meta-sign see Brian Rotman, *Signifying Nothing: The Semiotics of Zero* (Stanford, 1987), pp. 46-56.

41. In regard to theories of the relation between meaning and value, see Jean-Joseph Goux's *Symbolic Economies: After Marx and Freud* (Cornell, 1990). Another excellent resource can be found in Brian Rotman, see preceding note.

42. For more on "wideware," see "Cognitive Technology: Beyond the Naked Brain," in Clark (note 9), pp. 140-159. Related notions can be found in Bernard Stiegler's notions of mnemotechnics as described in "The Invention of the Human," *Technics and Time, Vol. 1: The Fault of Epimetheus* (Stanford, 1998), pp. 21-182.

43. The notion of an "image of thought" is first developed by Deleuze in *Difference and Repetition*, but is expanded extensively in "The Plane of Immanence" in *What is Philosophy?* by Gilles Deleuze and Félix Guattari (Columbia Univ., 1994).

44. For more on the relation between sync and complex systems science, see Steve Strogatz's *Sync: How Order Emerges From*

Chaos in the Universe, Nature, and Daily Life (Hyperion, 2nd ed., 2004). For how this relates to neural networks, artificial and living, see Cotterill (note 9).

45. For more on embodied and emergent cognition, see Melanie Mitchell, (note 7), pp. 115-85, Shaun Gallagher's *How the Body Shapes the Mind* (Oxford, 2006), Rolf Pfeifer and Josh Bongard's *How the Body Shapes the Way We Think: A New View of Intelligence* (Bradford, 2006), and *Philosophy in the Flesh: The Embodied Mind and its Challenge to Western Thought* (Basic Books, 1999). For more on emergent and distributed cognition theories, particularly in relation to genetic algorithms and multi-agent systems, see Jacques Ferber's *Multi-Agent Systems: An Introduction to Distributed Intelligence* (Addison-Wesley, 1999).

46. For more on the relation between sync and complex systems science, see Strogatz (note 44). For more on how these issues relate to neural networks, artificial and living, see Cotteril (note 9).

47. The notion of a "reptile brain" is a massive simplification. However, the cortico-adrenal circuits of the limbic system, including the amygdala, are largely responsible for the aggressive and paranoid defense mechanisms described in this text. For a book-length discussion of these circuits, in relation to the oxytocin and vasopressin circuits which modulate these, see Joseph LeDoux's *Synaptic Self: How Brains Become Who We Are* (Penguin, 2002). For more on the evolutionary consequences of these issues, see the following note.

48. For more on the evolution of cooperation, particularly in relation to game-theory, see the highly influential book *The Evolution of Cooperation* by Robert Axelrod (Princeton, revised, 1997). For a more biologically oriented yet equally complex development of these and related notions, see Martin Nowak and Roger Highfield's *Supercooperators:*

Altruism, Evolution, and Why We Need Each Other to Succeed (Simon and Schuster, 2011).

49. On the linguistic turns in contemporary philosophy, Michael Losonsky's *Linguistic Turns in Modern Philosophy* (Cambridge, 2006), the final two chapters in particular, pp. 190-252. For more on how these issues relate to wider cultural concerns, see the chapters on "Postmodernism and Philosophy" and "Postmodernism and Critical Theory," by Stuart Sim and Georges van den Abbeele, respectively, in *The Routledge Companion to Postmodernism* (ed. by Stuart Sim, Routledge, 3rd ed., 2011).

50. For more on the critique of totalization in post-structuralism, see Catherine Belsey, *Post-Structuralism: A Very Short Introduction* (Oxford, 2002), p. 99.

51. The foundations crisis in mathematics is described at length in Morris Kline's *Mathematics: The Loss of Certainty* (Oxford, 1980) and Jeremy Grey's *Plato's Ghost: The Modernist Transformation of Mathematics* (Princeton, 2008). The classic reference on the decline of "grand narratives" in science and beyond is Jean-François Lyotard's *The Postmodern Condition: A Report on Knowledge* (Univ. of Minnesota, 1984). The notion of the "society of the spectacle" is found in Guy Debord's *The Society of the Spectacle* (Zone, 1995). For more on Alexandre Kojève's notion of the "end of history" see Shadia Drury's *Alexandre Kojève and The Roots of Postmodern Politics* (Palgrave, 1994), pp. 41-66, as well as Francis Fukuyama's *The End of History and the Last Man* (Avon, 1992).

52. On the relation between paradigms and anomalies in science, see Thomas Kuhn's *The Structure of Scientific Revolutions* (Univ. of Chicago, 3rd ed., 1996). Ernesto Laclau's approach to social paradigm crises, strongly influenced by the work of Karl Marx and Jacques Lacan, can be found in *New Reflections on the Revolution of Our Time* (Verso, 1997). Lyotard's approach to paradigm changes in science and

beyond can be found in *The Postmodern Condition* (preceding note), while the relation between self-reference and feedback in dynamic systems can be found in Hofstadter (note 54).

53. In regard to the existence of various forms of skepticism in the ancient world and around the globe, including in ancient Chinese and Indian traditions, see *The Alternative Tradition: A Study of Unbelief in the Ancient World*, by James Thrower (De Gruyter, reprint, 2011). For a study of ancient Greco-Roman variants, with an emphasis on academic and Pyrrhonian varieties, see *The Cambridge Companion to Ancient Skepticism* (ed. by Richard Bett, Cambridge, 2010).

54. A wildly enjoyable presentation of issues related to paradoxes of self-reference, and how this relates to axiomatic foundations in mathematics, computation, and beyond, can be found in Douglas Hofstadter's *Gödel, Escher, Bach: An Eternal Golden Braid* (Basic Books, 1979). For more on how this relates to the history of mathematics, see Morris Kline or Jeremy Grey (note 51 for both). A philosophical account of how these relate to recursion in logic is George Spencer-Brown's *Laws of Form* (Dutton, 1979). More in relation to observation can be found in Niklas Luhmann's "The Paradox of Observing Systems" in *Theories of Distinction: Redescribing the Descriptions of Modernity* (Stanford, 2002), pp. 79-93, and in relation to self-organizing complexity in Ira Livingston's *Between Science and Literature: An Introduction to Autopoetics* (Univ. of Illinois, 2005), pp. 58-79.

55. Karl Marx's critique of commodity fetishism can be found in *The Marx and Engels Reader* (ed. Robert Tucker, Norton, 2nd. ed., 1978), pp. 215-25. The critique of reductionism in complex systems science can be found in the preface in Melanie Mitchell (note 7). On the difference between desire and craving in various strands of Buddhist thought, see

Carl Olson's *The Different Paths of Buddhism: A Narrative-Historical Introduction* (Rutgers, 2005), pp. 53, while for the relation to these notions and the critique of reification in the work of Nagarjuna, see pp. 154-6. The critique of the error of binding (*taqyid*) in the work of the Sufi philosopher Ibn 'Arabi is articulated in Michael Sells' *Mystical Languages of Unsaying* (Chicago, 1994), pp. 78-83, 90-115. A.N. Whitehead's notion of the "fallacy of misplaced concreteness" can be found in *Science and the Modern World* (Free Press, 1925), pp. 51-8. Hegel's critique of *Vorstellung*, often translated as "picture-thinking," can be found in Hegel's *The Phenomenology of Spirit* (trans. by V.A. Miller, Oxford, 1977), pp. 35-6, 440-80. Spinoza's critique of the imagination can be found in *Ethics* (Hackett, trans. by Samuel Shirley, 1992), pp. 42, 91.

56.   David Graeber does an excellent job of tracing the relations between these issues in *Debt: The First 5,000 Years* (Melville House, 2012), pp. 307-360. This can also be profitably read alongside the genealogy of the relations between the development of money, mathematics, conceptions of spatiality in art, and notions of personal individuality in Rotman (note 40), as well as that of the intertwining of the birth of Western capitalism and expansionism, conquest, and enslavement in Cedric Robinson's highly influential account in *Black Marxism: The Making of the Black Radical Tradition* (Univ. of North Carolina, reprint, 2000), pp. 1-164.

57.   Jeff Hawkins, for example, describes what the brain does as "memory prediction," see *On Intelligence: How a New Understanding of the Brain Will Lead to the Creation of Newly Intelligent Machines* (Times Books, 2004). Pattern-completion also describes the manner in which animal brains are able to guess and forget, in a manner similar to Hopfield networks (see note 9).

58.   An excellent introduction to theophanic pantheism can be

found in Tom Cheetham's account of this in Henry Corbin's reading of Ibn 'Arabi in *The World Turned Inside Out: Henry Corbin and Islamic Mysticism* (Spring Journal Press, 2003).

59. For a critique of contemporary multinational capitalism and neoclassical/neoliberal economic theory from the perspective of modern evolutionary theory and complex systems science, see Eric Beinhocker's *The Origin of Wealth: Evolution, Complexity, and the Radical Remaking of Economics* (Harvard Business Review Press, 2007), Mark Taylor's *Confidence Games: Money and Markets in a World Without Redemption* (Univ. of Chicago Press, 2008), and Benôit Mandelbrot and Richard L. Hudson's *The Misbehavior of Markets: A Fractal View of Risk, Ruin, and Reward* (Perseus, 2004).

60. More on the differences between unfettered capitalism and evolution can be found in Beinhocker (preceding note), pp. 261-414, and in Graeber (note 56), pp. 260-1.

61. The metaphor of Buddhist teachings as a raft can be found in Olson (note 55), p. 21. On the metaphor of the ladder in Ludwig Wittgenstein's *Tractatus*, see Joachim Schulte's *Wittgenstein: An Introduction* (SUNY Press, 1992), pp. 44, 66.

62. The notion of crystallization describe here has much in common with Gilles Deleuze's notion of the crystalline regime, as described in *Cinema II: The Time-Image* (Univ. of Minnesota, 1989), pp. 126-136. For more on the theorization of physical crystallization on which this is based, see the summary of Gilbert Simondon's thought on these issues, as described in Combes (note 34), pp. 6, 14-23.

Notes to "Networkologies: A Manifesto"

1. There are other philosophies which use networks in various ways, though none of these base themselves explicitly on networks, and all differ substantially from this project. For

more on philosophies with networked aspects, see Bruno Latour and John Law's work on actor-network theory, as described in Bruno Latour's *Reassembling the Social: An Introduction to Actor-Network Theory* (Oxford, 2007). For a text which brings out the networked side of the work of Gilles Deleuze, see Manuel De Landa's *Intensive Science and Virtual Philosophy* (Continuum, 2002).

2. "To him who looks at the world rationally, the world looks rationally back." Georg Wilhelm Friedrich Hegel, *Reason in History* (Prentice Hall, 1996), p. 13.

3. Soft-computing will be explained in my forthcoming text *The Networked Mind: Artificial Intelligence, Soft-Computing, and the Future of Philosophy*. For more on how these issues relate to fuzzy control systems, see Arturo Sangalli's *The Importance of Being Fuzzy* (Princeton, 1998). More on these technologies in general can be found in Andrea Tattamanzi and Marco Tomassini's *Soft Computing: Integrating Evolutionary, Neural, and Fuzzy Systems* (Springer, 2001).

4. For a clear and accessible overview of many of the interpretations of the experimental evidence of quantum physics, including those related to histories, time-symmetry/ smearing, decoherence, many worlds, and Feynman's famous diagrams, see Victor Stenger's *Timeless Reality: Symmetry, Simplicity, and Multiple Universes* (Perseus, 2000), pp. 107-275, or Murray Gell-Mann's *The Quark and the Jaguar: Adventures in the Simple and the Complex* (Henry Holt, 1994), pp. 135-176. While Gary Zukav's *The Dancing Wu-Li Masters: An Introduction to the New Physics* (Harper, 2001, reissue) is now slightly dated on recent findings, and has some minor issues with its use of non-Western philosophy, it nevertheless probably remains the most user-friendly yet comprehensive overview of quantum physics and relativity theory in print, and a recommended starting point for those with no prior background. David Bohm's approach to quantum

physics in relation to notions of implicate folding can be found in *Wholeness and the Implicate Order* (Routledge, reprint, 2002). The networked side of quantum physics, and how this can destabilize more reifying approaches to spacetime and quantum "particles" can be found nicely summed up in Zukav, pp. 239-279. Multi-level selection theories in biology can be found in Edward O. Wilson's *The Social Conquest of the Earth* (Norton, 2012), and a relational approach to chemistry is articulated in Philip Ball's *Designing the Molecular World: Chemistry at the Frontier* (Princeton, 1994).

5. For Bruno Latour's highly influential study of science as practice see *Science in Action: How to Follow Scientists and Engineers Through Society* (Harvard, 1988). For more on Brian Rotman's semiotics of mathematics, see *Ad Infinitum* .... *The Ghost in Turing's Machine: Taking God Out of Mathematics and Putting the Body Back In - An Essay in Corporeal Semiotics* (Stanford, 1993). Isabelle Stenger's extended engagement with the history and philosophy of science can be found, for example, in texts such as "The Invention of Mechanics" in *Cosmopolitics I* (Univ. of Minnesota, 2010).

6. See note 15.

7. The notion of an "image of thought" is first developed by Deleuze in *Difference and Repetition*, but is developed extensively in "The Plane of Immanence" in *What is Philosophy?* by Gilles Deleuze and Félix Guattari (Columbia Univ., 1994).

8. A general introduction to artificial neural networks and their implications can be found in the chapter on "Connectionism" in *Mindware: An Introduction to the Philosophy of Cognitive Science*, by Andy Clark (Oxford, 2001). For a book which describes the theory behind artificial neural networks in imaginative, largely non-

technical language, see Marvin Minsky's *The Society of Mind* (Simon and Schuster, 1988). For more on the specific types of artificial neural networks and how they relate to the study of the brain, see Manfred Spitzer's *The Mind Within the Net: Models of Thinking, Learning, and Acting* (MIT, 1999) and Rodney Cotterill's *Enchanted Looms: Conscious Networks in Brains and Computers* (Cambridge, 2000). A book which relates these to complex systems science in a wide sense is Klaus Mainzer's *Thinking in Complexity: The Computational Dynamics of Matter, Mind, and Mankind* (Springer, 5th ed., 2007), especially pp. 227-300. For the classic, and still great, text on the historical and technical issues related to the development of artificial neural networks, see Abrahamson and Bechtel's *Connectionism and the Mind: Parallel Processing, Dynamics, and Evolution in Networks* (Blackwell, 2nd ed., 2002). Those seeking a contemporary account of the massive successes of artificial neural networks, also at times called "deep learning" should see "Scientists See Promise in Deep-Learning Programs," by John Markoff, *The New York Times*, November 23, 2012. For more on how the basic wiring types of artificial neural networks simulate basic aspects of animal cognition, see pp. 26-7, 119-35 in Spitzer (*ibid.*) for induction in back-propagation networks with hidden layers, pp. 170-4 for pattern completion memory in Hopfield networks, pp. 97-106 for recognition and categorization in Kohonen networks, and pp. 174-6 for temporal integration in Elman networks. A slightly more technical account of these types and functions can be found in section 2.1 of "Connectionist Architectures" in Bechtel and Abrahamson, *ibid.*, pp. 19-28.

9.   On the manner in which the notion of the binary computer affected ideologies of what it means to think, see David Golumbia's *The Cultural Logic of Computation* (Harvard, 2009).

10. The notion of virtuality at work in the networkological

project is different from that of Deleuze and Bergson. The networkological project differentiates the notions of virtual and potential, while Deleuze and Bergson do not, with ramifications to be described in future texts.

11. The study of symmetry is essential to several fields of study in contemporary mathematics, but is most directly addressed by group theory. An accessible introduction to group theory can be found in "Symmetry: The Group Concept," by Ian Stewart, in *Concepts of Modern Mathematics* (Dover, 1995) pp. 95-112. A more advanced yet still accessible treatment can be found in the wonderfully illustrated *The Symmetries of Things* by John Conway, Heidi Burgiel, and Chaim Goodman-Strauss (AK Peters, 2008), or R. Mirman's *Group Theory: An Intuitive Approach* (World Scientific, 1995). Implications of these notions for physics can be found in Leon Lederman's *Symmetry and the Beautiful Universe* (Prometheus, 2004). The most basic description of the relevance of category theory for contemporary philosophy can be found in Norman Madarasz's introduction to Alain Badiou's *Briefings on Existence: A Short Treatise on Transitory Ontology* (SUNY, 2006), pp. 12-15. For a more traditionally mathematical approach, if one which presumes no prior knowledge, and which includes a basic introduction to topos theory, see F. William Lawvere's *Conceptual Mathematics: A First Introduction to Categories* (Cambridge, 2nd ed., 2009).

12. Process philosophy is introduced by Nicholas Rescher in *Process Philosophy: A Survey of Basic Issues* (Univ. of Pittsburg, 2000). For more on the most famous exponent of process in philosophy, see Robert Mesle's *Process-Relational Philosophy: An Introduction to Alfred North Whitehead* (Templeton, 2008). In regard to Whitehead's critique of over-reification as "the fallacy of misplaced concreteness," see *Science and the Modern World* (Free Press, 1925), pp. 51-8.

13. The classic history of complex systems science can be found in M. Mitchell Waldrop's *Complexity: The Emerging Science at the Edge of Chaos* (Simon and Schuster, 1993). A more recent overview of the field can be found in Melanie Mitchell's *Complexity: A Guided Tour* (Oxford, 2009), while the most accessible introduction is likely Neil Johnson's *Simply Complexity: A Clear Guide to Complexity Theory* (Oneworld, 2007). Another excellent, wide-ranging, and enjoyable introduction to complexity is Philip Ball's *Critical Mass: How One Thing Leads to Another* (Farrar, Strauss, and Giroux, 2004). For those wanting a more technical introduction, a good place to start is *The Computational Beauty of Nature: Computer Explorations of Fractals, Chaos, Complex Systems Science, and Adaptation*, by Gary William Flake (Bradford, 1998), as well as Yaneer Bar-Yam's *Dynamics of Complex Systems* (Perseus, 2006) and Sunny Auyang's *Foundations of Complex System Theories: In Economics, Evolutionary Biology, and Statistical Physics* (Cambridge, 1999).

14. For more on meta-stability, see, for example, Ball (preceding note), pp. 163-72, 292-3, 321-8.

15. Non-linearity, the mathematical unpredictability which occurs whenever more than two systems influence each other in a feedback relation, often described in terms of the famed 'three body problem' in physics, is discussed in Mitchell (note 13), pp. 22-26.

16. For a book-length treatment of autopoeisis and its many ramifications, see *Between Science and Literature: An Introduction to Autopoetics*, by Ira Livingston (Univ. of Illinois, 2006). A book-length treatment of emergence can be found in Steven Johnson's *Emergence: The Connected Lives of Ants, Brains, Cities, and Software* (Touchstone, 2001), or John Holland's *Emergence: From Chaos to Order* (Basic Books, 1999). A text on emergence which links these issues with many other philosophical and scientific concerns of this

project is Manuel De Landa's *Philosophy and Simulation: The Emergence of Synthetic Reason* (Continuum, 2011).

17. The phrase "how newness enters the world" is taken from Homi K. Bhabha's quite thematically different yet strangely resonant ruminations on this subject in "How Newness Enters the World: Postmodern Space, Post-Colonial Times, and the Trials of Cultural Translation," from *The Location of Culture* (Routledge, 2nd ed., 2004).

18. For those looking for a general introduction to the scientific study of networks, there are many excellent and user-friendly introductions, each emphasizing different aspects of this field in relation to complex systems science, including Albert Lazslo-Barbasi's *Linked: How Everything is Connected to Everything Else and What It Means* (Plume, 2003), Duncan Watt's *Six Degrees: The Science of a Connected Age* (Norton, 2nd ed., 2004). For those looking for a more technical introduction, see Mark Newman's *Networks: An Introduction* (Oxford, 2010). For texts which link complex systems science, networks, and issues in contemporary post-structuralist philosophy and cultural theory, see Mark Taylor's *The Moment of Complexity: Emerging Network Culture* (Univ. of Chicago, 2003) and Brian Rotman's *Becoming Beside Ourselves: The Alphabet, Ghosts, and Distributed Human Being* (Duke, 2008). Those looking for more on the mathematical study of networks as graph theory, see Martin van Steen's excellent, accessible, and self-published text *Graph Theory and Complex Networks* (van Steen, 2010).

19. An introduction to Bergson's notions of radical creativity can be found in his lecture series *The Creative Mind: An Introduction to Metaphysics* (Dover, 1946). Deleuze's take on this, in relation to Bergson and beyond, can be found in *Bergsonism* (Zone, reissue, 1990). Gilbert Simondon, a crucial influence on Deleuze, develops related notions in his theories of individuation. While most of Simondon's works

are being translated into English as of the printing of this book, the first full-length study of Simondon's work in English is Muriel Combes' *Gilbert Simondon and the Philosophy of the Transindividual* (MIT, 2012). For a text which brings Deleuze's Bergsonian philosophy together with complex systems science, see Manuel De Landa's *Intensive Science and Virtual Philosophy* (Continuum, 2002).

20. For more on the history of the notion of the "Big Bang" and quantum singularity, see "The Beginning of Time: When Exactly Was It?" in Paul Davies' *About Time: Einstein's Unfinished Revolution* (Simon and Schuster, 1996). More on how these notions may relate to the possibility of multiple universes can be found in John Gribben's *In Search of the Multiverse: Parallel Universes, Hidden Dimensions, and the Ultimate Quest for the Frontiers of Reality* (Wiley, 2010).

21. Quantum superposition or entanglement, in which quantum events are able to exist in multiple states in multiple space-times until they are disturbed and hence "decohere," smearing the quantum event and spacetime in each other, can be found, for example, in Stenger (note 4), p. 99. This strange notion, and its relation to the famed EPR and quantum eraser experiments, is the subject of many recent books, such as *The God Effect: Quantum Entanglement, Science's Strangest Phenomenon*, by Brian Clegg (St. Martin's, 2009). For more on these issues, see note 4.

22. More on quantum foam can be found in "Quantum Foam" in John Wheeler's *Geons, Black Holes, and Quantum Foam: A Life in Physics* (Norton, 1998). More on the construction of the continuum in mathematical analysis can be found in "Modern Analysis" in Jeremy Grey's *Plato's Ghost: The Modernist Transformation of Mathematics* (Princeton, 2008), pp.129-147. The difficulties related to attempts to divide quarks and their "fractal" manner of reproducing, similar to that of a lizard which regenerates its tail, can be seen in

Vincent Icke's *The Force of Symmetry* (Cambridge, 1995), p. 268.

23. For more on fractals, see Ian Stewart's *From Here to Infinity: A Guide to Today's Mathematics* (Oxford, 1996), pp. 222-242, or alternately, Benôit Mandelbrot's *The Fractal Geometry of Nature* (Freeman, 1983).

24. An introduction to transfinite set theory in a manner which resonates with the concerns of this work can be found in the section on "Set Theory" in the introduction by Oliver Felthman and Justin Clemmens to *Infinite Thought* by Alain Badiou (Continuum, 2005), pp. 12-17. For a more directly mathematical account, see Mary Tiles' *The Philosophy of Set Theory: An Introduction to Cantor's Paradise* (Dover, 1989).

25. For an accessible account of holographs, holography, and the implications of these notions, see Bohm (note 4), pp. 182-5.

26. The political implications of fractals, and their inability to be contained, are described by David Graeber in a citation I cannot locate, even if it ultimately goes back to that of Mandelbrot and his famous example with the attempt to measure the coast of England, for more, see note 23.

27. The description of inner spacetime as involving contractions and expansions of this sort is similar to that presented by Bergson in *Matter and Memory* (Zone, reissue, 1991). For more on the evolution of non-Euclidean geometries, see Grey, note 22.

28. See note 4.

29. On the relation of the arrow of time to entropy, along with the debates related to these issues, see Huw Price's *Time's Arrow and the Archimedes' Point: New Directions for the Physics of Time* (Oxford, 1997).

30. According to the general theory of relativity, gravity is the same as acceleration. Repulsive forces of various sorts, including momenta against the pull of gravity, are then what

keep the attractive force of gravity from collapsing the universe upon itself in a "Big Crunch." One form of momentum with very real implications on the quantum level is angular momentum, which manifests as what is generally called "spin," even though most researchers argue that it is only "as if" particles with spin are actually moving. This has led some to argue that spin is an example of how matter is little more than curved spacetime, thereby leading to the ability to describe the world of experience as a play of energy with itself, as described by Zukav (note 4), pp. 213-311.

31. For more on the notion of immanence in Deleuze, see, for example, *Pure Immanence: A Life*, by Gilles Deleuze (Zone, 2001).

32. More on non-orientability in topology can be found in Ian Stewart's *Concepts in Modern Mathematics*, (Dover, 1995), pp. 144-158.

33. Antonio Damasio's account of why emotions should be seen as the manner in which the brain feels the way it maps the body can be found in *Looking for Spinoza: Joy, Sorrow, and the Feeling Brain* (Harcourt Brace, 2003), pp. 83-136.

34. The semiotic issues mentioned here are discussed at length in *Semiotics: The Basics*, by Daniel Chandler (Routledge, 2nd ed., 2002). Beyond mainstream semiotics, the work of Yuri Lotman can be found in *Universe of Mind: A Semiotic Theory of Culture* (Indiana Univ., 2001), Thomas Seebock in *Signs: An Introduction to Semiotics* (Univ. of Toronto, 1994), Louis Hjelmslev in *Prolegomena to a Theory of Language* (Univ. of Wisconsin, revised, 1961), and Vilém Flusser in *Writings* (Univ. of Minnesota, 2002). The relation between the theories of Hjelmslev and the semiotics of Deleuze and Guattari can be found in Brian Massumi's *A User's Guide to Capitalism and Schizophrenia* (MIT, Swerve ed., 1992), pp. 47-92.

35. For an accessible introduction to information theory, see Charles Seife's *Decoding the Universe: How the New Science of*

Information is Explaining Everything from Our Brains to Black Holes (Penguin, 2007).

36. For more on epigenesis, see the section on "Genetic Regulatory Networks" in the section called "The Program of Life" in *What is Thought?* by Eric Baum, (MIT, 2004), pp. 52-66.

37. For a related approach to these issues, see Gilles Deleuze, *Cinema I: The Movement-Image*, (Minnesota: 1986), pp. 59.

38. For more on why language might be considered a prison house, see Fredric Jameson's *The Prison House of Language: A Critical Account of Structuralism and Russian Formalism* (Princeton, 1975).

39. For a more embodied approach to the question of the origins of mathematics, see George Lakoff and Rafael Nuñez's *Where Mathematics Comes From: How the Embodied Mind Brings Mathematics into Being* (Basic Books, 2001). For a semiotic and embodied approach to these issues, see Rotman (note 18). The powerful philosophy of mathematics of Gilles Châtelet is unfortunately difficult to find in English, though this is starting to change as his work becomes more influential. The primary work of his in English, which is unfortunately often out of print, is *Figuring Space: Philosophy, Mathematics, and Physics* (Springer, 1999). Fernando Zalamea is one of the most wide ranging and incisive new voices in philosophy of mathematics, and one whose networked approach to a wide variety of issues is highly resonant with many aspects of this project. For more on his work on networks, see *Adriana y Penélope: Redes y mixturas en el mundo contemporanéo* (Perfect Paperback, 2004). For his work on contemporary philosophy of mathematics, see *Synthetic Philosophy of Mathematics* (Urbanomic/Sequence, 2013).

40. An account of the questioning of the law of non-contradiction and excluded middle in logic can be found in Grey

(note 22), pp. 265-384. More on orientability can be found in note 32.

41. An excellent text on the evolution of language is Guy Deutscher's *The Unfolding of Language: A Guided Tour to Mankind's Greatest Invention* (Holt, 2006).

42. See note 44.

43. Similar ideas can be found in Brian Rotman's notion of money as meta-sign in *Signifying Nothing: The Semiotics of Zero* (Stanford, 1987), pp. 46-56.

44. The notion of machinology is based on the philosophy of Félix Guattari. For more, see "Machinic Philosophy: Assemblages, Information, and Chaotic Flow" in John Johnston's *The Allure of Machinic Life: Cybernetics, Artificial Life, and the New AI* (MIT, 2008), pp. 105-162. For more on the notion of mediology as developed by Régis Debray, see *Media Manifestos: On the Technological Transmission of Cultural Forms* (Verso, 1996).

45. Jean-Joseph Goux's work can be found collected in English in the book *Symbolic Economies: After Marx and Freud* (Cornell, 1990). David Graeber's work on a social action theory of value can be found in most condensed form in Chapters 4 and 7 of *Toward an Anthropological Theory of Value: The False Coin of Our Own Dreams* (Palgrave, 2001), pp. 91-116, 229-262. Jonathan Beller's work on attentional theories of value can be found in *The Cinematic Mode of Production: Attention Economy and the Society of the Spectacle* (Dartmouth Univ. Press, 2006). Octavian Ksenzhek's work on econo-physics can be found in *Money: Virtual Energy – Economy Through the Prism of Thermodynamics* (Universal Publishers, 2007). For more on the work of Doyne Farmer, see his page at the Santa Fe Institute at http://tuvalu.santafe.edu/~jdf/ SFI%20Template/About%20Me.html.

46. More on robustness can be found, for example, in Scott Page's *Diversity and Complexity* (Princeton, 2010), pp 3-21.

For a book-length treatment of this notion, see Andreas Wagner's *Robustness and Evolvability in Living Systems* (Princeton, 2007).

47. For more on metalepsis and prolepsis, see note 57 below.

48. Eric Baum articulates the notion that "thought is condensation" in regard to complex systems science, epigenetic networks, and contemporary artificial intelligence in his book *What is Thought?* (note 36), in particular, see pp. 92-3. Gilbert Simondon's influential evolutionary approach to technological development, and what this means in regard to his notions of thought and thinking, can be found in Combes (note 19). More on embodied cognition can be found in Mitchell (note 13), and in greater detail in pp. 115-185, Shaun Gallagher's *How the Body Shapes the Mind* (Oxford, 2006), Rolf Pfeifer and Josh Bongard's *How the Body Shapes the Way We Think: A New View of Intelligence* (Bradford, 2006), and *Philosophy in the Flesh: The Embodied Mind and its Challenge to Western Thought* (Basic Books, 1999). Emergent and distributed cognition theories, particularly in relation to genetic algorithms and multi-agent systems, can be found in Jacques Ferber's *Multi-Agent Systems: An Introduction to Distributed Intelligence* (Addison-Wesley, 1999).

49. Such a relational approach to the study of the evolution of neural networks draws heavily upon the holism characteristic of the influence of John Dewey, whose classic article on the reflex arc is still relevant today. For more on this, see "The Reflex Arc Concept in Psychology," in *The Essential Dewey, Vol. 2: Ethics, Logic, Psychology* (Indiana Univ. Press, 1998), pp. 3-11. Catherine Malabou makes related points on the role of neurons in regard to neuroplasticity in general in *What Shall We Do With Our Brains?* (Fordman, 2008), in particular pp. 6-8, while a general Deweyan approach to the intersection between theories of mind and neuroscience can

be found in W. Teed Rockwell's *Neither Brain Nor Ghost: A Non-Dualist Alternative to the Mind-Body Identity Theory* (Bradford, 2005). The most directly neuroscientific approach to these issues, with particular emphasis upon the manner in which interneurons evolve from the internalization of the need to control movement is Rodolfo Llinás' *I of the Vortex: From Neurons to Self* (MIT, 2011).

50. A great summary of the modern evolutionary theory at work in this project can be found in Eric Beinhocker, *The Origin of Wealth: Evolution, Complexity, and the Radical Remaking of Economics* (Harvard Business Review Press, 2007), pp. 187-217. For a more detailed account, see Martin Nowak's *Evolutionary Dynamics: Exploring the Equations of Life* (Harvard, 2006), Daniel Dennett's *Darwin's Dangerous Idea: Evolution and the Meaning of Life* (Simon and Schuster, 1995), Gerald Edelman and Giulio Tononi's *A Universe of Consciousness: How Matter Becomes Imagination* (Basic Books, 2008), and Edward O. Wilson's *The Social Conquest of Earth* (Norton, 2012).

51. The principle of least action in physics is the subject of Chapter 6, "Least Action," in John Taylor's *Hidden Unity in Nature's Laws* (Cambridge, 2001), pp. 175-190.

52. Gerald Edelman describes the motivational systems in the brain, such as those in neuromodulatory structures tied into the limbic system, as value systems. For more, see Edelman and Tononi (note 50), pp. 43-9.

53. For more on "wideware," see "Cognitive Technology: Beyond the Naked Brain" in Clark (note 8), pp. 140-159. Related notions can be found in Bernard Stiegler's account of mnemotechnics in "The Invention of the Human" in *Technics and Time, Vol. 1: The Fault of Epimetheus* (Stanford, 1998), pp. 21-182.

54. A book-length study of the coevolution of language and the brain is Terrence Deacon's *The Symbolic Species: The*

Coevolution of Language and the Brain (Norton, 1998).

55. Inclusive fitness is described at length in Wilson (note 50), pp. 143-182.

56. More on the limbic system in this sense can be found in Joseph LeDoux's *Synaptic Self: How Our Brains Become Who We Are* (Penguin, 2002).

57. Walter Benjamin's notion of a "tiger's leap into the past" can be found in "Theses on History" in *Illuminations: Essays and Reflections* (Harcourt Brace, 1968). The notions of metalepsis and prolepsis, in terms of classical rhetorical theory, can be found in Richard Lanham's *Handlist of Rhetorical Terms* (Univ. of California, 1991), pp. 91, 121. For more on these notions in the expanded sense intended here, and in light of Benjamin's approach to related issues, see Harold Bloom's *Kaballah and Criticism* (Continuum, reprint, 1981), pp. 35-56.

58. G.W.F. Hegel's complex notion that evil can be thought of as the manner in which particularity strives to maintain itself against the universal coming to consciousness of Spirit can be found in scattered and cryptic form in *Phenomenology of Spirit* (trans. by V.A. Miller, Oxford, 1977), pp. 473, 477, 588. For a commentary which can make sense of these difficult notions in a manner resonant with this project, see Jean-Luc Nancy, *Hegel: The Restlessness of the Negative* (Univ. of Minnesota, 2002), in particular, the section on "Freedom," pp. 66-75.

59. See "Everybody Wants to be a Fascist," from *Chaosophy: Texts and Interviews*, by Félix Guattari, pp. 154-175 .

60. The notion of radical listening described in this text has much in common with Guattari's notions of group therapy, various aspects of Buddhism, as well as the philosophy of Emmanuel Lévinas, Paulo Freire, and Enrique Dussel. See note 79 for more on Freire and Dussel, while for more on Guattari's group therapeutics, see Janell Watson's *Guattari's Diagrammatic Thought: Writing Between Lacan and Deleuze*

(Continuum, 2009), pp. 15-54. More on these aspects in Lévinas can be found in *Otherwise Than Being: Or Beyond Essence* (Duquesne Univ., reprint, 1998), and the section on "Substitution" in particular. Lest it be thought that these ideas are primarily Western, Tibetan notions of mother-meditation have much in common with these notions. For a Western translation of these ideas, see Robert Thurman's excellent guided Tibetan Buddhist meditation primer, *The Jewel Tree of Tibet: The Enlightenment Engine of Tibetan Buddhism* (Free Press, 2005), and for mother-meditation in particular, pp. 119-141. Two texts which work to bring together insights from various Buddhist and psychoanalytic therapeutic practices, with many ramifications for notions of individual and collective healing and growth, can be found in Mark Epstein's *Thoughts Without a Thinker: Psychotherapy From A Buddhist Perspective* (Basic, reprint, 2004), and *Psychoanalysis and Buddhism: A Dialogue*, edited by Jeremy Safran (Wisdom Publications, 2003).

61. An explanation of Spinoza's approach to these difficult issues can be found in Deleuze's glossary-like yet potentially life-changing *Spinoza: Practical Philosophy* (City Lights, 1988), in particular, the entries on "Affections," "Freedom," and "Power," pp. 39-41, 69-71, and 97-104, respectively.

62. A book length study of the notion of non-duality, which shows up in many forms in non-Western philosophy, is David Loy's *Non-Duality: A Study in Comparative Philosophy* (Prometheus, 1988).

63. Most of these notions are easily misinterpreted, should not have their literal meaning taken at face value, and have a highly complex relation to their respective contexts. The sources listed here present these complex notions in a sense resonant with that intended in regard to this aspect of the networkological project. The Stoic position can be found in Pierre Hadot's *What is Ancient Philosophy?* (Belknap, 2005),

pp. 128-9, 192-211. For more on Spinoza's *amor intellectus dei* ("intellectual love of god") a state often simply referred to as "beatitude," see Gilles Deleuze's discussion of beatitude in *Expressionism in Philosophy: Spinoza* (Zone, 1990), pp. 255-320, or in regard to Spinoza's notion of freedom in *Spinoza: Practical Philosophy* (note 61), pp. 69-71. For more on an interpretation of Hegel with much in common with that espoused by this project, see the section on "Freedom" in Jean-Luc Nancy, note 58. Sufi notions of the *fana'* (generally translated as "annihilation") can be found in William Chiddick's *Sufism: A Beginner's Guide* (Oneworld, 2007), pp. 43, 109, 178-200. Hindu notions of realizing that *Atman* is *Brahman* can be found explained simply yet thoroughly by Swami Bhaskarananda in *Journey From the Many to the One: Essentials of Advaita Vedanta* (Viveka Press, 2009). Vajrayana Buddhist notions of what it might mean to identify with the Buddhanature can be found, for example, in the extraordinary text "Shakyamuni Buddha Through Tibetan Eyes" by Tse Chokling Yongdzin Yeshe Gyaltsen, as found in Robert Thurman's *Essential Tibetan Buddhism* (HarperOne, reprint, 1996), pp. 62-94. More on the *tathagathagarbha* itself can be found in W. Donald Mitchell, *Introducing the Buddhist Experience* (Oxford, 2nd ed., 2007), pp. 146-9.

64. The notion of thinking emerging from its own simpler past forms is the subject of Hegel's *The Phenomenology of Spirit*. The overall interpretation of this controversial work with which this project has the most in common, however, can be found in Nancy's work on Hegel, see note 58.

65. On the linguistic turns in contemporary philosophy, see Michael Losonsky's *Linguistic Turns in Modern Philosophy* (Cambridge, 2006), the final two chapters in particular, pp. 190-252. For more on how these issues relate to wider cultural concerns, see the chapters on "Postmodernism and Philosophy" and "Postmodernism and Critical Theory," by

Stuart Sim and Georges van den Abbeele, respectively, in *The Routledge Companion to Postmodernism* (ed. by Stuart Sim, Routledge, 3rd ed., 2011).

66. On the relation between paradigms and anomalies in science, see Thomas Kuhn's *The Structure of Scientific Revolutions* (Univ. of Chicago, 3rd ed., 1996). Ernesto Laclau's approach to social paradigm crises, strongly influenced by Karl Marx and Jacques Lacan, can be found in *New Reflections on the Revolution of Our Time* (Verso, 1997).

67. Guattari's approach to pragmatics can be found for example, in a work such as *The Machinic Unconscious: Essays in Schizoanalysis* (Semiotexte, 2010).

68. For a wildly enjoyable presentation of issues related to self-reference and the issues which arise in attempts at axiomatic foundations in mathematics and beyond, see Douglas Hofstader's *Gödel, Escher, Bach: An Eternal Golden Braid* (Basic Books, 1979). For more on how this relates to the history of mathematics, see Morris Kline's *Mathematics: The Loss of Certainty* (Oxford, 1980) and Jeremy Grey's *Plato's Ghost: The Modernist Transformation of Mathematics* (Princeton Univ., 2008). A philosophical account of how these issues relate to recursion in logic can be found in George Spencer-Brown's *Laws of Form* (Dutton, 1979). More in relation to observation can be found in Niklas Luhmann's "The Paradox of Observing Systems" in *Theories of Distinction: Redescribing the Descriptions of Modernity* (Stanford, 2002), pp. 79-93, and in relation to self-organizing complexity in Ira Livingston's *Between Science and Literature: An Introduction to Autopoetics* (Univ. of Illinois, 2006), pp. 58-79.

69. The notion of crystallization described here has much in common with Gilles Deleuze's notion of the crystalline regime, as described in *Cinema II: The Time-Image* (Univ. of Minnesota, 1989), pp. 126-136. For more on the theorization of physical crystallization on which this is based, see the

summary of Gilbert Simondon's thought on this, as described in Combes (note 19), pp. 6, 14-23.

70. Quantum events can only be truly reified by mathematical fiction, a process called "renormalization." In fact, there is good reason to believe that the very notion of a distinct quantum particle is a fiction produced by reifying human worldviews. For more on the manner in which particles are ultimately abstractions, see Stenger (note 4), p. 155, and Zukav (note 4), pp. 237-279.

71. See Joachim Schulte, "Family Resemblance," in *Wittgenstein: An Introduction* (SUNY, 1992), pp. 110-114. This notion is similar in many ways to that of degeneracy in network structures, for more, see Peter Csermely's *Weak Links: The Universal Key to the Stability of Networks and Complex Systems* (Springer, 2006), pp. 108-9.

72. For more on Walter Benjamin's "constellatory" approach to historiography, see the "Epistemo-Critical Prologue" to *The Origin of German Tragic Drama* (Verso, 2009). For a secondary source on this, see "Allegory and Melancholy" in *Walter Benjamin: Critical Constellations*, by Graeme Gilloch (Polity, 2002), pp. 57-87.

73. For more on the psychological work of John Dewey see *Experience and Nature* (Dover, reprint, 2012), for R.W. Fairbairn, see *Psychoanalytic Studies of the Personality* (Routledge, 1994), pp. 28-182, and for Maurice Merleau-Ponty, see *The Phenomenology of Perception* (Routledge, reprint, 2002).

74. While many working in contemporary cognitive neuro-science and artificial neural networks advocate something like panpsychism, it is generally philosophers who have made use of this term. For an example of a contemporary philosophical discourse on panpsychism, see William Seager's "Consciousness, Information and Panpsychism" in *Explaining Consciousness: The Hard Problem* (ed. by Jonathan

Shear, Oxford, 1997), pp. 269-286. More on the notion of panpsychism in the history of philosophy, see David Skrbina, *Panpsychism in the West* (Bradford, 2007). Antonio Damasio is an example of a prominent neuroscientist who argues against mind/body dualism in what could be called a panpsychist manner, for example, in books such as *Descartes' Error: Emotion, Reason, and the Human Brain* (Penguin, 2005), or *Looking For Spinoza: Joy, Sorrow, and the Feeling Brain* (Harcourt, 2003). In addition, artificial neural networks themselves can be seen as part of a larger argument for panpsychism. David Bohm's endorsement of an essentially panpsychist perspective can be found in the book he wrote with Basil Hiley, *An Undivided Universe: An Ontological Interpretation of Quantum Theory* (Routledge, 1993), p. 386.

75. A text on pedagogy which has been enormously important to me in many ways, and one which is strongly influenced by Dewey, Vygotsky, and Freire, is bell hooks' *Teaching to Transgress: Education as the Practice of Freedom* (Routledge, 1994).

76. See *Relational Psychotherapy: A Primer*, by Patricia Young (Routledge, 2002), *The Intersubjective Perspective*, by Robert Stolorow, George Atwood, and Donna Orange (Basic Books, 2002), *Gestalt Therapy: A Guide to Contemporary Practice*, by Philip Brownell (Springer, 2010), and *Gestalt Therapy: 100 Key Points and Techniques*, by Dave Mann (Routledge, 2010).

77. The notion of "the commons," and the related verb "to common" or "communing," has a long and complex history. One place to start on this issue is Michael Hardt and Antonio Negri's *Commonwealth* (Harvard, 2009).

78. The notion of a discourse of the oppressed is based on many of the ideas developed in Chela Sandoval's *Methodology of the Oppressed* (Univ. of Minnesota, 2000), Paulo Freire's *Pedagogy of the Oppressed* (Continuum, reprint, 2000), as well as the

work of Gloria Anzaldúa. This notion also builds on that of the need for the development of a common language between oppressed persons to form a counter-hegemonic bloc able to compete with dominant power structures, as articulated in Ernesto Laclau and Chantal Mouffe's *Hegemony and Socialist Strategy: Towards a Radical Democratic Politics* (Verso, 2nd ed., 2001).

79. The notion of the manner in which oppressed persons can teach us the most about our society can be found, among others, in the works of Alain Badiou, Enrique Dussel, Paulo Freire. For more, see Dussel's *Philosophy of Liberation* (Wipf and Stock, 2003), "Equality and Justice" in Peter Hallward's *Badiou: A Subject to Truth* (Univ. of Minnesota, 2003), pp. 223-242, or Freire (preceding note).

80. For more on the notions of a subject and subjugated groups on which this is based, see Deleuze and Guattari's *Anti-Oedipus: Introduction to Schizoanalysis* (Routledge, 1999), pp. 103-106.

81. For a critique of classical economic theory from the perspective of complexity economics, see Eric Beinhocker's *The Origin of Wealth: Evolution, Complexity, and the Radical Remaking of Economics* (Harvard Business Review, 2006), Benôit Mandelbrot's *The Misbehavior of Markets: A Fractal View of Risk, Ruin, and Reward* (Perseus Books, 2004), and *Confidence Games: Money and Markets in a World Without Redemption*, by Mark Taylor (Univ. of Chicago, 1998).

82. For more on these notions, see *The Shock Doctrine: The Rise of Disaster Capitalism*, by Naomi Klein (Picador, 2008), and Beinhocker (preceding note).

83. For an incredible history of value that keeps an eye on our current situation, see David Graeber's *Debt: The First 5,000 Years* (Melville House, 2012). For a text which uses evolutionary and algorithmic methods such as those described in this text to rethink contemporary economic structures, see

Peter Barnes' *Capitalism 3.0: A Guide to Reclaiming the Commons* (Berrett-Koehler, 2006).

84. The notion of complexity as evolving at the "edge of chaos" is one of the fundamental notions of complex systems science, and is ultimately the same as meta-stability. For an approach to complexity which emphasizes this aspect, see Ilya Prigogine and Isabelle Stenger's classic and highly influential text *Order Out of Chaos: Man's New Dialogue with Nature* (Bantam, 1984).

85. See Žižek on Pascal for a similarly metaleptic approach to belief in, for example, "The Spectre of Ideology," in *Mapping Ideology*, ed. by Žižek, et.al. (Verso, reprint, 2012), p. 1-32.

86. For an example of a complex systems approach to political change, see the description of changing alliances in early twentieth century Europe in Ball (note 13), pp 285-287.

87. More on this notion can be found in the mini-article on my website called "The Human Mic As a Radical Transformation in Human Political Subjectivity," at http:// networkologies.wordpress.com.

88. On the notions of "empire" and "multitude," see Michael Hardt and Antonio Negri's *Multitude: War and Democracy in the Age of Empire* (Penguin, reprint, 2005). The notion of transindividuality originates with Gilbert Simondon, but is closely linked with that of transversality developed by Félix Guattari, and these notions permeate the works that Guattari wrote with Deleuze. For more, see Combes (note 19), pp. 25-50, and *Guattari's Diagrammatic Thought: Writing Between Lacan and Deleuze*, by Janell Watson (Continuum, 2012), pp. 23-32.

89. For more on classical anarchism, see Peter Marshall's *Demanding the Impossible: A History of Anarchism* (PM, 1992), while more on contemporary and post-anarchism can be found in *Postanarchism: A Reader* edited by Duane Rousselle and Süreyya Evren (Pluto, 2011) and *Contemporary Anarchist*

Studies: An Introductory Anthology of Anarchism in the Academy edited by Aster, et.al. (Routledge, 2009) or Saul Newman's *The Politics of Postanarchism* (Edinburgh Univ., 2011).

90. An introduction to theophanic pantheism in regard to the work of Ibn 'Arabi and Henry Corbin is Tom Cheetham's excellent *The World Turned Inside Out: Henry Corbin and Islamic Mysticism* (Spring Journal Press, 2003). The work of Frithjof Schuon presents a highly compatible perennialist take on these issues, for more, see *The Essential Frithjof Schuon*, ed. Seyyed Hossein Nasr (World Wisdom, 2005).

91. An excellent introduction to perennialist philosophies of the divine are Aldous Huxley's *The Perennial Philosophy: An Interpretation of the Great Mystics, East and West* (Harper Perennial, 2009), even if the most developed set of perennialist theorizations is likely that of Frithjof Schuon, for more see preceding note. For Sri Aurobindo's evolutionary version of advaita Vedantism, see *The Life Divine* (Aurobindo Ashram, 2010), while Pierre Teilhard de Chardin's evolutionary theology can be found in *The Phenomenon of Man* (Harper Perennial, 2008). Seyyed Hossein Nasr's excellent if at times orthodox theorizings on perennialism can be found in *The Essential Seyyed Hossein Nasr* (World Wisdom, 2007). One of the more important works of Ju Mipham can be found in *Mipham's Beacon of Certainty: Illuminating the View of Dzogchen, The Great Perfection* (trans. by John Petit, Wisdom: 2002), while a full length study on the implications of his more radical ideas in regard to their context can be found in Karma Phuntso's *Mipham's Dialectics and the Debates on Emptiness: To Be, Not to Be, or Neither* (Routledge: 2010). A fascinating introduction to the thought of Jiddu Krishnamurti can be found in his conversations with physicist David Bohm, collected in *The Ending of Time* (Harper and Row, 1985). While the game-

theoretic approach of Robert Wright's *The Evolution of God*
(Back Bay, reprint, 2010) may at first seem in conflict with
many of these notions, this project will work to show why
this is in fact not the case. For more on liberation theology,
one of the most influential texts has been Gustavo Gutiérez's
A Theology of Liberation: History, Politics, and Salvation (Orbis,
Revised, 1988). A good place to start on process theology is
Bruce Epperly's *Process Theology: A Guide for the Perplexed*
(Continuum, 2011).

92. Whitehead argues that God acts as a "lure" to greater
complexification in regard to each "occasion" in the
universe. For more, see Brian Epperson's *Quantum Mechanics
and the Philosophy of Alfred North Whitehead* (Fordham,
reprint, 2012), p. 101.

93. See Jean-Luc Marion, "Idols and Icons," *God Beyond Being:
Hors-Texte* (Univ. of Chicago, 1991), pp. 7-24.

94. For more on the notion in Spinoza that "we do not yet know
what a body can do," in relation to Deleuze's interpretation
of this in particular, see Deleuze's *Spinoza: Practical
Philosophy*, note 61, pp 17-22.

95. The notion that all electrons in our universe may be refractions of the same particle, and the reasons for this, was first
suggested to Richard Feynman by John Wheeler. For more
on this notion, see Richard Feynman's Nobel Prize lecture at
www.nobelprize.org/nobel_prizes/physics/laureates/
1965/feynman-lecture.html. More on entanglement and
decoherence in regard to the smearing of spacetime and
particles within each other can be found in note 21.

96. More on the mathematics of zero can be found in Charles
Seife's *Zero: The Biography of a Dangerous Number* (Penguin,
2002), and Brian Rotman's *The Semiotics of Zero* (note 43). The
manner in which our universe could have been the result of
a vacuum fluctuation can be found in Stenger (note 4), p. 98.

97. Buddhist notions of *shunyata* ("emptiness") and *tathata*

("suchness") are discussed at length in David Loy's *Nonduality: A Study in Comparative Philosophy* (Perseus, 1998), particularly pp. 42-68. More on the *tathagatagarbha* can be found in W. Donald Mitchell's *Introducing the Buddhist Experience* (Oxford, 2nd ed., 2007), pp. 146-9. Isaac Luria's school of Kaballism is described in Gershom Scholem's *Major Trends in Jewish Mysticism* (Shocken, 1946), pp. 244-286, but for more on the philosophical implications of his notions of voiding, see Bloom (note 57), pp 16-19. For more on spacing, deferral, and originary repetition in the works of Jacques Derrida, see "Spacing and Temporality" in Julian Wolfrey's *Derrida: A Guide for the Perplexed* (Continuum, 2007), pp. 58-62, or alternately, "Différance" in *The Margins of Philosophy*, by Jacques Derrida (Univ. of Chicago, pp. 1-28).

98. See Jakob von Uexküll's *Foray Into the World of Animals and Humans* (Univ. of Minnesota, 2010).

99. More on double articulation in relation to language can be found in *A Thousand Plateaus: Capitalism and Schizophrenia* (Univ. of Minnesota, 1995), pp. 27, 40-1. For more on how these issues relate to that of disjunctive synthesis, see Brian Massumi's *A User's Guide to Capitalism and Schizophrenia* (MIT, Swerve ed., 1992), pp. 47-92.

100. The notion that links are extended nodes, and nodes contracted links, is common within the network literature.

101. The notion of abduction in the work of C.S. Peirce can be found in the introduction to *The Cambridge Companion to Peirce* edited by Cheryl Misak, (Cambridge, 2004), pp. 16-18.

102. For more on these notions, see my mini-article on my website entitled "On Descriptive Philosophy: Or Beyond the Linguistic Turn, A Networkological Approach" http://networkologies.wordpress.com/2011/03/29/on-description-or-beyond-the-linguistic-turn-post-scriptum/.

103. See note 6.

104. Nietzsche argued all philosophy was the "unconscious and involuntary autobiography" of its authors, see "The Prejudices of Philosophers," from *Beyond Good and Evil*, in Walter Kaufmann's *Basic Writings of Nietzsche* (Random House, 2000), especially the section on pp. 197-9.

Contemporary culture has eliminated both the concept of the public and the figure of the intellectual. Former public spaces – both physical and cultural – are now either derelict or colonized by advertising. A cretinous anti-intellectualism presides, cheerled by expensively educated hacks in the pay of multinational corporations who reassure their bored readers that there is no need to rouse themselves from their interpassive stupor. The informal censorship internalized and propagated by the cultural workers of late capitalism generates a banal conformity that the propaganda chiefs of Stalinism could only ever have dreamt of imposing. Zer0 Books knows that another kind of discourse – intellectual without being academic, popular without being populist – is not only possible: it is already flourishing, in the regions beyond the striplit malls of so-called mass media and the neurotically bureaucratic halls of the academy. Zer0 is committed to the idea of publishing as a making public of the intellectual. It is convinced that in the unthinking, blandly consensual culture in which we live, critical and engaged theoretical reflection is more important than ever before.